The World Labour Market

A History of Migration

Lydia Potts
Translated by Terry Bond

Zed Books Ltd
London and New Jersey

The World Labour Market: A History of Migration was first published in English by Zed Books Ltd, 57 Caledonian Road, London N1 9BU and 171 First Avenue, Atlantic Highlands, New Jersey 07716, in 1990.

The German language edition was first published as *Weltmarkt für Arbeitskraft: Von der Kolonisation Amerikas bis zu den Migrationen der Gegenwart* by Junius Verlag GmbH, Hamburg, Stresemannstrasse 375, Postfach 50 07 45, 2000 Hamburg 50 in 1988.

Translation by Terry Bond
Cover design Sophie Buchet
Typeset by Photosetting and Secretarial Services, Yeovil, Somerset
Printed and bound by Billings and Sons Ltd, Worcester

British Library Cataloguing in Publication Data

Potts, Lydia *1957–*
    The world labour market : a history of migration.
    1. Personnel. Migration, history
    I. Title   II. Weltmark für Arbeitskraft. [*English*]
    331.12791

    ISBN 0-86232-882-9
    ISBN 0-86232-883-7 pbk

Library of Congress Cataloging-in-Publication Data

Potts, Lydia, 1957–
    [Weltmarkt für Arbeitskraft. English]
    The world labour market : a history of migration / Lydia Potts : translated by Terry Bond.
        p.   cm.
    Translation of: Weltmarkt für Arbeitskraft.
    Includes bibliographical references.
    ISBN 0-86232-882-9.—ISBN 0-86232-883-7 (pbk.)
    1. Alien labor—History.   2. Forced labor—History.   I. Title.
HD6300.P6813   1990
331.12'791—dc20   89-25041
                        CIP

Contents

Tables

Illustrations

Diagrams

Maps

Introduction

Some observations on 'aliens research' in the Federal Republic of Germany

The employment of foreign workers (both male and female) in West Germany passed its peak almost 15 years ago, yet even today the Republic still employs 1.5 million workers from Turkey, Italy, Greece, Yugoslavia and other countries and plays host to more than two million family members. Nor is West Germany in any way an exceptional case with regard to the number of migrant workers – people who have left their countries of origin in order to find work abroad – that it employs. It should be regarded instead as typical of the highly industrialized nations.

The employment of migrant workers has been and still is the subject of intense debate in West Germany, and the political and academic debates surrounding the many aspects of this issue have received a great deal of attention. Since West Germany, and indeed other host countries, first declared such 'aliens' to be a problem in the light of the economic crisis and growing unemployment, there has been no end of discussion on the subject in the media and in academic circles. The literature on this theme is now so extensive that the great number of works published each year begs the question of whether all aspects of the problem have not already been probed and whether yet another study does not merely increase the volume of material on the subject, which can in any case no longer be ignored, without being able to provide any new insight. One concise dictionary of foreign labour published in Switzerland states, 'The literature [on the subject] is now so plentiful and so diverse that it would be presumptuous for anyone to attempt yet another version of the main fields of research' (Auernheimer, 1984, p. 60).

Against this background I do not intend to attempt anything approaching a comprehensive presentation or classification of the various tendencies and lines of research, nor do I propose offering any explanation of one or more of the specialized research areas such as government policy relating to aliens, the legal, educational or welfare aspects of employing migrant workers, criminality amongst aliens, hostility towards aliens, the integration into society of aliens and so on. Instead, I mean to highlight what I consider to be some of the deficiencies of the debate on labour migration. Indeed, these were the starting point for this study, which looks in particular at the processes and structures which provide the setting in which millions upon millions of people have for centuries been scattered throughout the world as workers – and only as such, that is to say, reduced to their function as mere suppliers of living labour power. The fact that – for various reasons – this is not a theme touched upon by 'aliens research' forces me to introduce an inevitable note of criticism of that discipline.

Whereas in the 1960s the word *Gastarbeiter* was the euphemism typically used to describe workers recruited from abroad, in the 1980s Germans talk almost exclusively of 'foreigners'. Nor is this merely the language of everyday life, politics and the media. A glance at the title pages of the countless books and essays on the subject reveals that it is also the language of academia. What is the significance of this? Whereas the term *Gastarbeiter* still brings to mind industrial production and the importation of labour power, the term 'foreigner' has no such overtones. It does not distinguish, for example, between those of different social or ethnic origins or between the various reasons for mobility. Tourists, commercial travellers, refugees, those seeking asylum, people from Switzerland as well as from Ghana or Turkey are all – or so it might seem – covered by the same term. Strictly speaking, all non-Germans are foreigners, and the result of this ethnocentric outlook is that the real problems inherent in the transfer of people in the form of living labour power are not defined, but instead concealed. A further consequence is that 'aliens research' concentrates – logically when one considers the term – on the study of the individual 'alien'. His or her 'integration', socialization, proficiency in the language, family structures, religious and political orientation, academic and professional qualifications and so on are examined for the purposes of deducing behavioural patterns that might aid teachers, social workers, policy-makers and administrative bodies. Bibliographies and statistics on the subject show that particularly in the 1980s, publications and research projects have concentrated on social and educational fields.

What, then, are the theoretical foundations that underlie 'aliens research'? As an academic field it is relatively new; the causes and patterns of the transfer of labour power, the history of labour migration and the formulation of migration theory have never aroused any great interest. Nor, as far as I am aware, has any international comparative study or overall account of the process of labour migration today been carried out in a West German context, at least not in any field other than the directly political.

Consequently, even today the academic debate on labour migration is still essentially dealing with the issue as if the recruitment of migrant workers were a phenomenon exclusively, or at least largely, attributable to West Germany's development after World War Two and in particular to those periods of peak prosperity which are now a thing of the past.

Meanwhile the whole issue has taken on a distinctly Germano-Turkish flavour. Politically this has manifested itself in the *Rückkehrförderungsgesetz*, a law intended to promote the repatriation of migrant workers from non-EC countries, and in negotiations on if and when Turkey, as a future EC member country, should have free access to Western European labour markets. There has been serious discussion of whether West Germany's problem in this area might not, in fact, be a 'Turkish problem' rather than a 'foreigner-related problem'. One eminent academic rejects this suggestion and maintains that the problems caused by the presence of the Turkish population in West Germany, and in particular its inability to integrate, have not arisen as a result of that population's ethnic or cultural characteristics, but are instead primarily 'situational', by which he means related to geographical concentration, the fact that the Turks have only recently entered West Germany, and so on.

Such illustrations of the level of debate indicate that the theoretical groundwork so vital to academically well-founded commentary and opinion has so far been inadequate. Only a relatively small proportion of the literature on the subject provides a starting point for such theoretical work, and such starting points as exist are essentially to be found in two strands of the debate with very different approaches.

One such strand has spawned several genuinely sociological studies that seek to develop a conceptual framework that can then form the basis of further analysis. Its central concepts are those of assimilation, integration, segregation, stratification and minorities. Migratory trends are often examined individually and in some cases comparisons drawn. Such studies include works by Esser (1980), Harbach (1976), Hoffmann-Nowotny (1970, 1973, 1981) and Heckmann (1981), all of whom subscribe to this school of thought.

Politico-economic analyses, on the other hand, are more concerned to discover the actual causes of migration, its effects both in the foreign worker's country of origin and in the host nation, and the link between migration and capitalism or imperialism. Such analyses regard migration as a structural process, and works from this school include *Ausländerbeschäftigung und Imperialismus* (The employment of foreign workers and imperialism) from 1971, and those by Geiselberger (1972) and Nikolinakos (1973). In general, the two strands of the debate do not overlap, chiefly due to the incongruity between their respective conceptual frameworks and lines of inquiry.

This second school of thought is, however, suffering from visible stagnation. Its major works were completed in the early 1970s and they have not been followed by others because they were insufficiently debated at the time and contained methodological errors the effects of which can still be felt today. Nikolinakos (1980), for example, sets himself the task of developing a 'theory of migration under late capitalism'. It is a characteristic feature of labour migration, however, that it does not occur under 'late capitalism', but is inseparably linked to the process of industrialization. 'Late capitalism' is, therefore, precisely the wrong starting point, since it is not then possible to refer back to a theory of labour migration in earlier times.

Moreover, the politico-economic strand of the debate is, in the final analysis, ahistorical. For example, in their 1980 study (p. 7) Blaschke and Greussing write, 'The history of industrialization is also the history of labour migration. One of the features of developing capitalism is its tendency to transform all labour markets into one labour market of world proportions.' Yet the anthology that opens with this notion contains no mention of its origin or its impact on the formulation of theory.

The year 1984 saw the publication of an anthology (Griese, 1984) with the promising title *Bilanz und Kritik der Gastarbeiterforschung und der Ausländerpädagogik* (A survey and critique of *Gastarbeiter* research and educational studies in immigration). The anthology demonstrates that the weaknesses of the debate to date have not gone unnoticed, but its critique of the central issues is radical only in appearance and is ultimately rooted in the prevailing model of *Gastarbeiter* research and opinion. It ends with the following self-criticism:

> We must say 'no' more often to lucrative financial offers which go hand in hand with career advancement and prestige, and instead edu-
> cationalize 'aliens policy', politicize 'aliens labour' and moralize academic study and research. In short, we must turn the whole field of 'educational research into immigration' on its head. (Griese, 1984, p. 219)

Unfortunately, the above impetuous plea for the abolition of the term 'alien' and its compounds is not even accepted in the writer's own work.

It is unclear what 'educationalization of policy' might mean, and one is always sceptical of calls to 'moralize academic study'. Such a stance, rather naïve in this form, obscures the fact that it is material interests that cause migration and shape the lives of migrant workers and their families, and that those same material interests also exert a certain degree of influence on research and academic study. The value of calls to deprofessionalize the work done with migrant workers and their families is particularly dubious when such calls are made by professional 'aliens educationalists'. 'If other professionals can create the basic conditions under which "aliens" can organize themselves and articulate their own interests, then that is sufficient in the way of politico-educational work' (Griese, ibid.).

On balance, then, the above survey of '*Gastarbeiter* research' and 'educational studies in immigration' testifies to the fact that no fundamental advances in the content of such research, such methodology or objectives should be expected.

A glance beyond the borders of West Germany reveals that some of the problems encountered there by people researching labour migration – the lack of a theoretical and historical basis, the restriction of the debate to one country, and the dearth of international comparative studies – are not exclusively West German problems. The Director of the New York Center for Migration Studies characterizes the debate in the USA as follows:

> To sum up, it should be said that in the USA international migration is
> not normally a subject debated in connection with international politics,
> North–South relations, or the new world economic order. The
> development of sound theories which explain the phenomenon of
> migration still requires a certain amount of work. The majority of
> studies are based on a representative sample and either concentrate on
> the study of a particular group of immigrants or are restricted to the
> USA. (Tomasi, 1982, p. 40)

In West Germany, as in the USA, the study of labour migration is not in
any way linked to the theory of development or the study of developing
nations, yet it is just such a link which might provide important impetus for
all three fields. If one considers the phenomenon in relation to development
and underdevelopment one gains new insights into the whole question of
migration; the inclusion of labour migration in theoretical analyses of
development (or imperialism) might also eliminate fundamental shortcomings in this field. The debate on the 'new international division of
labour' is a perfect illustration of my point.

The new international division of labour and the world market for labour power

The existence of a world market for labour power was first discovered in
West Germany in the 1970s, during the debate on the politics and theory of
development, and in particular as a result of a study on the new
international division of labour (Fröbel, Heinrichs and Kreye, 1977). The
authors of the study evolved a thesis which maintained that in addition to
the considerably older, more frequently discussed world markets for goods
and capital, world markets in production sites and labour had also been
emerging during the 1970s, this having been made possible by the
fragmentation of the productive process, the development of transport and
communication technology, and the 'virtually inexhaustible potential of
available labour' in the developing nations. The authors stressed that 'The
materialization of these three prerequisites (and other, less central
conditions) has permitted the emergence of a world market for labour
power, a truly international industrial reserve army, and a world market
for production sites' (ibid., p. 30). In 1975, claim the authors, around
725,000 workers in the developing nations were employed in factories
producing for the world market, in free production zones, and on other
sites. Of these, 420,000 were in Asia, 40,000 in Africa, and 265,000 in Latin
America (ibid., p. 613).

Ten years later this figure has more than doubled. In a follow-up study
the authors estimate that such workers now number more than 1.8 million,
of which well over 50 per cent are women. In addition, a more or less

equally large number of workers are involved in producing for the world market outside foreign holding companies or export production zones, making a total of 3.6 million people employed in the developing nations to produce industrial goods for the world market (Fröbel, Heinrichs and Kreye, 1986, p. 448). These figures are supported by other, official studies.

It is not only the fact that goods manufactured in factories producing for the world market and in free production zones are sold exclusively on the world market, but also the scale of the activity and in particular its distribution over three continents – with centres in East Asia and the Caribbean – that justify talking in terms of a world market for labour power. On the other hand, although there may indeed have been important changes in the international division of labour since the 1970s which have affected workers in both the developing and industrialized nations, geographical shifts in production and the establishment of free production zones in the developing nations do not themselves cause the *emergence* of a world market for labour power. These factors merely extend such a market in that they enable industrial production to take place and to be profitable (at least for the most part) in the home countries of those supplying so-called 'cheap' labour.

One hidden 'labour import' into Europe and the USA began long before geographical shifts in production took place. Ever since the colonial penetration of Asia, Africa and Latin America raw materials, agricultural products and handicrafts have been produced by 'cheap', almost cost-free labour in those regions for the benefit of the various colonial powers and sold on the world market. This worldwide production was likewise organized from Europe or the USA. Like geographical shifts in production, this process allows the transfer of objectified or dead labour power. Through the import or export of various goods a world market for labour power is created that deals in indirect labour power; people, as the providers of labour power, as living labour power, are not (or not necessarily) transferred themselves.

However, the fact that labour migration has always been a global phenomenon proves that the world market for labour power also existed in an immediate and direct form for a considerable length of time before geographical shifts in production began to take place and on a much larger scale. It is estimated that there were at least 20 million migrant workers in the world in 1980, and that more than half of these were from the developing nations.

The world market for labour power – historical development, present-day structures, and developmental analysis

The world market for labour power in its direct form emerged not as a result of present-day migration, but hundreds of years ago. Living labour power has been transferred in large quantities and over long distances since the end of the 15th century.

This study will attempt to trace that process. The journey will span the enslavement of the Indians that followed the conquest of America, the various forms of forced labour and forced migration in Latin America, Asia and Africa, African slavery, the coolie system used to despatch the people of Asia all over the world, and finally present-day labour migration and the brain drain, the exodus of academics from the developing nations.

Regarded thus, the world market for labour power appears to be a universal structure with a history of several hundred years. In the course of that history every inhabited continent and almost every society on earth has been drawn into the world market – although with differing, even opposing functions. For the original inhabitants of America and Australia, and the residents of Asia and Africa this has meant extermination, abduction, and exploitation. For at least part of the white people's world it has meant material wealth.

The system under which the workers of the world are transferred across its surface appear, at first sight, very different. Closer inspection reveals that to some extent at least they build on each other and interlink both temporally and geographically, that experience of the one form is used to develop new forms, that time and time again, even in the recent past, humankind has reverted to older, apparently obsolete forms. The history of the world market for labour power – as we understand the term – is, of course, not primarily the story of free wage labour; often the worker concerned was neither 'free', nor paid a wage. Both in the 20th century and before, essentially compulsion and force have shaped its evolution.

Women play an important part in the labour market. Although in terms of labour migration, slavery, and coolie labour they constituted a minority (as a rule around one third), they were no less affected by the structures of the world market for labour power than men: their reproductive function and its control has been the subject of particular attention and has attracted various measures during every stage in the market's development. Women have suffered exploitation not only in the productive process, but also in the reproductive process, and this in the most extreme forms imaginable. Moreover, the women left behind in their country of origin have borne the brunt of often forced emigration in very specific ways.

It is not possible to trace the history of the world market for labour power through several centuries and through all its various forms and structures in one study in such a way as will allow detailed consideration of the multitude of very different processes it encompasses, their causes and their effects on the societies concerned. The aim of this study can only be to plot the evolution of an initial, crude concept. Thus it offers an overview of the most important stages in the world market for labour power and slots the term into its historical and theoretical context.

The study concentrates on giving an account of the world market for labour power in its direct forms, that is to say, those forms which require or include the transfer of human beings. It points out the links, similarities and differences between these various forms and attempts to clarify those forms of exploitation specific to female workers (as far as the literature on the subject permits). Chapters 1 to 5 offer an historical analysis of the processes of the world market for labour power in its direct forms, beginning at the end of the 15th century and extending to the present day, Chapter 6 considers the extent to which theories of development and migration deal with these structures and processes, and finally Chapter 7 draws together the elements of a preliminary theoretical analysis of the world market for labour power.

1. Origins: the Spanish Colonization of America (1492 –1700)

Until the beginning of the modern age the world known to Europeans was essentially limited to Europe and some outlying areas on the Mediterranean. Within a few decades in the late 15th and early 16th centuries the picture had changed radically: European ships landed on the Caribbean islands and in North, Central, and South America, rounded the Cape of Good Hope, for the first time ever reached India by sea from Europe, and circumnavigated the world. During this same period Europe was in the throes of another fundamental transformation, namely the emergence of the capitalist mode of production. Centuries later this new mode of production was to bring about the industrialization of Europe and North America, but its early manifestation was in 'primitive accumulation', the accumulation of wealth in a few hands. This was a prerequisite for the transformation of money into capital and therefore for the subsequent development of trading and industrial capital. For the great majority of the population of Europe primitive accumulation meant the forcible and violent expulsion of peasants from the land and the isolation of direct producers from their means of production.

However, domestic exploitation, the exploitation of the population of one's own society, was only one of the two pillars upon which primitive accumulation rested. The new 'discoveries' made possible the large-scale exploitation of foreign lands, and it was against this background that the world market for goods, and later also that for capital, emerged. The fact that a world market for labour power also emerged is generally overlooked yet from the very beginning, the populations of conquered territories were a vital element in their European colonizers' calculations.

With this in mind, there now follows an account, by way of example, of the birth of Spanish America and the systems developed there for exploiting Indian labour power. Spanish America is an ideal example, not merely because it was the first large colonial empire of the modern age, but also because, at least in the 16th and 17th centuries, it was the largest. Huge areas of this empire were densely populated and to begin with constituted an inexhaustible reservoir of labour power. Spanish America was conquered and penetrated at a time when feudalism was still flourishing in Spain, but when the conditions which would pave the way for the emergence of capitalism were also developing. According to Marx (*Capital*, vol. 1, p. 145), 'The modern history of capital dates from the creation in the 16th century of a world-embracing commerce and a world embracing market.'

Riches from the Spanish colony first flowed back to Spain, but were then distributed througout Europe by interested merchants of various nationalities, including Germans (e.g. the emporia of the Welser and Fugger families). Shipments from America were often registered in Seville only as a formality and then, since the Crown had pledged them in advance, despatched to their owners in the rest of Europe.

Conquest, plunder and the depopulation of America

'The first American to discover Columbus made an unfortunate discovery indeed.'

Georg Christoph Lichtenberg (1742–99)

In 1492 Columbus landed on an island in the Bahamas, taking it to be an offshore island belonging to Japan. Thus begins the history of the conquest of America, the history above all of a trail of plunder and murder of enormous dimensions which was to last for decades. The Spaniards found the islands of the Caribbean and the American mainland to be densely populated. In a contemporary account of the province of Nicaragua the priest and future bishop Las Casas wrote:

I cannot speak highly enough of the fertility, the healthy climate, the charm, the prosperity, and the extraordinary population. It was truly amazing to see the host of villages situated in the province. They appeared to stretch for three or four miles and were rich with glorious fruits, which is no doubt why it was hardly possible to count the number of their inhabitants. (Las Casas, 1981, p. 35)

Elsewhere he writes:

Those regions which were unknown before the year 1541 were swarming with living creatures, like bees in a hive. It seemed as though God had planted the whole, or at least the greater part, of the human race in this one tract of land. (Ibid., p. 9)

During the decades that followed, the Spaniards, using the islands of the Caribbean as a base, conquered successively larger sections of the American mainland. In the north they pushed as far as Florida in 1510 and California in 1535, in the south they ventured as far as the Strait of

Magellan in 1519–20. They also destroyed the Maya, Aztec, and Inca Empires; the Inca Empire alone took in the highlands of the central Andes in their entirety, from present-day southern Columbia via Ecuador and Peru to Bolivia, the Peruvian coast, and parts of Chile and northwest Argentina (Engl, 1975, p. 17). Within a mere 50 years the Spaniards occupied all those major regions that were to belong to Spanish America until the beginning of the 19th century, when they each became independent in quick succession.

The Spanish *imperium* was established step by step. Detachments of generally not more than a thousand soldiers conquered territory after territory; bloodbaths became an accepted tactic. Many contemporary accounts described such action, for which the conquistadors developed a specific, euphemistic terminology ('depopulate, waste, harass, destroy, and conquer'). 'It was a kind of principle. Their first move would be to inflict a massive bloodbath or *matanza* [butchery] on the large Indian population so that the people would tremble on hearing the name "Christ" as if before true devils' (Friederici, 1925, p. 475).

The conquistadors hoped above all to carry off large amounts of gold. This was the main goal upon which even Columbus's sights were set as he travelled the world on his voyages of discovery. On 12 November 1492 he wrote in his diary:

> for there are, without doubt, huge amounts of gold in these territories, and it is not without reason that the Indians whom I am taking along say that there are places on these islands were gold is dug up from the earth and where the people wear it around their necks, in their ears, and on their arms and legs. And their rings are very thick rings too.

It simply did not occur to the conquistadors to concern themselves with anything other than the hunt for gold, silver, precious stones, and pearls. When Cortez, the future conqueror of the Aztec Empire, first set foot on Hispaniola (Haiti) the Spanish governor offered him land for a *hacienda*. He refused the offer with the words, 'I have not come here to work the land like a peasant, but to search for gold' (Friederici, 1925, p. 404). Ultimately the Indians came to believe that gold was the white man's god.

During their first few years in Spanish America the conquistadors did not acquire a great deal of booty, even though they robbed the natives of all that they possessed. The amount of gold they acquired remained insignificant until they reached the great urban cultures of the American mainland. In Peru and Mexico, for instance, they amassed large quantities through extortion or force. In 1533 the captured Inca Atahualpa offered Pizarro a room measuring 24 feet by 17 feet and over 8 feet high filled with gold in exchange for his release. The Spaniards accepted the offer and actually received more than they had demanded, for in front of the house they found a pile of gold as high as a man. They divided the treasure up amongst themselves and the Inca was strangled. The quest for gold continued with great success (see Engl, 1975, pp. 103ff).

In order to procure actual or suspected treasures, the Spaniards entered the conquered territories with unimaginable and senseless violence, often directed against the entire population. At the beginning of his *Report on the Devastation of the West Indian Lands* Las Casas sums up the conquistadors' behaviour towards the Indians thus:

> For forty years they have done nothing, and today they still do nothing, but slaughter, garrot, inflict pain upon, torment, and torture them, as well as exterminate them by means of a thousand different kinds of the most gruesome atrocities in the world, both new and obscure, the likes of which have never been seen, heard, or read of before and of which I shall give a few examples below. (Las Casas, 1981, p. 12)

Las Casas describes the consequences of such campaigns: 'As a result, of the more than 3 million people of the island of Hispaniola whom I once saw with my very own eyes there are only 200 natives left today.' He goes on to say that not only the people of Haiti but also the inhabitants of San Juan (Puerto Rico) and 30 of its neighbouring islands, Jamaica, Cuba, the Bahamas, and various other islands met the same fate.

> It is a certain and true fact that in those forty years more than 12 million men, women, and children were led to the slaughter in the most foul and gruesome manner through the aforementioned tyrannical and fiendish methods of Christians. In fact, we would not be wrong if we were to quote the number at 15 million.

These words sum up the first stage of colonization in Spanish America, a colonization whose principal effect on the 'discovered' territories was the annihilation of large sections of the population, indeed of whole nations.[1] The Spaniards' behaviour set a standard for countless later colonizations in America, Africa, Asia and Australia, regardless of whether the objectives of such colonizations were gold and silver, ivory, rubber, uranium or diamonds. It was irrelevant to the colonizers whether the inhabitants of the territories to be taken for the 'motherland' defended themselves or not.

Immediately after this relatively short phase, in which the only fate that the population and therefore the labour force could expect was annihilation and which ended as soon as direct pillage and plunder as sources of income threatened to dry up, the conquistadors discovered that Indian labour power was indispensable to them.

This realization did not mean that the programme of extermination was over – overwork as a further form of ethnocide was still to come – but from among the ranks of the conquistadors and from the state itself voices were raised in support of maintaining the labour force as a source of present and future wealth. Adopted for the first time in Spanish America, this strategy has since been employed in many other European colonies.

Indian slavery

> 'It is true, they do not hang everyone! For without the Indians it would never have been possible to mine gold and silver in the regions of Peru...'
>
> (Céspedes, 1982, p. 64)

Columbus planned to supply slaves to the motherland in return for breeding cattle, seeds and foodstuffs from Spain. 'Indian slaves' he wrote, 'could provide cheaper labour for Europe and compensate for the financial expenditure required on overseas expeditions' (Konetzke, 1965, p. 166). During his second voyage in 1495 he took a number of Indians back to Spain in order to sell them there. Although the plan was initially approved by the Crown, permission was suspended a few days later.

The policy of the Spanish Crown towards the enslavement of the Indian peoples was to be nothing if not contradictory. Although there were no large-scale transfers of Indian slave labour to Europe, as Columbus had intended, slavery was the first and in those early days the most important method by which the population in Spanish America was subjugated and exploited. The practice was alternately permitted, restricted, and forbidden by the Crown.

Why did the conquistadors need slavery? Simply because in the long run their expectations and those of the Spanish rulers who took a share in the profits of colonization could not be met from plunder alone. The longer the conquest and colonization lasted, the more interest the Spaniards showed in the labour power of the Indians. In addition to providing personal and domestic services, they demanded that the Indians produce basic foodstuffs and extract gold and silver, for these metals formed the backbone of the Spanish colonial system.

As early as 1494 Columbus began to have gold extracted from the river sand on Hispaniola (Haiti); even then it was normal to use forced labour and literally to work the labourers to death. Naturally, workers could only be recruited by force, and slavery was a form of force already known to the Spanish conquerors and regarded by them as suitable for this purpose. At the end of the Middle Ages slavery was generally considered justifiable in Europe in the following cases:

1. that of prisoners taken in the course of a just war;
2. that of people who had been slaves in their countries of origin;
3. when tribute arrears were paid off through the supply of slaves; and
4. in the case of those who committed offences against the law, morality, or custom (see Kossok and Markov, 1955–56, p. 236).

It was these latter provisions more than any other that served as a pretext for slavery during the colonization of America. This was because ever since Pope Alexander VI Borgia had undertaken his division of the world in 1493 the inhabitants of all known and unknown regions to the east of a specified line had been regarded as Portuguese and all those to the west of the line as Spanish subjects, although individually they were to be regarded as freeborn citizens.

Initially, then, there was no legal basis for the enslavement of the Indian peoples by the conquerors of America, but legalization soon followed. After 1503 the colonizers were legally entitled to enslave any insurgent Indian and in general all those who took up arms against Christianization. In 1504 it became legal to enslave the *indios caribes*, since these were cannibals. As Caribs, the inhabitants of the north coast of South America and its numerous offshore islands, as well as the Lesser Antilles, now faced enslavement, and Venezuela soon became known as the Slave Coast. In 1525 the Emperor further extended the list of those who could be legally enslaved. In a codicil to her will in 1500 Queen Isabella had commanded that no one

> should dare to seize and enslave any Indian from those islands or from that mainland for the purposes of transporting them to this my kingdom, nor for the purposes of despatching them to any other region of the world. Nor should they suffer any injury to body or property.

Nevertheless, in 1505 the Spanish Crown began to profit from slavery, just as it had profited from plunder by means of the double tithe. In 1511 slavery was abolished, not out of any opposition to the institution itself, but because it was recognized that abolition would expand the labour force and therefore increase the colonies' yields and the Crown's income (Häbler, 1895, p. 183).

The year 1513 saw a clearer definition of which Indians could be regarded as having been enslaved in a just war. Henceforth any conqueror entering a new territory would have to read out the so-called *requerimiento*, a long tract which preached the story of the creation and demanded immediate subjugation to Pope and King and acceptance of the Christian faith. Anyone refusing to comply would be enslaved.

The rather loosely worded regulations covering the taking of slaves are, however, no guide to what actually happened. Friederici quotes the following story:

> When Alonso Pérez de Tolosa set out from Venezuela for New Granada every village which the troops came across on the way fell victim to a surprise raid. More often than not a village would be attacked without warning at dawn with the help of horsemen and bloodhounds. There was no question at all that the stipulated *requerimiento*, by means of which the Indians were to be offered peace, friendship and voluntary subjugation, would be read out. The men, those who were unable to escape, were slaughtered or enslaved, the women raped, and they and the children carried off as slaves – at least those who could walk. The

villages were thoroughly looted, and the former owners forced, as slaves, to lug the booty after their masters! ... The chieftains were burned alive, impaled, or torn apart by the dogs, the remainder of the male prisoners killed or enslaved. All others, even newborn babies, were branded as slaves and taken away in a long, continuous chain (*corriente*) in neck irons. The young girls and pretty women were immediately shared out amongst the soldiers for the purpose of rendering them personal services. (Friederici, 1925, pp. 468ff)

Even when it was actually read out, the *requerimiento* was merely a formality, in the same way as the term *indios caribes* was interpreted differently according to each situation.

A typical example of a method used to enslave the Indians is quoted by Häbler:

To some extent the rapidly increasing depopulation of the Greater Antilles may be put down to slave hunts. On the other hand, it served as a pretext for further extending the quest for slaves. Although even the decrees which provided for the transportation to Hispaniola of the populations of most of the islands of the Lesser Antilles did so on the understanding that these Indians would be considered free workers, they nevertheless played a fairly fundamental part in extending slavery for, as the move did not depend on the free will of the Indians concerned, even the slightest hint of refusal to leave their native soil usually provided the pretext for applying the law on armed resistance against Christianization. (Häbler, 1895, pp. 182f)

Forced migration of the kind described here was quite common even in the first few decades of Spanish colonial rule. Indians were also transported to Hispaniola from the Bahamas (*islas inutiles*), 60,000 of them between 1509 and 1519 alone. By 1519 only 800 of these were still living. Such people were not regarded as slaves, but as *naborias perpetuos*, lifelong forced labour not tied to the land. Even if one ignores the fact that such an arrangement was, in effect, the same thing as slavery, it is still not clear what distinguished *naborias perpetuos* from slaves in law (Simpson, 1966, p. 178).

The peoples of the Lesser Antilles, Peru and Nicaragua met the same fate as those from the *islas inutiles*, so called because the Spaniards regarded them as being of no use. Nicaragua supplied Panama and Peru with thousands of slaves, of whom fewer than one in 20 survived, for shipment amounted to a death sentence. The population of Nicaragua was reduced by four fifths: one third were sent abroad and the remainder died in other ways (Sherman, 1971, pp. 25f).

For decades such practices continued unchecked. They had their opponents, the best known of whom was Las Casas, but no effective measures were taken against such forced labour for a long time. In 1526 a decree was issued stating that Indians could only be declared slaves by the governor or the King's officials and could only be branded with the official iron, yet it was 1530 before the first general ban on enslavement was issued and even that applied only to new enslavements. Existing owners were obliged to register their slaves within 30 days. Nevertheless, the colonists opposed these provisions so strongly that they were rescinded in 1534.

In 1537 a papal bull expressly pronounced the Indians 'full people' and in 1541 the purchase of slaves by Spaniards was forbidden. In 1542 the *Leyes Nuevas* (New Laws) in Spanish America both banned the enslavement of further Indians and ordered the release of those already enslaved illegally. In order to prevent their dying out, the text of the laws concerned itself in particular with Indians employed in the pearl fishing industry, which made much use of Indian slaves, and with those employed as bearers (see Engl, 1975, p. 280).

Such laws were an expression of the conflict between the Crown and the conquistadors. Whereas the latter were interested in the private deployment and control of the labour force and short-term profits, the Crown – not least in order to counteract the conquistadors' attempts at gaining independence – had an interest in state control of the labour force and in the long-term maintenance of this source of wealth, i.e. in the reproduction of labour power.

It was another two generations before a halt was called to Indian slavery as a general practice in Spanish America, not least because the administrators responsible for overseeing the application of the law were themselves slave-owners (Sherman, 1971, p. 29). Even after 1542 there were, from time to time, new illegal bouts of enslavement in Spanish America. There were also several legal exceptions to the ban on slavery. In 1608 the captured inhabitants of Chile were enslaved – men and boys from the age of ten and a half and women and girls from the age of nine and a half. Not until 1674 was it decreed that Chile's Indians should no longer be treated in this way (Konetzke, 1965, p. 171).

Indian slavery was the first large-scale system in the history of capitalism to exploit the workers of conquered territories outside Europe to any great extent. Although the Portuguese enslaved the Africans as early as 1445 and did so until roughly the middle of the 16th century, the Indian slavery which followed the discovery of America by far exceeded the enslavement of the African peoples, both in terms of its scale and of its significance.

From an historical point of view, the forced migration of the African peoples was both a prerequisite for and an essential characteristic of their deployment as slaves, yet the practice of shipping workers against their will was also applied to Indian slaves. Indeed, this is one of the reasons that Indian slavery in Spanish America must be regarded as a preliminary stage in the development of the world market for labour power in general and of the transatlantic slave trade in particular.

The ban on Indian slavery of 1542 and its wide acceptance in Spanish America in the subsequent decades did not grant the Indians personal freedom, nor did it eradicate or even limit the over-exploitation of their labour power. If anything, the opposite is true: the *encomienda* and the *mita*, which replaced Indian slavery as the major form of forced labour, by far overshadowed it. For a long time these systems were also more important than African slavery, which only entered its major phase on their abolition.

The forced recruitment of Indian labour: scale and techniques

Alongside Indian slavery and after its abolition, various systems of forced labour were developed and employed in Spanish America. Some derived from the Spanish feudal system, others sprang from Incan institutions or resembled wage labour. In addition there were several forms of hidden forced labour, such as poll taxes and enforced consumption.

The ideological basis shared by these various systems was the assumption that work is a moral duty and has a civilizing effect. As Kontezke points out:

> The first legal provision which stipulated that the Indians had a duty to work was contained in a decree issued by Queen Isabella in 1503. The ruler referred to reports that the natives of the island of Haiti did not want to work, even for wages, but preferred to live as vagrants and eschewed contact with the Spaniards by fleeing, with the result that the Spaniards could find no one to work the land or extract gold. It was now the Queen's wish that the natives be converted to the Christian faith and should, for this purpose, have contact with Christians. Indians and Spaniards were to live together and help each other so that the island might be cultivated and its sources of wealth tapped. Thus the decree provided that the natives could be forced to work and to have contact with Spaniards. (Konetzke, 1965, p. 173)

Even in the 20th century the use of Christianity to legitimize forced labour was a feature common to all colonizations. Academic study of missionary work has not only revealed an alliance between the Crown, the conquistadors, and the Church, but also that the justifications for such procedures were not questioned until centuries later:

> The first task of the Spanish conquistadors and colonizers in the New World was to gather together the Indians, who had hitherto been living wild, and settle them in village communities. This was vital if government and colonial officials were to rope the Indians into the productive process at all and if missionaries were to be guaranteed any degree of success in their work. (Specker, 1951, p. 1)

Table 1
Tributary Indian households (*tributarios*) and Spanish households (*vecinos*) in Spanish America, 1574

Territory	Tributarios	Vecinos
1. Hispaniola	100	962
2. Cuba	292	326
3. Jamaica	0	0
4. Puerto Rico	0	280
5. Venezuela, Cumaná	53,150	203
6. Margarita	No figures	50
7. Trinidad	4,000	0
8. Northeast Brazil*	No figures	0
9. Guatemala	53,694	760
10. El Salvador	14,202	710
11. Honduras	16,155	360
12. Nicaragua	11,337	420
13. Costa Rica	No figures	83
14. Panama	169	745
15. Nuevo Reino de Granada	134,200	1,425
16. Santa Marta	2,400	137
17. Cartagena	7,514	308
18. Popayán	69,800	298
19. Quito	102,200	859
20. Lima	21,217	2,115
21. Huánuco	49,973	300
22. Trujillo	49,582	670
23. Huamanga	46,875	600
24. Cuzco, Puno	110,220	900
25. Arequipa	21,725	425
26. Charcas, Santa Cruz	124,000	853
27. Tucumán	No figures	200
28. Buenos Aires	No figures	–
29. Paraguay	80,000	380
30. Chile	95,400	1,513
31. Mexico	338,872	4,020
32. Tlaxcala, Puebla	201,185	3,150
33. Oaxaca	106,815	380
34. Yucatán, Tabasco	52,371	278
35. Michoacán	96,158	815
36. Nueva Galicia	13,390	1,099
Total	**1,876,996**	**25,624**

* The towns of Belém and San Luis in Northeast Brazil were owned by Spain.

Source: Slicher van Bath, 1979, p. 57.

The tribute

Virtually every inhabitant of America whom the Spaniards were able to conquer was forced to work. Tribute registers reveal the scale of the process and show that the Spaniards succeeded, in less than 100 years, in harnessing a potential labour force the enormity of which was quite remarkable for those times. Table 1 shows the number of Indians registered as liable to the tribute in various parts of Spanish America in 1574.

A tribute was a poll tax the payment of which would take various forms. It could be paid, for example, in the form of gold platters or gold dust, salt, maize, corn, coca, chickens, eggs, fish, or other foodstuffs, as well as in the form of cotton woven goods, gold, silver or labour. Indian men over the age of 16 or 18 were registered as *tributarios* (tributaries), although registration and payment was not uniform. In many regions, for instance, there were large numbers of *indios de guerra*, Indians who had not yet been conquered, and unlike the *indios de paz*, who had already been conquered, the *indios de guerra* refused to pay the tribute. The heads of Spanish families and households were registered as *vecinos*. A typical Indian or Spanish family consisted of four or five people. Thus the fact that 1.9 million Indians were registered as tributaries suggests that the total number of people conquered was somewhere in the region of 8.5 million: 8.5 million people whose labour power was completely or partly at the disposal of the colonizers.

In addition to the conquered Indian workforce, there were already an estimated 31,000 to 40,000 African slaves in Spanish America by 1574.

A comparison with the population of the motherland at the same time reveals the importance of the 'foreign' labour force: in 1541 Spain had a population of only 7.4 million (Zavala, 1962, p. 51). There were far more Indians than Spaniards working to make Spain rich.

The tribute was, however, only a very small part of the products and services which the Indians had to supply. The Spanish colonial empire was founded upon the *ecomienda* in the agricultural sector and the *mita* in the crucial mining sector.

The *encomienda*

Like that of Indian slavery, the birth of forced labour, in particular the *encomienda* (from the Spanish *encomendar*, meaning 'to entrust') can be traced back to the time of Columbus's voyages. At first the conquistadors seized Indians at random to work for them, something that Columbus sought to restrict 'by attempting to prevail upon individual caziques to place their people at the disposal of the Spanish settlers for one or two years so that essential work might be carried out' (Konetzke, 1965, p. 173).

The *encomienda*, which developed rapidly, was derived from the Spanish feudal system and consisted of the Crown assigning a certain number of natives from the conquered territories to deserving conquistadors. The *encomendero* was responsible for the Christianization of those *indios encomendados* tied to his land, and these had to supply both the fruits of their labour and their labour power itself. Under the *encomienda* the natives formally retained their personal freedom.

Not only did the *encomienda* share the birthdate, so to speak, of Indian slavery, it also shared the contradictory attitude of the Spanish Crown to its excessive use and abuse. Simpson characterizes the *encomienda* thus:

> As developed in the Antilles, the encomienda was at first (up to the passage of the New Laws of 1542) the delegation of the royal power to collect the tribute from, *and to use the personal services of*, the King's vassals (the Indians). The encomendero undertook to look after the welfare of his charges and to educate them in the proper (Spanish) norms of conduct, as well as to discharge the usual feudal obligations of bearing arms in the King's defense. In reality, at least the first 50 years of its existence, the encomienda was looked upon by its beneficiaries as a subterfuge for slavery (Simpson, 1966, p. xiii)

The *encomienda* was applied very differently in the different parts of Spanish America, particularly as regards the nature and the quantity of goods to be delivered and work to be done.

The Laws of Burgós of 1513, which constituted the first attempt at a standardized body of legislation on the Indian issue, stipulated that under the *encomienda* Indians should work for nine months of each year for the Spaniards and for the remaining three months of the year should be obliged to till the land and do wage labour. No *encomendero* would be permitted to have more than 150 or less than 40 *indios encomendados* at his disposal. Three quarters of the yield from the *encomienda* would devolve to the *encomendero* and the Crown would receive the remaining quarter.

There was a great deal of disagreement over the hereditary nature of the *encomienda*, which was normally granted for three generations, i.e. up to and including the conquistador's grandchildren. The question remained unresolved until the *encomienda* had outlived its usefulness. The system was abolished by law in 1720, but had already lost a large degree of its significance by this time.

Nevertheless, for the greater part of Spanish rule in America the *encomienda* was the system that permitted the most extensive appropriation of Indian labour power. It was the life nerve of Spanish colonization in America. 'Except for a few favoured groups ... all Indians who were not slaves were given in encomienda, so that the members of every ordinary family were subjected to compulsory labour of one sort or another' (Kloosterboer, 1976, p. 81). The privileged groups alluded to above were those members of the former ruling class who co-operated with the Spaniards. One of the many reasons that the conquistadors found the Indian nobility so useful was its ability to control the conquered population.

The *mita*

'... the silver extracted in Potosi would have been sufficient to build a bridge long enough to link Spain with these *"Indias"* ... A bridge of silver, yes indeed, but parallel to that one could have built another bridge, just as long as the first, out of bones ... out of the bones of the *mita* Indians who died in the mines ...'

(Céspedes, 1982, p. 64)

In economic terms mining, above all the mining of gold and silver, formed the backbone of Spanish colonialism. Unlike Portuguese Brazil, the agricultural sector in Spanish America did not produce goods for export to the motherland and other European countries. Its major concern was to guarantee the extraction of precious metals.

Just as the gold mines in Haiti, which were worked by Indian slaves and had been opened by Columbus, fell into decline the Spaniards 'discovered' rich deposits of silver in Potosi. In 1545 they began to mine there, and by 1573 Potosi boasted a population of 120,000 and was the largest town in the world after London. By 1650 the population had soared to 160,000, but the increase was wholly a result of silver mining. When the deposits were exhausted the town disappeared: by 1825 there were only 8,000 inhabitants.

In the meantime Potosi was a place of untold luxury, and great riches flowed from there to Spain and the rest of Europe. Between 1549 and 1555, 250 tons of silver – 68 per cent of world production at that time – were extracted in Potosi each year. One fifth of all precious metal mined belonged to the Spanish Crown in the form of the double tithe or *quinto*, and according to incomplete official data from the Board of Trade in Seville, 16 million kilograms of silver – three times as much as the entire European reserves – were unloaded in the port of San Lúcar de Barrameda between 1503 and 1660.

The workers who staffed the mining industry were Indians, and were forced into the mines for the first few decades by the *encomienda*.

Encomenderos would bring their Indians to that God-forsaken region and either sell them literally to the mine owners, or put them into a mining company as their share of the capital. In those days anyone who had been granted an *encomienda* was sitting on a goldmine. Nor did those Spaniards who were not busy bundling their Indians off to Potosi have cause for complaint. The value of their property ... had risen tenfold overnight, for Potosi had caused a profitable market to open up for the natural produce supplied by the *indios encomendados* in settlement of the tribute. (Kornberger, 1980, p. 9)

Eventually this particular source of labour power proved insufficient, and the Spaniards resorted to an Incan institution which had originally been a specific form of village teamwork. When the mine owners demanded an additional labour force of 4,500 in 1574 the viceroy introduced the so called *mita*. It was ruled that no *mita* Indian who had worked in a mine for a week could be forced to do so again for another two weeks, since the working conditions at 4,000 metres were extreme. In order to secure a daily workforce of 4,500 it was therefore necessary to bring a total of 13,500 workers to Potosi. The surrounding districts were each placed under an obligation to provide one seventh of their men between the ages of 18 and 50 for one year. After a year in the mines no worker was to be called upon again for seven years. Like those regulating slavery and the *encomienda*, the rules governing the *mita* appeared positively humane in comparison with the actual practice which built up around them.

Silver mining at an altitude of 4,000 metres was strength-sapping work, even during the first few years, when the mines were opencast and the silver could be melted in clay furnaces according to the Incan method. The introduction of the *mita* coincided with the move towards deep mining and the use of quicksilver, which meant that even inferior silver could be mined profitably. To the miners, deep mining meant exposure to constant changes in temperature, from the cold on the *altiplano* to the heat at a depth of several hundred metres. Carrying the silver ore on their backs, they climbed primitive ladders lit by candles, and regularly they fell. Underground there were countless accidents. To the Spaniards, the use of quicksilver represented technical advance, to the Indian workers it meant massive doses of a deadly poison.

> The *mita* resembled a machine with which to crush Indians. The quicksilver used for the purposes of extracting silver by amalgamation was just as likely, if not more likely, to poison the workers as were toxic gases. It caused hair and tooth loss and brought on uncontrollable shaking fits. Those suffering from quicksilver poisoning, the 'quick-silvered', dragged themselves through the streets begging for alms... Because of the smoke from the smelting furnaces no grass or seed grew within a radius of six miles from Potosi, and the gases were no less fatal to the human body. (Galeano, 1980, pp. 52f)

In order to survive just a short time in these conditions the workers consumed huge quantities of coca. Each year Spanish traders brought 100,000 baskets containing a million kilograms of coca leaves to Potosi. The miners paid over their paltry wages for coca and spirits instead of buying food, simply to help them endure their deadly drudgery.

Few *mitayos* lived long enough to return home after their allotted year in Potosi. Barely one fifth survived their first year in the mines. By 1660, when the *mita* had still been in existence for less than a century, the provinces on the *altiplano* had lost 80 per cent of their tributaries. Not one seventh, but up to one third of the men liable to work found themselves in the town of Potosi as a direct result of compulsion.

Yet decreases in the population did not lead to a relaxation of the *mita* but rather to its extension to other provinces; as the output of silver fell the mine owners did not dispense with their *mitayos*, but instead hired them out to others.

The archbishop of Lima, Melchior de Linan (who died in 1704) was in no doubt

> that those precious metals were steeped in the blood of the Indians, that if one were to squeeze the money which had been made out of them more blood than silver would drip out, and that if the compulsory *mita* were not abolished the provinces would be altogether ruined. (cited in Konetzke, 1965, p. 202)

By the end of the 18th century Potosi, the *cerro rico* or 'rich mountain', had itself gone to ruin, and in 1812 the *mita* was abolished. Within the space of 300 years the over-exploitation of the labour force that had accompanied the mining and working of silver ore had cost the lives of a total of eight million forcibly recruited Indian workers (Galeano, 1980, p. 51).

Further methods of acquiring Indian labour
In addition to slavery, tribute work, the *encomienda* and the *mita*, which were undoubtedly the major methods of forcibly recruiting Indian labour, countless other methods were in use in Spanish America. Their nature, names, and dimensions varied from region to region and from year to year. One method by which the Spaniards indirectly deprived the Indians of their labour power was the *reparto mercantil*. Particularly after the decline of Potosi, which had formed a large market, the Indians were forced by Spanish officials to buy, at exorbitant prices, specified quantities of goods which often had no value in use to them at all. Kornberger writes:

> A few even went as far as to force the Indians to buy articles such as the Greek classics, dictionaries of economics, silk stockings, spectacles, and razor blades, for which the beardless Indians had no use whatsoever. (Kornberger, 1980, p. 16)

Several major methods of appropriating labour directly are described briefly below.

1. Transport: tambo, camarico, boga
In an attempt to make up for Spanish America's lack of infrastructure and means of transport the Spaniards enlisted the Indians to carry out transport duties (*tambo* and *camarico*) and ship's duties (*boga*) (Friederici, 1925, p. 486). According to the Spaniards' needs, Indians were employed as bearers or to drive whatever beasts of burden they might own themselves. These duties were additional to their regular work, and over great distances their harshness equalled that of mine work. One 16th-century account

reads:

> By the end of the journey the poor Indians have few cattle left. The majority do not survive the trip and perish, the remainder are cut and weak. By then the Indians have sacrificed their entire fortunes and their own labour, made the journey there and back at their own expense, and have not been available to tend house and home. Despite all this, and this is the worst aspect of it all, they are not excused a single penny of their regular tribute. (Engl, 1975, p. 363)

2. *Domestic service:* yanacona

In addition to the above *ad hoc* methods of recruitment, there were further, institutionalized methods whose objectives were the permanent exploitation of the Indian labour force. Such types of service were covered by the term *yanacona*. 'The word is derived from the Quechua language, in which it referred to a person who worked as a serf in the Incan royal household' (Konetzke, 1965, p. 196). It was used in Spanish America for the various kinds of service into which the Indians were drawn, in particular for domestic service. In the West Indies and in Mexico such servants were known as *naborias*, and Indian servants working in the town houses of landowners in central and southern Peru were called *pongos*. Like agricultural workers tied to the land (*huasipungos* in Ecuador) or those who did the most menial work, such as latrine cleaners (*huataruna*), such servants received no wages. On the bottom rung of the ladder stood the *arrendir*, who worked in turn for the *yanacona*. A few forms of *yanacona* lasted into the 20th century as hereditary servitude (Dieterich, 1981, p. 167). It was, for example, not until 1952 that the *pongeaje* was officially abolished in Bolivia, and in Ecuador comparable forced labour relations existed until the 1970s.

3. *Agriculture:* repartimiento, gananes *and* tlaquehuales, peonaje

One of the methods of recruiting workers for the agricultural sector was the *repartimiento*. The term is sometimes also used to describe the *encomienda* or one of its specific forms (see Konetzke, 1965, pp. 184, 191), but in its narrower sense it describes the post-1549 obligation of rural communities to supply workers to build towns, to regulate water supplies, and to work as agricultural labourers etc. Such workers were controlled by the Crown or, more significantly, by its agents (Grieshaber, 1979, p. 111). Like the *mita*, the *repartimiento* officially relied on the rotation of the labour force.

The *repartimiento* was particularly important in Mexico because of the country's demographic development. In 1518 Mexico had a population of around 25 million. In the course of the conquest and colonial penetration 50 years later, 90 per cent of that population was wiped out, leaving only 2.5 million people still living, and by 1605 this figure had more than halved to one million. It was 1803 before the population once again reached three million (see Grieshaber, 1979, p. 111).

Over a long period, then, workers became increasingly scarce. Not until the slow increase in the population of the 18th and 19th centuries were big landowners who had appropriated property during the demographic decline able to command the services of a growing number of workers who themselves had no access to farmland or other means of production.

It was quite usual until the end of the colonial age for Indians to be forcibly assigned to landowners and this practice was given new impetus in the second half of the 18th century, when the state began to promote an upturn in the economy. Even so, the *repartimiento* was unable to provide big landowners with sufficient workers at any time during Spanish rule (Konetzke, 1965, p. 206).

As a result, the big landowners conducted additional, private recruitment campaigns, and Mexico's labour system experienced a shift from the *encomienda*, through the state-controlled *repartimiento*, to private recruitment. From the beginning of the 17th century big landowners who wished to recruit labour privately would have their bailiffs forcibly round up workers in the *pueblos* (villages).

> Their practice was generally to force money or cattle onto the gullible inhabitants on credit. Since these people were naturally unable to repay such excessive sums of money, the landowner then had an excuse for forcing his debtors to work on his *hacienda*. (Trautmann, 1981, p. 358)

By employing *gananes*, as permanent Indian employees were known, and *tlaquehuales*, who were itinerant workers, the landowners also made use of certain forms of wage labour.

Their major concern was to tie down the scarce labour force, and this they accomplished by paying out advances on wages and loans and forcing the recipients into debt servitude, or *peonaje*. The system, which resembled hereditary debt bondage in that debts devolved to the next generation, was operated widely.

At the beginning of the 20th century *peonaje* was the lot of most Latin American Indians. One estimate for 1911 suggests that one third of the population of Mexico, 80 per cent of the country's agricultural workers, were living under conditions of hereditary debt servitude at that time (Ennew, 1981, p. 13). The Anti-slavery Society regarded such conditions as a form of slavery.

4. *Mining:* naborios[2]

Gold and silver mining in Mexico reached its peak just as Potosi went into decline. During the second half of the 18th century the Guanajuto and Zacatecas mines were the most important in America: in the period between 1760 and 1809 they produced gold and silver to the 1968 value of $5,000 million (Galeano, 1980, p. 47).

Whereas the labour system operating during the major phase of silver mining in Potosi was the *mita*, Mexico's dominant system was a specific form of wage labour practised by the *naborios*.

> The typical Mexican mineworker was officially a free man, geo-
> graphically mobile, and well paid. It was also typical for him to come
> from among the ranks of the *naborios* (free Indians), Indians who were
> not affected by the *encomienda*, the *repartimiento*, or slavery, and often
> by no other system of production. As a class, the *naborios* were born of
> the cataclysmic annihilation of the native population and the economic
> structures which followed the conquest. (Chapa, 1981, p. 513)

The mineworkers received board, lodging, and a wage in the form of
money. In addition, they were entitled to the *pepena*, whereby the best
pieces of ore extracted each day belonged to the worker who made the
highest bid. Later a form of piecework pay in its original form was
introduced whereby a mineworker received a share of the ore which he
extracted over and above a certain level (*partido*).

Chapa points out that the *naborios* working in the mines earned
considerably higher wages than those working on the land. In fact, as those
employed in the Mexican mines during the colonial period were also more
productive than those working under the *encomienda* and *repartimiento*
systems, they must have been well-qualified, well-paid wage workers
(Chapa, 1981, p. 517).

Indian women: forced labour and the forced reproduction of labour power

Academic works on the history of Spanish colonization seldom contain
information about the living and working conditions of Indian women.
The few which mention the female half of the colonized society rarely
contain accounts which deal with Indian women as workers.

Such accounts as exist reveal that women worked in the mines, served as
bearers, toiled on the land, and wove for their colonial masters. The laws of
Burgós, although they were scarcely ever applied, did make reference to the
plight of women and stipulated that they should not be sent to work in the
mines after their fourth month of pregnancy, but instead should be
assigned only light domestic work. Clauses added to the laws after they had
been enacted stated that married women should not be forced to work in
the mines, or anywhere else, unless their husbands were in agreement
(Simpson, 1966, p. 35).

The wording of these protective measures indicates that a considerable
proportion of minework must have been carried out by women, including
pregnant women. Reporting the extent to which female Indian bearers were
over-exploited, the chronicler Pedro Pizarro wrote:

> ... the women from the highlands bore their loads on their backs, just as
> the men did, and carried the tribute wherever their masters commanded.

It was sometimes the case that women in transit with such loads would give birth in the open fields. They would go some way from the road and after the birth they would go in search of a source of water with which to wash the child and themselves. Then they would pick up the newborn baby, place it on top of their load, and go on their way. I have seen that myself many a time! (cited in Engl, 1975, p. 366)

One *ordenanza* passed by the governor of Tucumán in 1576 obliged all Indian women between the ages of 10 and 50 to spend four days each week and ten months each year working for the *encomendero*. On each workday they had to assemble at the marketplace at dawn to pray. They would then be sent to the place where they would do their weaving. Depending on the time of year, this obligatory personal service would last 11 to 14 hours a day (Dieterich, 1981, p. 151). Sherman (1971, p. 25) points out that every form of forced labour to which Indian men were subjected also applied to women and children.

Reports from Mexico and Guatemala reveal that the Indians complained that women were not only forced to do domestic and other work, but also to stand in for their husbands if they were ill, even though women were exempt from the legal obligation to do forced labour.

In Peru such practices were more common still. *Mita* Indians, for example, often had to travel great distances to Potosi. Their families would accompany them and were largely exposed to the same strains and living conditions as the men. One eyewitness reported how 2,000 Indians from one area a hundred miles from Potosi undertook the journey with their wives and children with the result that a total of 7,000 people were in transit for two months. Each family had at least eight to ten llamas in tow, some as many as thirty or forty. In total some 30,000 animals accompanied the families for the purposes of transporting foodstuffs and shelter. Of the 7,000 people who arrived in Potosi, only 2,000 returned home. The rest either died in Potosi or were compelled to remain there because they did not own enough beasts of burden or foodstuffs for the journey back (Kloosterboer, 1976, pp. 91f).

The services which Indian women were expected to render the conquistadors were not, however, restricted to the production and transportation of foodstuffs, textiles, and precious metals. Indian women were also on the receiving end of specific exploitation in the sexual sphere and with regard to the reproduction of the labour force, which at the same time their conquerors were busy wasting and exterminating.

The literature on the subject has sparked off a great deal of discussion of the physical beauty and sexual appeal, or otherwise, attributed to the *indias* by their conquerors (see Friederici, 1925, pp. 212f and Konetzke, 1965, pp. 86f). Mention is made of a 'tribal or racial smell' of regions 'where a whiter skin increases a woman's allure and charm' and of 'natural racial repulsiveness'. Friederici, for instance, gathers together and compares comments on the women of at least 14 separate tribes, islands etc. throughout America (Friederici, 1925, pp. 212f).

These comments, some of which sound positively idyllic, are a transfiguration of that which Indian women, without distinction, were forced to do for the Spaniards from the very beginning of the conquest: to satisfy their sexual desires. As a rule this meant rape, forcibly imposed marriages (the purpose of which was to acquire title to property) and the rendering of personal and domestic services of all kinds. The resulting blend of Spaniard and Indian, and later African, slaves accounts for the population of people of mixed descent now dominant in Latin America.

Women as compulsory gifts
Early on in Spain's conquest of America the conquistadors received women from the native population, these having been presented 'as voluntary or more or less compulsory gifts to the conquerors marching through the country, or handed over in settlement of the tribute or as spoils of war' (Friederici, 1925, p. 500). These girls and women were designated as washerwomen, bakers, cooks or chicha cooks, but also as chambermaids and bedmaids. As a result of Cortez's activities in this field it became part and parcel of the technique of the *conquista* to extort women and girls from the natives (Friederici, 1925, p. 501).

Forcibly imposed marriages
Another method by which the Spaniards were able to procure women was that of forcing or virtually forcing them into marriage. The primary objective of such marriages was the acquisition of title to property belonging to the caziques. Spaniards would marry the sisters or daughters of caziques and would thereby secure land and workers for themselves through their children, since succession often passed through the women in the family (Friederici, 1925, pp. 499, 267).

This device for acquiring land and workers through marriage was recommended both by the Church and by the Crown. A directive from the year 1513 states clearly that, 'In this way all Caziques would quickly become Spaniards and a great deal of expense would be avoided' (Konetzke, 1960, p. 139).

The procurement of women by force
According to Friederici:

> the conquistadors procured far more women for themselves by force than by both of these methods. The forcible abduction of women from villages, from their huts, from the plantations, and from the paths... was commonplace... and the Crown knew it. All such women were forced to satisfy the crude sensuality and lust of the conquerors... During the civil wars the wives of those killed were forcibly married off to the soldiers of the victorious army... Castellanos gives an extremely vivid account of the activities of soldiers from Peru, each of whom travelled with an entire company of female attendants... for women

and horses... were the things which the soldiers were keenest to find. (Friederici, 1925, p. 504)

At another point Friederici writes:

Not a few women and girls were distributed as booty to the Spanish soldiers under the laws of war or were bought as slaves, at least for as long as Indian slavery was still permitted. Such Indian women were placed at the complete disposal of their white masters.

Such accounts would appear to tell the whole story, yet the same sources which document the wholesale rape of the Indian women also maintain that these women took part 'of their own free will'. Friederici (1925, p. 264), for example, begins, 'Since Indian womankind everywhere, weak and in need of love, seemed from the very beginning to be rather favourably disposed towards the Europeans and preferred them to their own men...'. Konetzke goes even further:

Very often a white man did not need to resort to force or seduction in order to procure sex. The Indian women complied with the Europeans' wishes and gave themselves willingly and wantonly. They preferred these foreign invaders, whose strength and superiority made a great impression on them, to the men of their own race. It is said of the native women of Brazil that they considered it a great honour to have sexual relations with the Christians. The first mestizo children would be gazed at in wonder and admired by the mother's entire Indian family. Indian women demonstrated a great devotion and loyalty to their white masters and lovers. Even Indian women who had been abducted preferred to stay with the Spanish soldiers than to return to the members of their own family who came in search of them. (Konetzke, 1965, pp. 89f)

A few pages on the author makes similar claims about the attitudes of women brought to America as slaves from Africa. He also places relationships between Indian women and both Spanish conquistadors and African men forcibly removed from their own countries on the same level:

Some negroes also married Indian women, for the latter preferred these to men of their own race. The fact that Indian women gave themselves so freely to the negroes, whose cheerful and lively temperament they found attractive, expedited the mixing of the races which gave birth to the Sambos or Ochinos, known as Cafusos in Brazil. (Konetzke, 1965, p. 94)

Statements like these – and there are many more – document the sexist and racist nature of male- and European-dominated historiography, which considers only a few, isolated and fragmentary accounts of the lives and work of Indian women to be worth reporting.

The reproduction of labour power
The result of the sexual exploitation of Indian women was the emergence of a new source of labour power reared by them. According to the graphic account given by Friederici (1925, p. 590):

> The Spaniards in the colonies were extraordinarily productive with this mass of women ... In many areas of Spanish America these concubinary relationships, common-law mixed marriages, and legal mixed marriages saved the native population from extinction or extermination. The number of Spaniards, however, who initiated and continued with this mixing process was relatively very small ...

The offspring of these Spaniards did not inherit their fathers' status, but formed a new grouping within society. Mestizos suffered discrimination in Spanish America in many ways. Such discrimination was justified both on downright racist grounds and on the grounds that mestizos were generally born out of wedlock, for the Spaniards seldom married Indian women. The colonial rulers adopted the motto 'A white woman for a wedding, a mulatress for bed, and a black woman to do the work' (cited in Prien, 1978, p. 82).

Mestizos were also without rights, or at least badly handicapped, when it came to inheritance and rarely had access to educational establishments and ecclesiastical or government posts. Many well-respected trades, such as that of the goldsmith, silversmith, gold-beater, blacksmith and veterinary surgeon, did not allow mestizos to become master craftsmen. They were not permitted to carry arms or to 'be seen at the side of people of high rank', and had no vote. In fact, the relationships between Spaniards and Indian women produced a source of labour power which was extensive, 'cheap' and, moreover, hierarchically structured.

The criteria for determining a person's position within this hierarchy were racial. Mestizos were located above Indians, since they were not required to pay the tribute, and above people of African origin, but beneath Spaniards. The multitude of variations which became possible is set out in an official classification containing the accepted order of rank.

Spanish man and Indian woman beget mestizo,
mestizo man and Spanish woman beget castizo,
castizo and Spaniard beget Spaniard,
Spanish man and negro woman beget mulatto,
Spaniard and mulatto beget morisco,
morisco and Spaniard beget albino,
Spaniard and albino beget torna atrás,
Indian man and torna atrás woman beget lobo,
lobo man and Indian woman beget zambaigo,
zambaigo man and Indian woman beget cambujo,
cambujo man and mulatto woman beget albarazado,
albarazado man and mulatto woman beget barcino,

barcino man and mulatto woman beget coyote,
coyote man and Indian woman beget chamiso,
chamiso and mestizo beget coyote mestizo,
coyote mestizo man and mulatto woman beget ahí te estas.
(from Röhrbein and Schulz, 1978, p. 4)

By the end of the colonial era 30 per cent of the population of South America were of mixed race (Konetzke, 1965, p. 95), almost all of them the disinherited sons and daughters of Spaniards, refused access to means of production of every kind and deprived of every opportunity to climb the social ladder. Socially, economically and legally speaking they were neither Spaniards nor Indians and belonged neither to the colonized nor to the colonizers. Gradually people of mixed blood, whose origins lie in a form of exploitation directed exclusively at Indian women, began to replace the exterminated Indian labour force. Today they form the majority among the people of Latin America.

The earliest enslavement of the African peoples

The Spanish American colonial empire was not founded exclusively on the exploitation and annihilation of the Indian labour force. Soon after the conquest of the New World the first blacks were imported by their masters as house slaves. During the first half of the 16th century the Crown repeatedly granted licences allowing several hundreds or even several thousands of African slaves to be brought to America. Even those who viewed the world more critically than most, such as Las Casas and the Hieronymite monks, who observed the destruction of the Indians and hoped to avoid their eventual extinction, pleaded for the importation of Africans, whom they regarded as more robust and more suitable for hard physical labour. As the Indian population declined, the transatlantic slave trade burgeoned. According to one estimate, there were some 40,000 African slaves in Spanish America by 1570. Eighty years later in 1650 this number had risen to around 857,000, and by the end of the colonial era to approximately 2,347,000 (Konetzke, 1965, p. 76).

Prior to the introduction of the *mita* the profitability for the mining industry of black slaves was the subject of a great deal of debate in Spanish America. Wolff (1964, p. 161) writes:

Geronimo de Soria, a mine owner and *encomendero*, put forward an exact calculation in a memorandum. He quoted the price of a pair of slaves as 600 to 800 *castellanos* in Potosi and Porco and calculated the annual yield from their work at 750 *pesos*. Considering the costs, primarily of supervision, of subsistence, and of providing tools, he calculated an annual deficit of 150 *castellanos* per negro which the treasury would have to absorb, thus scotching the very suggestion that negro labour in the mines might be moderately profitable.

The first point to note here is that Geronimo de Soria assumed for the purposes of his calculation of profitability that every slave would perish after only a year or so working in the mines, as did the Indians. Individual mine owners' experience of black slaves confirmed this. The second point to note is that it is clear from the calculation that systems of forced labour that were based on the exploitation of the Indian labour force were as profitable as they were above all because the replacement of the labour force did not require any kind of additional investment on the part of the colonial rulers. As we have already seen, it was the Indian populations in the various provinces that were charged with finding replacements for the *mita* Indians who died in the mines.

Thus in Peru during Spanish rule African slaves were kept in the house mainly for show, or might be employed in a few trades. In coastal regions they were employed as agricultural labourers. Minework, however, devolved primarily on the Indians, since their labour power was 'cheaper'.

Further factors that raised the cost of deploying black slaves were their fierce resistance and regular escape. Armed bands of escaped slaves known as *cimarrones* and occasional uprisings (in Puerto Rico in 1526, in Panama in 1531 and in Mexico in 1537) even led to bans on the import of African slaves into Spanish America.

In fact, the form of slavery to which the African peoples were subjected and which later shaped the world market for labour power was initially developed not in Spanish America but in the Portuguese colony of Brazil, although in general Brazil always lagged way behind the Spanish colonial empire in terms of importance. For a long time no deposits of silver or any other precious metal were discovered in Brazil, and the Portuguese were only able to recruit workers from among the Indian population, which lived chiefly as hunters and gatherers, with great difficulty and then only in small numbers.

Thus in Brazil Indian slavery remained the most common method of exploiting the native labour force for considerably longer than it did in Spanish America. Nevertheless, Indian slavery was only able to satisfy a small proportion of the region's demand for labour, and very early on the import of African slaves formed the economic basis of the colony. 'Black slaves, brought originally from Africa to work on the sugarcane plantations of the northeast', writes Russel-Wood (1982, p. 28), 'became the corner-stones of the Brazilian economy.' By around 1600 Portugal had transformed Brazil into one huge sugar plantation. Estimates of the total number of Africans who had been transported to Brazil before the ban on slave-trading imposed in the region in 1850 range from 3 million to 18 million. Although originally imported for the plantations, African slaves were also deployed in large numbers in the Brazilian mines, though these were opened relatively late. It is estimated that no less than 600,000 blacks were employed in the Brazilian mining industry during the 18th century (Davidson, 1966, p. 16).

Illustration 1
Slave brand marks from notary's documents registered in Lima
(Bowser, 1974, p. 82)

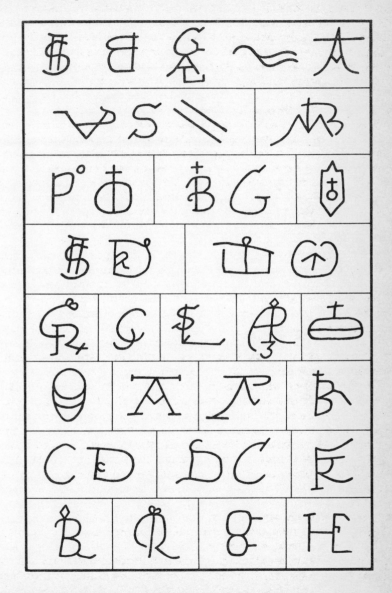

(A series of brand marks such as those in the first line shows that the slave
has changed owner one or more times.)

The effect of the colonization of America on the world market for labour power

At the beginning of the 18th century the Spanish American *imperium* began to disintegrate. Spanish rule was either replaced by new states or, as was the case primarily in the Caribbean and Central America, the Spaniards were ousted by other colonial powers such as Holland, England and France.

This political upheaval had little effect on the lives of the Indian workers. Their Spanish colonial rulers became Peruvian, Ecuadorian or Mexican land and mine owners, and the new English, French and Dutch colonial rulers were barely distinguishable from their Spanish predecessors.

The changes on the world market which accompanied this political upheaval did, however, affect labour systems. Whereas Spanish America had previously engaged in agricultural production almost exclusively for the limited American domestic market, at the beginning of the 18th century it became generally accepted in colonized America that production on plantations should be orientated towards the world market. The majority of the plantation economy's workers were African slaves. In this respect Brazil's role was that of an outrider.

> It was the Portuguese who introduced ... America to sugar plantations and the black slave problem. Later, the English and French established large-scale sugar industries in the West Indies, and the industry also expanded into the southern parts of the English colonies on the American mainland.' (Fieldhouse, 1965, p. 24)

It is impossible to overestimate the importance of Spanish rule for the emergence and development of the world market for labour power. First of all, a great variety of labour systems – as already described – were developed and operated in Spanish America, and in many respects these were the forerunners of methods employed by subsequent colonizers in other continents. Secondly, the Spaniards did not merely exploit the native Indian labour force, they also exterminated it. Densely populated regions farmed by the native population do not lend themselves to the establishment of a plantation economy, and so, in order to make room for the huge plantations, the Spanish embarked upon a programme of genocide, the slaughter of whole nations, the almost complete annihilation of a reservoir of labour power which had appeared inexhaustible at the outset of colonization. As a consequence, the importation of labour power from other continents became not only an option, but an absolute necessity if profitable production were to be maintained.

The extent of depopulation in America
Figures have already been quoted for Mexico which suggest that the decline in population in that country was in the ratio of 25:1. Other authors assume a population of 11 million at the time of the conquest and a low of 1.5

million people in 1650 (Frank, 1968, p. 134), a ratio of around 7:1. This discrepancy offers a brief insight into the disagreement between academics as to the extent of depopulation. Dobyns assumes a ratio of between 20:1 and 25:1 for the whole of America, on the basis of which the population of America before the conquest must have been between 80 and 110 million (cited in Smith, 1970, p. 452). According to Konetzke (1965, p. 104), on the other hand, the most competent scholars in this field are convinced that the population at the beginning of the conquest was a minimum of 8.4 million and a maximum of 50 million Indians. I do not intend to add to this controversy. What is certain is that even if one takes an average of the various calculations the scale of the depopulation of America still stretches the bounds of the human imagination.

The causes of depopulation

Academic disagreement in this area does not, however, merely revolve around the extent, but also the causes of depopulation. Whereas Las Casas, for example, maintains that most of the deaths occurred as a result of Spanish atrocities, more recent literature asserts that 'the disastrously high incidence of death among the Indians' was 'much more a natural occurrence than the result of human wrong' (Konetzke, 1965, p. 106). One 1984 work puts it thus:

> The fact that entire Indian nations were wiped out by diseases introduced from Europe indicates the fundamental significance of epidemiological factors in early colonial history. It reminds us that the course of history was shaped by natural events over which contemporaries had no control and which they did not understand themselves. (Wirz, 1984, p. 17)

I have no wish to dispute the suggestion that diseases introduced from Europe contributed to the extermination of the Indians, but it should not be permitted to obscure the fact that the crucial factors were the barbaric methods used to conquer and oppress the Indians, forced labour, the working conditions, and the loss of culture. Resisting colonization also cost many Indians their lives, particularly after colonial penetration. Suicide, individual or collective, was often their only way out.

Friederici (1925, pp. 298ff) describes a series of such incidents. The many forms of suicide that the Indians employed included the taking of vegetable poisons, jumping from a great height, and refusing all nourishment. In addition:

> The Indians of Brazil, particularly the mission Indians and those who had been enslaved, were able to bring about their own deaths by folding back their tongues and blocking their windpipes. Another form of suicide was rooted in the mental condition known as 'moral depression' whereby an Indian who had resolved to die actually did so in the shortest

possible time without making any external effort to occasion or accelerate his death.

Entire tribes are known to have preferred collective suicide to subjugation, and Friederici cites a whole series of examples, including one case involving '4,000 men and countless women and children'.

A further form of resistance which cost large numbers of Indians their lives was their attempt to conduct an economic war against the Spaniards.

> Thus when the Indians of Haiti, Honduras, Popayán, and other places agreed in their desperation not to grow anything more, in order to force the intolerable tyrants out of the country through lack of food, many of the hated invaders did indeed die, but so too did many more of the natives... and for every ten Spaniards who died there must have been hundreds or thousands of natives to depart this life. (Friederici, 1925, p. 574)

Indian women were endowed with some knowledge of abortion methods, and it is more than likely that these also were employed as a form of resistance and contributed to the fall in population.

Another fact which denies the 'complicity of natural events over which man has no control' is that the Spaniards could see very well that the labour force was reducing in size. They knew too that the cause of this was over-exploitation. Official documents contain repeated references to this, and legislation enacted for the protection of the Indians was an attempt to counter over-exploitation. The Crown and certain sections of the Church endeavoured to guarantee the profitability of the labour force on a long-term basis, but were unable in the final analysis to prevail upon any generation of conquistadors. The interests of the latter were restricted to their own lifetimes and they were not prepared to run the risk of losing their share of the profits.

Thus the over-exploitation which was a feature of colonial labour systems not only continued as the population declined, it also intensified. The question of labour was riddled with contradictions. On the one hand there was an awareness of the fact that the Indians constituted the real wealth of the colony: 'Without *indios*, no Indies' (*Sin indios no hay Indias*) (see Dieterich, 1981, p. 136). On the other, this very wealth, which had undoubtedly appeared inexhaustible in the early days, was destroyed – ultimately through a disregard for economic objectives.

The colonization of America by Spain and Portugal gave birth to the first great colonial empires in the history of capitalism. It was here that 'foreign' labour power was used and exterminated in grand style for the first time ever in an attempt to precipitate primitive accumulation in Europe. The second pillar upon which primitive accumulation rested was not merely international trade, pillage, and plunder, but also the systematic use and exploitation of the labour power of non-European peoples.

The labour systems developed in Spanish America and Portuguese Brazil were the forerunners of the world market for labour power. They paved the way for its first stage, African slavery, and thereby for the first ever large-scale, transcolonial transfer of labour.

Notes

1. This is the case even if the figures quoted are too high. Knight (1978, p. 5), for example, estimates that there were in total no more than three quarters of a million people living on the islands of the Caribbean. Nevertheless, Las Casas's account points out the dimensions of the programme of genocide and the methods used.

2. Chapa's understanding of this term is obviously at variance with that of Konetzke (1965), Häbler (1895) and others. The following details are supplied by Chapa.

2. The Age of Slavery: the Transcontinental Forced Migration of the African Peoples (1700–1850)

'I do not know whether coffee and sugar are vital to Europe's happiness, but I do know that these two foodstuffs have plunged two continents into misery. America has been rendered devoid of human life for the purposes of acquiring land on which to grow them. Africa has been depopulated for the purposes of acquiring a nation to tend them.'

J. H. Bernardin de Saint Pierre, 1773

From about 1700 onwards the enslavement of the African peoples was the principal method by which European societies appropriated foreign labour power for their colonies. By the time the transatlantic slave trade ended in the first half of the 19th century, it had produced probably the largest forced migration in the history of the world. The African labour power that it made available was deployed mainly in the Caribbean, Brazil and the Southern states of the USA, although the course of slavery in these three regions differed considerably. In the Portuguese colony of Brazil, slavery reached its peak around 1650. Whereas more than two thirds of the entire population were slaves between 1530 and 1650, this figure had fallen to 48 per cent by the end of the 18th century and to only 15 per cent by 1872. At this point 1.5 million of Brazil's 9.9 million inhabitants were enslaved Africans. In the Caribbean and the USA, slavery as a labour system did not reach its peak until the 18th and 19th centuries.

By that time Spain had lost its dominant position in the Caribbean and essentially retained only Cuba. The remaining islands and adjacent mainland were shared by various other European powers: Holland's territories included Surinam, Curaçao and Bonaire; France owned Martinique, Haiti, Guadeloupe and French Guiana, and Denmark ruled over several islands. Great Britain, which in addition to Jamaica, Barbados, Antigua, Trinidad, the Bahamas and Bermuda had also taken possession of many smaller islands and parts of the mainland, was now the dominant power in the region.

From the end of the 17th century, each island was typically home to a small group of white residents and a number of slaves many times greater whom they controlled. In Jamaica in 1835 there were 20,000 whites and 310,000 slaves. In Barbados the ratio had reached 17,000 to 47,000 by 1683, and by 1825 the island boasted 15,000 whites and 78,000 slaves. In 1834 Antigua had 2,000 white inhabitants and 29,000 forcibly imported African dwellers, and in Martinique there were 9,000 whites and 78,000 people of African descent (Patterson, 1982, pp. 358ff, pp. 477ff).

As is well known, the future founding states of the USA were also originally British colonies. In 1860 34 per cent of the entire population of the Southern United States of America, or 94 per cent of all blacks living there, were slaves: 3.8 million people out of a total population of 11 million. Although slaves accounted for a lower *percentage* of the total population in the slave states of the USA – the most important of which were Virginia, South and North Carolina, Georgia, Mississippi, Alabama and Louisiana – than they had done in Brazil during its principal slave years, the slaves in these states nevertheless constituted a considerably higher proportion of the *total* number of enslaved African workers than their Brazilian counterparts had ever done.

The above brief overview reveals that although as a system central to the acquisition of labour, slavery was first introduced, developed and tested in Brazil, it reached the most dynamic and extensive stage of its development, appreciably later, in the Caribbean, and in particular in the USA.

> Paradoxically, the capitalist form of the slave economy did not reach its peak until after the abolition of the transatlantic slave trade, and then not in a colony, but in a new country whose leading politicians thought of themselves as pioneers of the bourgeois right to freedom: in the USA, more precisely in the American Southern states between the years of 1830 and 1862. (Wirz, 1984, p. 128)

This chapter deals in detail with the transatlantic slave trade and provides an assessment of the scale and consequences of the transport of labour power from Africa. It outlines the methods of recruitment and mode of transport used and the criteria on which selection was based. There follow several sections on slavery in the Caribbean and in the Southern states of the USA, which aim to explain the differences between and common features of these, the foremost slave-owning societies in modern times, with particular reference to the deployment and importance of African labour power.

The enslavement of the African peoples is probably that aspect of the world market for labour power about which most has been written. Consequently, the following paragraphs are not intended to document the current state of research in this field, nor do they discuss the many contentious issues that it has raised. Instead they are intended to outline those aspects that are characteristic of African slavery as a stage in the world market for labour power.

The transatlantic slave trade

Portuguese sailors began to enslave the African peoples as early as the first half of the 15th century. Whilst sailing along the African coast in search of a sea route to India, they established bases and began trading with the natives, who supplied them with gold and ivory. Gradually, however, the Africans themselves became the commodity most sought after by the Portuguese. They were transported primarily to Europe, where the majority were sold as house slaves, but some found their way into the various trades.

The discovery of America opened up a whole new market, a market in which demand was constantly on the increase. The greater the demand for workers, the more profitable the transatlantic trade became and the greater the competition between the nations of Europe. By the middle of the 16th century, Portugal had lost its monopoly and faced competition from the Dutch, French, English, and various others. During the 18th century, the most important countries involved in the slave trade ranked as follows (Wirz, 1984, p. 25):

1.	England	(41.3%)
2.	Portugal	(29.3%)
3.	France	(19.2%)
4.	Holland	(5.7%)
5.	British North America/USA	(3.2%)
6.	Denmark	(1.2%)
7.	Sweden and Brandenburg	(0.1%)

The transportation of slaves to America soon developed into a complex triangular trade from which the European ports profited greatly. This triangular or circular trade consisted of European ships travelling to Africa laden with cheap, often valueless barter goods, taking on slaves, transporting these to America, selling them, buying up the produce of American slave labour, such as sugar, rum, indigo, rice, coffee and cotton with the proceeds and finally selling these goods at a huge profit in Europe. It continued in this way until its abolition and was dominated by the English. Liverpool, London and Bristol were the major ports out of which it operated.

The duration, development and scale of the slave trade

Although the enslavement and transportation of Africans by Europeans spanned a period of more than 400 years, from 1445 to 1870, the vast majority of enslavements and shipments took place between 1700 and 1850, the period during which first the 'Sugar Islands' of the Caribbean and then the cotton plantations of the Southern states of the USA were at the height of their success. Whereas only around 3 per cent of all slave shipments from Africa took place before 1600 and roughly 16 per cent in the 17th century, more than 52 per cent of all shipments of Africans across the Atlantic took place in the 18th century. Most of these carried slaves to America. The remaining 28.5 per cent of enslavements and transportations took place in the 19th century, the century in which most slave-owning societies abolished slavery and the transatlantic slave trade itself was outlawed (Wirz, 1984, p. 36).

Estimates of the number of slaves imported into America range from 10 to 20 million. The total number of Africans affected, including all those who perished during slave raids or during transportation, is thought to be between 40 and 200 million, although the higher figures often take into account the oriental slave trade, which began long before its European counterpart.

The effects of the slave trade on the societies of the African continent were extreme. The forcible supply to America of workers for the plantation economy and the mining industry were the principal cause of depopulation in African coastal regions. Between 1580 and 1680, before the slave trade reached its peak, 1.5 million people were transported from Angola and the Congo. Some estimates put the figure at 4 million for Angola alone (Loth, 1981, p. 53). For 200 years from 1650 to 1850, the total population of Africa remained static, whereas during the same period the populations of Europe and Asia more than doubled (Rodney, 1976, p. 82). What is more, the decline in population which Africa experienced consisted predominantly of

Diagram 1
A schematic overview of the development of the transatlantic slave trade

(after Ph.D Curtin)

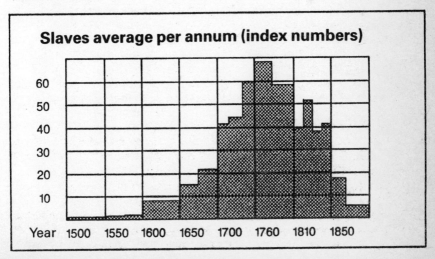

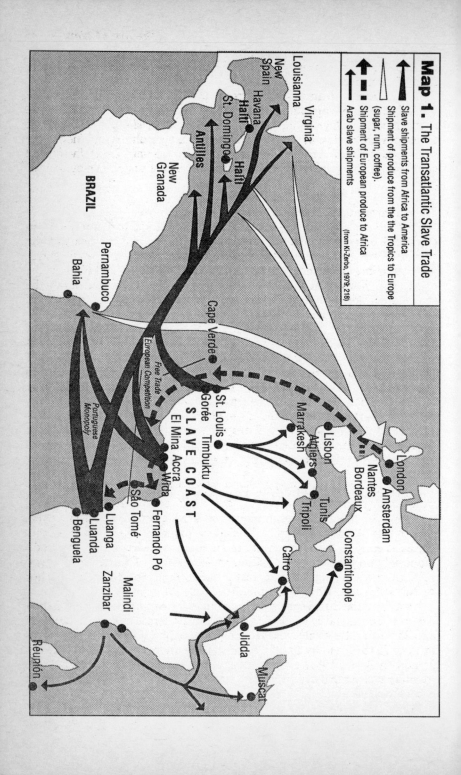

Map 1. The Transatlantic Slave Trade

Slave shipments from Africa to America

Shipment of produce from the Tropics to Europe (sugar, rum, coffee).

Shipment of European produce to Africa

Arab slave shipments

(from Ki-Zerbo, 1978: 218)

Louisianna
New Spain
Havana
St. Domingue
Haiti
Antijles
Virginia
New Granada
Haiti
BRAZIL
Pernambuco
Bahia

Cape Verde
European Competition
Free Trade
Portuguese Monopoly

St. Louis
Gorée
Timbuktu
Marrakesh
El Mina
Accra
SLAVE COAST
Wida
São Tomé
Fernando Pó
Benguela
Luanga
Luanda

Lisbon
Nantes
Bordeaux
London
Amsterdam

Algiers
Tunis
Tripoli
Cairo
Constantinople

Jidda
Muscat
Malindi
Zanzibar
Réunion

the loss of strong, healthy young men and women at the most productive time of their lives.

In addition to transportation itself, the Africans also had to suffer possibly even more appalling attendant phenomena such as slave raids, the flight of entire village communities and tribes, the disintegration of social structures, the decline of craftsmen's trades and agriculture, and the decline and disruption of African domestic trade by barter. These factors all contributed appreciably to the development of the underdevelopment of Africa.

The recruitment, selection, and transportation of slaves

At the time of the transatlantic slave trade Africa had not yet been colonized or penetrated by any European power, and the heart of the continent was completely unfamiliar to the Europeans. As a result, slaves were procured from the fortified bases that had been established on the coast or on offshore islands. A similar system had been operated during the Portuguese monopoly of the slave trade. Later the English, French, and others built their own fortresses.

Davidson (1966, p. 80) distinguishes three phases in the recruitment of African slaves, each characterized by the different methods of recruitment adopted. During the first phase slaves were captured by means of acts of piracy. These developed during the second phase into 'warlike ventures undertaken with the agreement of local chieftains' and ultimately, during the third phase, into a 'more or less amicable partnership' whereby the natives embarked upon expeditions in order that they might take prisoners who could then be sold to the Europeans. As well as selling prisoners of war, the chieftains also enslaved their own subjects. The Europeans traded cheap jewellery, cloth, sometimes gold, spirits and weapons in exchange for people.

The areas of Africa in which slaves were captured were mainly on the west coast, these being the most convenient due to their geographical proximity to America. Mozambique and Madagascar were also affected, since North American ships had sailed to Madagascar and various other places as early as the 17th century in an attempt to circumvent England's monopoly on the purchase of slaves in West Africa. During the 17th and 18th centuries Portugal, having lost ground in the rest of Africa, supplied Brazil with slaves from Mozambique (Loth, 1981, pp. 90, 92).

First of all the Europeans would assemble the captured Africans in their bases. Then the slaves would be valued. The preferred age was between 15 and 25 and a slave's value was reduced by one third if he or she was aged 8 to 15 or 25 to 35 and by a half if he or she was under 8 years old or between 35 and 45 (Loth, 1981, p. 55). In the West African Atlantic seaports the worth to a slaver of a male prisoner was up to 25 per cent higher than that of a female slave.

The choice prisoners were known as *pièces d'Inde*. These had to be aged between 15 and 25, to be free of defect, with all their fingers and teeth, without membranes over their eyes, and in excellent health. They had, of course, also to be male, although a woman with a child under the age of 3 was similarly regarded as a *pièce d'Inde*. Two children aged between 3 and 7 years were also valued highly, and three children aged between 8 and 15 had a value equal to that of two *pièces d'Inde*. To talk of a *pièce d'Inde* is to talk of a specific currency, since this was the term used to describe a piece of Indian cotton measuring 10 to 15 ells in length (Ki-Zerbo, 1979, p. 224; Wirz, 1984, p. 31). Judgement was often pronounced on the slaves' state of health by a doctor permanently stationed at the base concerned or by a doctor who was a permanent member of the ship's crew.

According to an account rendered by one slave ship captain, the procedure for selling slaves was as follows. First, the slaves would be paraded by the African middlemen in order of their value. The ship's doctor would then examine them thoroughly in order to ascertain whether they were in the best possible physical condition. In addition, he would make them jump up and down and stretch out their arms and would examine the insides of their mouths in order to ascertain their age. Beforehand the vendors would have completely shaved the heads of all of the slaves so that grey hairs on the head or in the beard could not betray the fact that some were older than claimed. They would also have rubbed palm oil into their wares, with the result that an old man was distinguishable from a middle-aged man only by the condition of his teeth.

Next the slaves would be examined to make sure that none of them was suffering from smallpox or any sexually transmitted disease with which they might infect the whole cargo. One captain observed, ' . . . our doctor was therefore compelled to examine the most intimate parts of the men's and women's bodies with the utmost care, something which is a great disgrace, but which cannot be avoided' (Mannix, 1971, p. 46).

After having been examined, the slaves sold would be branded with the mark of the relevant shipping line. They would then wait at the base, sometimes for a long time, for the journey to America. It was quite usual for the slaves, naked and chained together in pairs, to be stowed away in their hundreds like freight (Loth, 1981, pp. 103f).

The slavers had elaborate techniques for loading slave ships. On the coast of Guinea competition raged between two schools of thought: that of the 'tight-packers' and that of the 'loose-packers'. The latter worked on the assumption that the slaves on their ships should be allowed a certain amount of space so that they could get somewhat better food and could move around a little, since a greater number of them would then survive the journey and the profit would be higher. The 'tight-packers' worked on the basis that although more slaves died during the approximately two-months' crossing if they were squashed together in the smallest possible space, the profit ultimately proved higher because of the larger cargo which could be accommodated.

The 'tight-packers' had the upper hand, especially after 1750 (see Mannix, 1971, pp. 104f), and countless slaves perished on the crossing through illness, malnutrition or through participation in acts of resistance. Sometimes the captain would even get rid of slaves himself. When the duty payable on the importation of slaves into Brazil became so high that it exceeded the sale price of the 'inferior' slaves, the latter were simply thrown into the sea. Captains who continued to transport human beings across the Atlantic after the slave trade had been outlawed often threw their freight overboard when faced with the imminent seizure of their ships.

It is reasonable to assume that around one third of the slaves transported by the Dutch (Postma, 1979, p. 260) and on average around 15 per cent of those transported by the French (Klein and Engerman, 1979, p. 266) died during the crossing.

Despite the deaths, profits from the slave trade were high, and the price of slaves rose steadily over a long period. During the 17th century the Royal African Company expected to be able to unload slaves at four times their purchase price (Wirz, 1984, p. 33).

The wealth of many European ports was founded on such profits, yet the most important aspect of slavery was not the slave trade, but the deployment of African labour power in America. In principle, whatever the slave traders received on the sale of their 'Indian pieces' was their share in the profits that would be realized through the deployment of the labour power which they sold.

Slavery in the Caribbean

The slave economy in the Caribbean reached its peak at the end of the 18th century. At this time the so-called Sugar Islands were so vital to the French that whereas they were prepared to surrender Canada to the English, they were not willing to hand over their islands in the Caribbean (Wirz, 1984, p. 93). Britain's income from trading with the West Indies is thought to have been four times higher than its income from trading with the rest of the world as a whole (Davidson, 1966, p. 66).

The plantation economy was inseparably linked with the enslavement of the African peoples, and slavery was the labour system it used to facilitate the large-scale production of agricultural goods for export under factory-like conditions (a high degree of capital appropriation, half of which was for the purchase of slaves, extensive division of labour, and high labour intensity) (see Wirz, 1984, p. 107).

During the 16th and 17th centuries debt bondage was also widely used to recruit European workers. Davidson (1966, p. 52) writes:

However, the demand for workers for the West Indies and for the mines in Central America increased rapidly. The conquerors' first reaction was to enslave the native populations, the 'Indians', and these they literally hounded to death. Then they turned their attention once again to Europe and attempted to overcome the shortage which had arisen with

Illustration 2
The layout of a slave ship
(Mannix, 1971, pp. 146ff)

Notes on Illustration 2

The illustration on the opposite page comes from 1791 and shows how slaves were stowed on the Liverpudlian slave ship *Brookes*. The men were stowed on the right-hand side (C), the women on the left (G), and boys in the centre (E). The plan on the left shows a six-feet wide platform on which slaves were arranged 'like books on a shelf', and where they were unable even to sit up. The deck itself (right-hand illustration) is completely covered with rows of bodies.

The extent to which the illustration reflects the reality of travelling in slave ships is confirmed by contemporary reports, according to which the *Brookes* may be regarded as typical of the Liverpudlian slavers. Under a law passed in 1788 and intended to 'humanize' the slave trade, the ship was permitted to transport 454 slaves. Plans were available for many slave ships, and that for the *Brookes*, which consisted of a blueprint of the ship and a host of little black figures, demonstrates how 451 slaves could be stowed. There is no room for the other three slaves that the ship was permitted to transport, yet several witnesses, among them a former ship's doctor on the *Brookes*, testified before the British Parliament that before the 1788 law the ship had made voyages with more than 600 slaves on board.

Other, similar illustrations confirm that this was neither an unrealistic nor an extreme case. It was normal for slaves to be stowed in such a way that they often had less room on the ship than they would have had in a coffin. Nor was it unusual for ships to transport 600 or 700 slaves on one crossing. These would be chained to rough wooden surfaces so that on a rough crossing the skin on their elbows could be chafed to the bone. The women on the slave ships were easy pickings for the seamen. In addition to overcrowding, the slaves had to put up with sadistic punishments, little and bad quality food, and insufficient drinking water (see Mannix, 1962, pp. 104ff).

Often extra decks were built into trading ships in order to accommodate more people. In 1981, Negt and Kluge (p. 343) reproduced the illustration opposite under the title 'The Concept of Realism'. The sub-heading reads: 'Plan to accommodate 451 slaves on the 350-ton ship *Brookes*. The plan is unrealistic. If transported in these conditions all the people would die.'

bondsmen from their own countries, whose status barely differed from that of slaves. When this also proved insufficient they turned their attention to Africa, where they finally found the solution to their problems.

In 1645 Barbados had a white population of around 36,000, of whom approximately 10,000 were held in debt bondage. In addition, there were 6,000 slaves. By 1680 the white population had fallen to 17,000, of whom roughly 2,000 were bondsmen, whereas the African slave population had risen to 46,000 (Wirz, 1984, pp. 95f).

Like the slaves, Europeans held in debt bondage worked under extreme conditions, but unlike the Africans they regained their freedom when their contracts, whose duration was strictly limited, expired (see Wirz, 1984, p. 105). Slavery was, in fact, so widespread that its quantitative aspects considerably reduced the significance of debt bondage.

At the end of the 18th century there were more than a million African slaves living in the French and British Caribbean alone. Their legal status was that of 'things', a fact reflected not only in the English term 'chattel slavery', in which the word 'chattel' means 'possession', but also laid down explicitly in the laws regulating slavery in the French Caribbean. Article XLIV of the *Code Noir* of 1685, which remained in force until 1848, stated: 'We hereby declare that slaves are to be regarded as chattels and as such are part of a man's estate...' (cited in Buch, 1976, p. 23). This status as non-persons was characteristic of the lives of forcibly imported Africans.

Table 2
The French and the British slave population in the Caribbean, 1710–1814 (thousands)

	French	British
1710	88	148
1730	169	219
1750	265	295
1770	379	428
1790	675	480
1805	175[a]	585[b]
1814	178	755

[a] Excluding Haiti, St Lucia and Tobago.

[b] Excluding St Lucia, Tobago, Demerara and Berbice. The figure rises to 715,000 on inclusion of all the aforementioned territories and to 620,000 on inclusion of St Lucia and Tobago alone.

Source: Drescher, 1977, p. 34

The majority of the African slaves in the Caribbean were deployed in the fields. The managerial rule of thumb was that one slave was needed per morgen [approximately two acres – trans.] of sugar cane.

From the mid-18th century onwards, field slaves were divided into three groups, known as 'gangs'. The first and most important contained the strong, adult men and women, the second older slaves, pregnant women, nursing mothers and youths, and the third children. The crack of the overseer's or driver's whip determined the pace at which they worked. Violence and threats were omnipresent.

The limited promotion opportunities open to slaves lay on the one hand in switching to skilled work, for example in one of the craftsmen's trades or sugar refining, which was particularly tiring, and on the other in domestic service. Advancement of this kind was associated with better nourishment, better clothing and better accommodation, but more important it meant liberation from the rhythm of work in the fields. Such opportunities opened up for only a small minority of slaves (see Wirz, 1984, pp. 108f).

Gradually the slaves took over responsibility for supplying their own foodstuffs. On the Sugar Islands, with their monocultures and independence from the mainland, slaves were often given insufficient and monotonous food by the slave owners. In Jamaica the situation improved when the Africans were given land which they were permitted to cultivate on Sundays, Sundays not being working days, and whose yield belonged to them. In law they were unable to acquire property.

According to A. G. Knox, the food grown by the slaves in Jamaica in 1832 accounted for no less than 27 per cent of the island's entire agricultural output and therefore also represented a significant proportion of the food consumed in the white towns. (Ibid., p. 115)

Permitting slaves to meet their own food requirements was, however, a relatively late development, and should not blind us to the fact that the plantation economy of the Caribbean was based on the extreme attrition of human labour power. One third of all Africans imported into Jamaica died within three years of their arrival, and in the French Antilles the figure was more than half. As a rule owners expected a slave to be written off within five years (Wirz, 1984, pp. 97, 108).

The plantation owners of the Caribbean tended to buy adult male slaves. Only a third of those purchased were women, and these fetched a lower price. In Barbados, female slaves fetched only 80 per cent of the prices their male counterparts commanded; in Jamaica the figure was 75 per cent and in Nevis 87 per cent (see Galenson, 1979, p. 248).

For a long time African labour was so cheap and its delivery so smooth that the question of short- and long-term reproduction seemed, to the plantation owners of the Caribbean, unimportant. This attitude had a negative effect on the accommodation, clothing and foodstuffs they provided, the methods of punishment they used, the degree of overwork to which they subjected their slaves and social organization on the plantations.

In 1807 the slave trade was outlawed, and the supply of workers for the plantations essentially cut off. The initial reaction of the planters in the British Caribbean was to establish a slave trade between the colonies of the British West Indies. Between 1807 and 1833 thousands of slaves from islands such as Barbados, which had been settled early on and whose soil was well nigh exhausted, were shipped to newly acquired islands such as Demerara and Trinidad, where the soil was three or four times more fertile and the value of a slave twice as high as in the 'old' colonies (Eltis, 1972, p. 55).

Their second, more important strategy, which they had been pursuing ever since the birth of the abolitionist movement, was an attempt to reproduce black labour power on their own plantations. For reasons of economic rationality 18th-century Caribbean slave owners had shown no interest in the offspring of female slaves. On St Domingue, for example, the fact that only 50 per cent of a mother's labour power was available to the slave owner for a period of 18 months (towards the end of her pregnancy and during lactation) meant a loss of £300 which could not be offset by a 15-month-old child (Hall, 1971, p. 24). It was more profitable, therefore, to buy labour imported from Africa. At the end of the 18th century all this changed.

In 1798 a committee of the parliament of Tobago proposed that the following measures be adopted in order to reduce the importation of slaves:

- A customs duty to be levied on all imported slaves over the age of 25, but the importation of female slaves aged between 8 and 20 to be rewarded by means of a bonus.
- Female slaves to be forbidden by law to take their children into the fields with them, and childcare facilities to be provided on every plantation.
- A comfortable home to be provided on marriage at the expense of the slave owner for young couples, and these to be given cattle to the value of $16–20.
- In addition to their usual Christmas gifts, midwives to receive $1 for every child delivered alive.
- Women not to be required to work in the fields for at least five weeks after giving birth, and then only with written permission from a doctor.
- Mothers of six or more living children to be exempted from work in the fields, and each year six people in a position of responsibility on the plantation with the highest natural increase in the slave population to receive a bonus of between $50 and $100 (Williams, 1962, pp. 60ff).

These endeavours to mobilize the reproductive capacity of black women in a controlled manner were reflected in the planters' changed attitude towards abortion and infanticide. In the early days these had been encouraged, but when the supply of labour from Africa threatened to dry up and did not recover, such acts were forbidden by law. According to Reddock, when the female slaves were required to bear children they refused to do so for approximately five years (Reddock, 1983, p. 130).

The following excerpt from the diary of a West Indian planter written at the beginning of the 19th century demonstrates the interest which the Caribbean slave owners exhibited, after the abolition of the transatlantic slave trade, in the reproduction of slaves on their own plantations. It also shows the way in which black women resisted, and that their action was not widely understood by the slave owners:

> This morning a young, strong, healthy woman miscarried in the eighth month of her pregnancy (neither through any fault of her own nor as the result of an accident), and this is the third time that such misfortune has befallen her. There have been no other signs of pregnancy during the course of the year, and no more than eight out of 150 women are on the breeding list. They are all well dressed and well fed, at no time overworked, and become exempt from every form of labour as soon as they are placed on the breeding list. They are also treated with the greatest possible care and leniency, are rewarded for carrying children the full term, and are therefore anxious to have some. I do not know why they do so badly. Whatever the reason, one thing is certain, and that is that the children do not come. (Cited in Aufhauser, 1974, p. 55)

Slavery in the USA

> 'He [the English king, George III] has waged a cruel war against human nature itself, violating its most sacred rights of life and liberty in the persons of a distant people who never offended him, captivating them and carrying them into slavery in another hemisphere, or to incur miserable deaths in their transportation thither. This practical warfare, the opprobrium of *infidel* powers is the warfare of the *Christian* king of Great Britain. [Determined to keep open a market where men should be bought and sold,] he has prostituted his negative for suppressing every legislative attempt to prohibit or restrain this execrable commerce.'
>
> Thomas Jefferson, Original Draft of the
> Declaration of Independence, 4 July 1776.
> This passage was deleted from
> the final version by agreement.

> 'I have long marvelled that the original draft was not published. In all probability the reason for this is its vehement philippic against negro slavery.'
>
> John Adams, second President of the USA, 1822
> (cited in Wagner, 1947, pp. 72f)

Like many whites, the first 20 Africans to set foot in Jamestown, North America, in 1619 were mainly common bondsmen; only in the decades following their arrival were distinctions between black and white bondsmen institutionalized and African slavery introduced. The state of Virginia did not legally recognize slavery until 1661, relatively late in the day (see Franklin, 1983, pp. 67f), but thereafter black workers were no longer able to regain their freedom on expiry of their contracts, as were white debt bondsmen, and the status of their children depended on whether their black mothers were slaves or free. Over the next few years and decades comparable laws were passed in other British colonies on the North American continent.

Debt bondage remained a relatively important means of recruiting European workers throughout the 17th and 18th centuries. At the end of the colonial age 30 per cent of the white male population of the nascent United States were held in some kind of bondage, 10 to 15 per cent of them in debt bondage (Meuschel, 1981, p. 41).

Slavery did not reach its peak in North America until after the foundation of the USA, in fact some time between 1832 and 1862. During the 18th century the cultivation of tobacco, indigo, rice and sugar had led to the development of a plantation economy in the Southern states and after 1790 these states' leading product was cotton. Soon it was the USA's top export:

> By 1810 cotton was the country's leading export. Henceforth it would account for half, or more, of all American exports. Ultimately the USA's switch to the cultivation of cotton proved an even stronger economic justification for slavery in the USA than anything which had gone before. (Wirz, 1984, p. 136)

The cotton produced in the USA by black workers was of great importance to the expanding English textile industry, the leading branch of England's developing industrial sector, since it was this industry's basic raw material.

Not only were black workers responsible for what would remain the USA's top product until the 1940s, they also played a vital role in bringing into use the new land regularly needed to extend cotton production, and especially in cultivating the soil. Yet although they thus contributed to the rise of the USA as a world power, they were not considered as people even here, but as the goods and chattels of their owners. Not until slaves became legally responsible for their misdemeanours and crimes was there any recognizable legal difference between slaves and cattle (see Meuschel, 1981, p. 33).

Unlike those in the Caribbean, only a small proportion of the slaves in the USA had been imported from Africa. According to Curtin, little more than 400,000 Africans were imported into the USA between 1700 and 1861 (Curtin, 1970, p. 140). At most 6 per cent of the total number of slaves who were shipped across the Atlantic were destined for the USA. As early as the 18th century the slave population in the USA reached the stage at which its growth was 'natural' (see Wirz, 1984, p. 130), with the result that by the time slavery was abolished only around one in ten of the slaves living in the USA had been imported from Africa.

One of the factors which influenced the 'natural' growth of the slave population was that it reduced the cost of acquiring child labour, a commodity which had proved useful for the cultivation of cotton (Hall, 1971, p. 152).

The plantation owners set about breeding black labour in a systematic fashion, and in several states of the USA they were so successful that they even exported this 'product'. South Carolina, for instance, exported slaves to the value of $4 million annually (cf. Genovese, 1972, p. 330), and in 1836 Virginia exported 40,000 slaves and earned $24 million in the process. 'It was, in fact, a huge undertaking, permitted and protected by law, publicized in the newspapers, and recognized as a legitimate branch of production and trade!' (Wilson, 1969, vol. I, p. 101). According to contemporary evidence, the sale of slaves from Virginia accounted to a considerable extent for the wealth of that state and encouraged the further breeding of slaves in order to ensure that the black population there remained sufficiently large. Writing in 1831–2 a Professor Dew (cited in ibid., p. 100) described Virginia as a 'negro-raiser' for other states.

The buildings in which slaves were sold in Maryland and Virginia were highly fortified places, equipped with iron thumbscrews and gags, and decorated with cow hides which were often bloodstained. It was a feature of this trade that black parents had no rights at all to their offspring: 'A year after the importation of slaves from Africa ceased, a court in South Carolina ruled that female slaves had no legal right at all to their children' (Davis, 1982, p. 11).

Whereas in the Caribbean women normally constituted a minority within the slave population (although there were a few plantations which predominantly deployed female labour), the distribution of the sexes in the USA was generally balanced, since women were an indispensable part of the reproductive process. As was the case elsewhere, the majority of both male and female slaves in the USA were agricultural labourers – in the mid-19th century seven out of eight slaves, men as well as women, worked in the agricultural sector.

Women were not granted any privileges as a result of their reproductive role. On the contrary:

> Whenever it was appropriate to exploit them as if they were men they were treated like asexual creatures, but when it was appropriate to exploit them, torment them and oppress them in a way only possible when dealing with women they were confined to their specifically female roles. (Davis, 1982, p. 11)

One example was given by Moses Grandy, writing on the lot of the slave mother:

> On this particular estate nursing mothers, who had to leave their newborn babies at home, suffered so much when their breasts filled with milk that they were unable to keep up with the other workers. I have seen

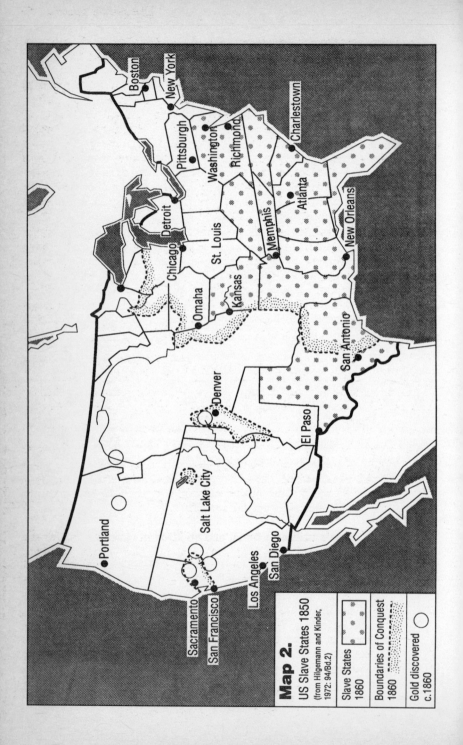

Map 2.
US Slave States 1850
(from Hilgemann and Kinder, 1972: 94/Bd.2)

Slave States
1860

Boundaries of Conquest
1860

Gold discovered
c.1860

Boston
New York
Charlestown
Pittsburgh
Washington
Richmond
Atlanta
Detroit
St. Louis
Memphis
New Orleans
Chicago
Omaha
Kansas
San Antonio
Denver
El Paso
Salt Lake City
San Diego
Portland
Los Angeles
Sacramento
San Francisco

overseers beat them with such brutality that milk and blood flowed from their breasts simultaneously. (Cited in Davis, 1982, p. 14)

The reproductive capacity of female slaves was highly prized, and girls who could be expected to bear 10, 12 or 14 children were much sought after. Nevertheless, they did not profit from the ideological exaltation of motherhood propagated in contemporary white society, but were regarded as tools and breeding stock whose value could be precisely calculated according to their breeding performance. Nor were they exempted from working in the fields, for they were regarded, like men, as full labour units, and only those who were specifically destined for breeding or nursing were occasionally classified as something other than full labour units. Children were counted as quarter labour units.

Even during pregnancy women were not excused from their work in the fields, but had to maintain the same work pace as the men. Women with newborn babies sometimes bound their offspring onto their backs in order not to have to leave them unattended.

Nor were pregnant women spared floggings. Instead, a hole would be dug in the ground, the size of which depended on the size of their unborn babies and over which they would then have to lie. In this way the future black worker would not, if at all possible, be lost.

The most severe punishments which could be meted out to a man were flogging and mutilation. Women, as well as being flogged and mutilated, were also raped. Rape was, to be precise, a naked expression of the slave owner's economic power and the overseer's control over the black woman as a worker. (Davis, 1982, p. 12)

In addition to working as agricultural labourers and in the reproductive sector, black women were also deployed as slaves in coalmines and ironworks, for woodcutting, and in the construction of railroads. Just how important female slaves were to the economies of the Southern states is clearly reflected in the following paragraph:

The slave owners utilized women and children in various ways for the purposes of increasing the competitiveness of goods produced in the Southern states. For one thing it cost less to capitalize and keep enslaved women and children than to employ the best trained men. John Ewing Calhoun, a textile manufacturer from South Carolina, estimated that the cost of keeping slave children was only two thirds that of keeping adult cotton-spinners. Another Carolingian estimated that the difference between the cost of keeping a female and a male slave was greater still than the difference between the cost of maintaining enslaved and free workers. The fact that the business community spoke out so plainly on the subject, supports the argument that by deploying child and female labour they were able to reduce their production costs considerably. (Stwobin, cited in Davis, 1982, p. 235)

Overview:
African slavery and the world market for labour power

1. Scale	at least 10 to 20 million Africans entered America as slaves
2. Chronology	1445–1870. Main phase: 1700–1850
3. Places of origin	the west coast of Africa, Madagascar
4. Destinations	Brazil, the USA, the Caribbean
5. Recruitment	by force; slave hunts also undertaken by African and Arab middlemen
6. Selection criteria	1. health: frequently examined by doctors: height, build, have they survived smallpox (pockmarks), condition of the teeth etc. 2. age: between 15 and 25 3. sex: one third female, two thirds male per shipment, some children
7. Transportation	on foot, slave ships
8. Distribution	via the slave market, lower prices for women and children than for men
9. Nature of work	primarily agricultural, some mining; physically tiring, often dangerous working conditions, working day compulsorily extended to the physical limits, child labour
10. Reproduction	direct (daily): phase 1: through distribution of food phase 2: through the provision of gardens primarily tended by women (Caribbean) Replacement of the labour force: phase 1: through new shipments from Africa phase 2: through attempts at breeding new slaves (USA)
11. Legal status and political rights	legally chattels, the property of slave owners, no freedom of movement, able under exceptional circumstances to keep small amounts of money
12. Social organization	as required by the slave owners: without relatives or with part of the family, as whole families: homes (often communal barracks) segregated from the white population, badly built and equipped
13. Ideological justification	educational aspect of work, Christian-izaticn, redemption from lack of culture and barbarism

After the abolition of slavery

Slavery was abolished in the USA in 1865, yet this did not mean that the four million black workers living there (cf. Franklin, 1983, p. 273) would henceforth enjoy the same rights as did white citizens.

The economic preconditions for equal rights did not exist in the USA, nor were they pursued, and blacks failed even to gain equality in the eyes of the law. Instead, a whole catalogue of measures was developed in order to prevent genuine emancipation. Setting out these measures, Kloosterboer (1976, pp. 57ff) begins with laws passed in the Southern states of the USA, whose objectives were to maintain the availability to the plantation owners of black workers. The most radical of the Black Codes, which varied from state to state, were developed by Louisiana, South Carolina and Mississippi. These forced virtually all 'coloureds' to work for whites, forbade 'vagrancy' and imposed large fines and prison sentences on offenders to boot. Should a black American be unable to pay his fine, he was obliged to work for anyone who would pay the fine in his stead. If he had run away from an employer then that employer would have first refusal on paying the sum and would thereby be assured of his worker. In general, then, any black American unable to pay a fine could be hired out to work for whites. 'Civil officers' were officially obliged to apprehend and return any black worker who had run away. Where runaways were apprehended by members of the public, the reward paid was deducted from the black worker's future wages. Anyone found guilty of encouraging black workers to flee or of aiding and abetting a runaway could reckon with a fine or prison sentence.

A second measure intended to tie the black labour force to the plantations was the apprenticeship system, whereby black minors whose parents were not willing or not in the position to support them remained on the plantations as apprentices. The parents' consent was not necessary.

Third, steps were taken to make it more difficult for black Americans to lease land. Moreover, they were not permitted to have any occupation other than that of plantation worker or domestic servant. The North opposed this last measure, yet despite being declared null and void by a constitutional amendment in 1866, the rule remained in practice in areas where it was supported by a majority of the white population.

Kloosterboer concludes her list by pointing out that very few former slaves were in a position to acquire land of their own. When slavery was abolished in the USA more than half of that country's land was under public ownership. None was given away, and although property prices were low, former slaves could not afford to buy.

Common to all these measures is that they were designed to maintain the availability for work of black Americans, who, no longer slaves, had no option but to sell their labour power to whites as wage workers in order to make a living. Only when measures adopted in the Southern states threatened the availability of workers for the industrialization that was just beginning within its own borders did the North intervene.

Slavery in the USA had several features in common with British West Indian slavery. First, they shared the same colonial origins and, second, they both demonstrated a certain intransigence, which continued to make its presence felt after abolition and distinguished these two systems of slavery from their Latin American, Brazilian counterpart.

In the Latin American colonies the practice of Indian slavery meant that not every slave was an African. Very early on it also became the case that not every African was a slave, since even during the slave era it was possible for blacks to secure their freedom. Some estimates suggest that at the time of emancipation there were already three times more free blacks than enslaved blacks living in Brazil, and that in 1827 Spanish-ruled Cuba was home to 20,000 free black inhabitants – more than lived on all of the British Caribbean islands put together (Tannenbaum, 1972, p. 31).

Furthermore, there was a great deal of mixing of the races in Latin American societies, with the result that the hierarchical structure of society according to race was more complex, less static and less definitive. In the British colonies and the USA, on the other hand, the division of society into black and white remained even after the abolition of slavery.

Naturally, there were also differences between British Caribbean and US slavery. Not least as a result of their considerably greater dependence on the transatlantic slave trade, which had been outlawed at the beginning of the century, the Caribbean islands abolished slavery several decades earlier than the USA. The coolie system was a crucial factor in their ability to do so.

Thus slavery was abolished in 1834 in the British colonies, although only children under the age of six were freed immediately, whilst the remaining blacks had to complete a four- to six-year 'apprenticeship' on the plantation belonging to their former owners. Those who could afford to do so were permitted to buy themselves out of this obligation early – a provision designed to act as an incentive to the blacks to seek wage labour in their free time (Kloosterboer, 1976, p. 3). The so-called apprenticeship was often a period of extra exploitation, since the former slave owners no longer regarded the labour force as chattels and its loss was therefore no longer of concern to them.

When the first batch of former slaves completed their apprenticeships in 1838 it became clear that the Caribbean and British colonies elsewhere faced desperate shortages of labour. Even those former apprentices who remained on the plantations did not work as much as they had done previously, when working days of 18 or 19 hours were not uncommon (cf. Hall, 1971, p. 17), but instead secured their living in the main by working the small fields they had been allocated during the slave era in order to produce foodstuffs. They found additional wage labour largely unnecessary.

Accordingly, attempts were made in the Caribbean, as later in the USA, to tie the black labour force to the plantations by means of laws against 'vagrancy'. In most colonies they were not successful: British Guyana and many islands including Jamaica and Trinidad had free land which the Africans were able to settle and farm. In Jamaica, where more than half the former slaves of the Caribbean lived, over 60 per cent left the plantations at the end of their apprenticeships and settled the island's mountainous central regions. Nevertheless, they were often forced, both by taxes and because they were only permitted to settle land which was of no use to the whites, to seek additional, seasonal work on the plantations (Bogues, 1982, p. 48).

Even where former slaves were able to lease land from the plantation owners, the planters were able to retain at least part of the black labour force, since wages and ground rent were calculated in such a way that many free slaves quickly ran into debt and were forced into bondage (Kloosterboer, 1976, p. 8). On small, densely populated islands such as Antigua, St Kitts and Barbados former slaves were forced to remain on the plantations and continue to work for whites simply by a lack of alternative opportunities.

None of this, however, altered the fact that in general black labour power was now scarce and expensive in the Caribbean. The plantation owners reacted to this new situation, among other ways, by experimenting with new sources of labour. First, they recruited some 40,000 people, Portuguese from Madeira and Africans from the west coast of Africa (Roberts and Byrne, 1966, p. 127), but with sources of labour exhausted in these regions, ships were soon sailing back to the Caribbean all but empty (Green, 1984, p. 17), and workers continued to be scarce. Not until workers were imported from Asia was the problem finally solved. The coolie system, which was developed in the decades immediately preceding abolition, quickly replaced slavery and increased the supply of black labour power both in the Caribbean and in other colonies.

Slavery today

The 19th century saw the abolition of slavery as a legal institution. According to figures published by the Anti-Slavery Society, more than 300 international treaties were signed between 1833 and 1890 to this end. Yet there are still countless forms of exploitation in existence today that are covered by the collective term 'slavery' and also forms of over-exploitation which at the very least rival slavery.

According to a UN convention held in 1956, debt bondage, the exploitation of children, forcibly imposed marriages and so on are all modern forms of slavery. These and many other similar institutions can be found all over the world, and cautious estimates suggest that they affect around 15 million men, women and children worldwide (*Frankfurter Rundschau*, 5 September 1984).

One form of modern slavery found in the Americas is the arrangement whereby Haiti supplies the Dominican Republic with workers to harvest sugar cane. The former territory of Hispaniola is today divided into two states. One of them, the Dominican Republic, whose inhabitants are comparatively light-skinned, supplies the world market with sugar. Haiti, with its dark-skinned inhabitants known as 'Congos', acts as a reservoir of labour power and supplies the workers required to harvest the sugar cane. A quarter of a million Haitians live illegally in the Dominican Republic. At harvest time this labour force is supplemented by 15,000 workers purchased from the Haitian government for $4 a piece. The lack of rights and the degree of over-exploitation to which both groups of workers are subjected and the extreme conditions under which they are forced to live in the sugar cane fields do not differ in any respect from the slavery of past centuries (cf. Lemoine, 1983). Escape is impossible, since the Congos are immediately distinguishable from the lighter-skinned Dominicans.

Some observers even believe that over-exploitation, which manifests itself over generations in a decline in physical strength, may actually have increased since the abolition of slavery. Quoting from a report on Brazil published in 1980, Linhart (1980, pp. 49f) states:

> We paid a visit . . . to the owners of a sugar refinery. They received us on the veranda of their white, colonial-style residence . . . The *casa grande* (the big house) and the *senzales* (slaves' houses) have remained just as they were during the slave era. The manager of the refinery, the owner's son-in-law, gave us a detailed account of the difficulties facing sugar production in the northeast . . . We are trying to estimate the sugar production of the states of Pernambuco and Alagoas. 'Forty-three million 60 kilo packs,' says the manager, 'but from this harvest time on we are planning to change the size of the packs. We are going to reduce the weight of each sack to 50 kilos, because the people are too weak to carry them as they are. Ah! once upon a time things were quite different! The men were strong, and the sacks weighed 80 kilos.' . . . Down below the workers on the second shift enter the factory in small groups. Soon it will be two o'clock in the afternoon, and they have twelve hours of work in 'that infernal steam' in front of them.

Linhart goes on to quote a nutritional scientist who asserts that slaves in the colonial age received better nourishment than today's Brazilian population, since the slave owners naturally sought to preserve the labour power in which they had invested. In the period immediately after the abolition of slavery Brazil endeavoured to check the spread of hunger by allocating the agricultural labourers on the plantations small parcels of land which they were permitted to cultivate as their own, but these were abolished with the emergence of large factories and the export-orientated sugar monoculture. Malnutrition among adults and particularly among the children on the plantations is now reaching enormous proportions. It is they who grow the sugar cane on which Brazilian cars are run: 'The hunger in northeast Brazil,' writes Linhart (1980, p. 53), 'will keep cars all over the country running!'

The perpetuation of slavery in the country has also been noted by Brazilian officials. According to a document published late in 1986, the Ministry for Agricultural Reform and Development has discovered a total of 167 large estates on which agricultural labourers are still retained as slaves. They are predominantly deployed in arable farming. The government document refers to 194 deaths among the agricultural labourers of the Fazendas as a result of violence between May 1985 and November 1986. Checks carried out by the team of inspectors compiling the report revealed that 4,000 workers are held in slave-like conditions in the region of Rondônia in the southern part of the federal state of Amazonas alone. In September 1986 the Brazilian Minister of Labour announced that more than 5 million agricultural workers in Brazil had suffered as a result of violations of the country's labour legislation (*Frankfurter Rundschau*, 29 December 1986).

Such conditions are not peculiar to Brazil or Latin America. Millions of people are also affected on the Indian subcontinent. In October 1985:

A study carried out by a judge uncovered another case of so-called contract workers being imprisoned and treated like slaves by their employers. A judicial report . . . tells how 95 construction workers in the town of Joshiyara were locked into a narrow, dirty metal cage, were denied sufficient food and clean water, and were sometimes forced to work in tunnels filled with poisonous gases . . . According to the study, the workers had to sleep between containers full of cooking oil and vegetables and stocks of rice and wheat in a dark and dirty cage measuring barely 18m × 5m. Several were taken ill and lay on the floor without medical attention. A number of the workers' wages amounted to less than the equivalent of fifteen pence per day. Of the workers questioned by the judge some were not yet 14 years old. The gas had burned their eyes and caused loss of appetite and distended stomachs. (*Frankfurter Rundschau*, 5 October 1985)

The workers had run into debt and were therefore being held in debt bondage. Like many others, they had to pawn themselves to landowners, employers and moneylenders in order to settle family debts. In 1976 the Indian government went as far as to prohibit the pawning of labour power, but to all intents and purposes nothing has changed. Civil rights organizations estimate the number of people coming within the scope of the system at around 5 million. At the beginning of October 1985 the Indian government announced that it had ransomed 173,000 workers so far that year and that 131,000 of these had been rehabilitated – whatever that might mean. At the end of March 1987, news agencies reported that in the previous year the governments of a number of Indian federal states had freed 215,000 people, many of whom had already been held as virtual slaves by their employers for decades. When it comes to putting an end to slavery on the Indian subcontinent such measures are but a drop in the ocean.

Not one of the reports on present-day slavery quoted says anything about whether and to what extent women are affected by this form of compulsion and over-exploitation. There is, of course, no reason to assume that they are untouched by it. Indeed, it is exclusively women who are traded on the 'new slave market' (Schmidt, 1985). This market is concerned not with workers for the agricultural sector or mining, but with women and children as sex objects. It is organized internationally and sells women from Asian, African and Latin American countries to tourists, to Europe and to the USA. Even in cases where the sale results in marriage, it almost always means the woman being forced, to some degree, into prostitution. In 1983 the United Nations Economic and Social Council stated, 'Any trade in women and children is slavery. The trade exists, and its network of business contacts extends throughout the world.'

Slavery was not, as the examples demonstrate, eradicated by the ban imposed on the slave trade or by the abolition of slavery as a legal institution in the 19th century. Nevertheless, these measures marked an important turning-point in the history of the capitalist world market for labour power and the conclusion of the preliminary stage in its evolution. Although not a form of wage labour, slavery is still one of the basic features of capitalist development. In its most distinctive form it transformed black labour power into a commodity. Due to its transcontinental character and the participation of all the major European powers and the USA, an international trade grew up around slavery from which both the USA and Europe profited greatly, first and foremost in that they were able to use directly millions of male and female slaves, and second in that they earned profits from the slave trade and from selling the fruits of slave labour.

During its final phase, after 1820, slavery was superseded in many slave-owning societies by the coolie system. The original American labour force had been all but wiped out and the African peoples forced to migrate. Now it was the turn of the Asian peoples to become victims of exploitation and to be traded on the world market for labour power. The population of yet another continent was to be transformed into a reservoir of labour power and shunted around the world at will. Whereas early Latin American slavery and forced labour had relied on the direct threat and use of violence, which was then backed up for the purposes of enslaving the African peoples by forced migration, the coolie system represented a new departure to the extent that its main tactic was to combine economic pressure and institutional violence with migration and the direct application of physical violence.

3. Coolie Labour as a New Form of Slavery: the Asian Peoples on the World Market for Labour Power (1830–1920)

The emergence, characteristics and scale of the coolie system

'Their cost is not half that of a slave.'
> George Arbuthnot, a plantation owner in Mauritius, speaking to Robert Gladstone on 18 July 1835, after the first Indians had been brought to Mauritius (cited in Tinker, 1974, p. 63)

The derivation and meaning of the term 'coolie'
The coolie system (coolieism) came into being during the second quarter of the 19th century, even before the abolition of slavery.

Today the term 'coolie' is used to describe any overworked and exploited worker, for overwork and exploitation were the very essence of coolieism. There is still some disagreement as to the derivation of the term. The reason that so many possible derivations, some of which are quoted below, have been suggested is that each mirrors a different facet of the system. One suggestion is that the term 'coolie' is derived from a Chinese phrase meaning 'bitter strength' (Brockhaus, 1970), another that it is an Urdu word meaning 'slave' (Oxford, 1933). Both are examples of the way in which the term itself reflects the striking resemblance between coolieism and slavery: for a long time the coolie system was distinguishable from slavery only by its legal status.

A further explanation of the term is that it was originally the name of a tribe in western India known to the Portuguese in the 16th century, and that the latter may then have carried it to southern India and China. It is probable that it then came into use in southern India on account of its similarity to the Tamil verb 'to hire'. Its possible derivation from the name of this Indian tribe, whose members were described above all as thieves, robbers and plunderers, as degenerate and inferior, in short as a 'villainous race', is evidence of the racist tendencies which coolieism and slavery shared. Whereas under slavery it was African, or 'black' labour which was forced onto the world market, under coolieism it was the Asian – 'yellow' or 'brown' – labour force which was exposed to exploitation in the most far-flung corners of the world.

Elsewhere the word is again said to be derived from the name of a western Indian tribe, but this time the crucial factor is that 'its members often hired themselves out as workers abroad' (Meyer, 1975). Finally, the term 'coolie' is said to be a mutation of the Indian word for 'wage labourer'.

These last two alternatives tell us above all that coolieism did not exist in a void – especially with regard to its ideological self-justification. Like many other systems of exploitation, including various forms of forced labour in Latin America, its *modus operandi* was to take a region's indigenous structures, develop them along the lines required by that region's colonial rulers, and carry them to an extreme.

In 1925 Sartorius von Waltershausen defined the term 'coolie labour' thus:

> The term ... was soon being used widely throughout Eastern Asia and Australia to describe emigrants who had committed themselves by contract to work in distant parts for one season or for several years. Accordingly, it covers Indian, Malaysian, Chinese, Polynesian and Japanese coolies, most of whom work in countries situated in the Tropics, but governed by Europeans. For the most part they are employed on the plantations, but also work in the mines as navvies on various kinds of projects, such as railway or canal construction.

The literature in this field often draws no distinction between the terms 'indentured labour', 'contract labour' and 'coolie labour'. In fact, the term 'indentured labour' refers to a clearly defined contractual relationship whereby a migrant worker signs a contract in his/her country of origin which fixes the duration (as a rule five years, but sometimes eight or ten) and remaining terms of employment. It was not possible for an indentured labourer to terminate the contract before expiry, and an actual or alleged breach of contract rendered the worker liable to prosecution.

If, on the other hand, the plantation owner should fail to honour the contract, the worker's chances of enforcing a claim for the few rights granted by that document were slim. Not until relatively late in the day did a legal reform afford workers the opportunity of lodging complaints with the state authorities. Even then an appellant ran the risk of being punished in the likely eventuality that the complaint was dismissed.[1]

To all intents and purposes such contracts meant enslavement, often lasting a lifetime, since many of the workers died before their contracts had expired; others had to make up for the time spent in prison, on the run, or in hospital after the expiry of the agreed term, and still more were made to renew their contracts upon expiry, often under duress.

Indentured labour was anything but free wage labour. It may be seen in its true colours in the words of Sir Thomas Hyslop: 'We want Indians,' he said, 'as indentured labourers but not as free men' (cited in Kondapi, 1951, p. 7).

Asian workers were also recruited for exportation under systems other than indentured labour, such as the *kangany*, *maistry* and credit-ticket systems, all of which we shall examine in connection with emigration from India and China. As a rule, the term 'coolieism' may be regarded as a collective term for these various other systems. Coolieism was not, of course, the only method adopted by Europe for the purposes of harnessing the labour power of Asia for its own benefit. The 'state slavery' introduced when the Dutch colonized Java is just one noted example of a relatively early method aimed directly at exploiting the labour force other than by means of forced migration. As one of the major stages in the development of the world market for labour power in its *direct* form, however, it is the coolie system on which this chapter will concentrate.

The causes and function of the coolie system
After the abolition of slavery as a legal institution, the export of Asian workers became far more important to many of the colonial societies that formerly had owned slaves. For one thing it enabled them to stock up on black labour power, for another it created competition among the free black workers and therefore facilitated the holding down or further cutting of their wages.

This was not, however, the only function of the coolie system, for it was also of vital significance in those colonial societies such as Australia which had not previously acquired their labour power through the transatlantic slave trade.

Coolieism was a mixture of various labour systems and stood somewhere between slavery, forced labour and debt bondage on the one hand and free wage labour on the other. It contained elements of all these systems, and each of its various forms (indentured labour, credit-ticket system, etc.) differed from the others by the extent to which it was influenced by one or the other of those elements. The economic, social and legal similarities between slavery and the coolie system, especially in its preliminary phase, were unmistakable.

The abolition of slavery as a legal institution came during a period of intensive colonization in Asia and Africa, and as a result of that colonization a large proportion of the populations of both continents was transformed into workers for the capitalist metropole and forced to supply raw materials to the developing industries of Europe and the USA.

The colonization of previously uncolonized regions of Asia was the earlier of the two developments. The British colonial rulers had begun to prepare the ground for a massive liberation of workers back in the 17th century, yet in the 19th century many of these workers still had to be forced by means of direct compulsion to offer their labour as 'coolies' on the world market for labour power.

India has not always been a country whose major contribution to the world market was raw materials. In fact, from the beginning of colonial history until the beginning of the last century India not only supplied herbs and drugs, but also the fruits of its inhabitants' diligence in the industrial sector, textile goods such as mousseline and calico. (Pelzer, 1935, p. 10)

By the 19th century, British rule had virtually bankrupted India's economy. The very devices which caused underdevelopment in India also had the effect of assigning to the subcontinent the role of supplier to the world market of both raw materials and that commodity with which we are concerned, human labour power, for the world market for labour power was one of the markets which the colonial powers hoped to expand.

Those devices included robbery, war and plunder, but also certain economic and customs policies, the break-up of village communities, the dismantling of social structures and the neglect of public works. The fall into decay of the irrigation system, which is a prerequisite for agricultural production in many parts of Asia, and the simultaneous destruction of various handicrafts and nascent industries, all of which forced the population back onto the land, are just two of the processes which have regularly permitted famine to take a hold in India since the end of the 18th century. Famine raged in 1770, 1784, 1804, 1837 and 1861 in Bengal and northern India, and in 1877, 1878, 1889, 1892 and 1897 until 1900 in other parts of India. In 1834 Lord Cornwallis claimed that one third of the regions of Hindustan that were controlled by the East India Company and that had once been densely populated were now nothing more than jungles inhabited only by wild animals.

Thus at the beginning of the 19th century there were millions of Indian workers who no longer had access to the means of production. Their numbers increased with each famine.

Many other Asian countries received similar treatment, though not all had been claimed as a colony by a European power, as had India. Under the Treaty of Nanking in 1842, China surrendered Hong Kong to the British, and Canton, Shanghai, Amoy, Fuzhou and Ningbo were opened up to service the opium trade. At this time the capitalist nations regarded China as an inexhaustible source of cheap labour. Its ports not only handled opium imports, they also witnessed the export of Chinese workers to all parts of the world.

The second half of the 19th century saw the tapping of new reservoirs of living labour power in Asia: Oceania, Java and even Japan supplied coolies for colonial production in various parts of the world. These were employed to cultivate sugar, coffee, tea, rubber, tobacco and cotton on the plantations, to mine gold, diamonds and tin, as pearl divers, in the construction of railways, roads and canals, and also as domestic servants.

Coolie labour: its regions of origin and destination
As the rulers of India, the English had sole control over the second largest supplier of coolie labour in the world, the first being China. They used this reservoir of labour power first and foremost for their own colonies in America, Asia, Africa and Australia, but from time to time they also

The import of coolies: the host countries

British colonies:
British Guyana (Demerara) (1) (2)
Trinidad (1) and Tobago (2)
Grenada (1)
St Lucia (1)
St Vincent (1)
Jamaica (1)
Antigua (5)
Nevis and St Kitts (1)
Canada (British Columbia) (3)
Uganda (1) (2)
Natal (1) (2)
Transvaal (3)
Cape Province (1)
Mauritius (1) (2)
Australia (especially Queensland) (1)
New Zealand (1)
Fiji (1) (2)
British North Borneo (2)
Ceylon (1) (2)
Burma (1) (2)
Assam (1)
British Malaya (Straits Settlements
and Malay states) (1) (2) (3)

French colonies:
Réunión (1) (2)
Martinique (1) (2)
Guadeloupe (1) (2)
French Guiana (Cayenne) (1) (2)
Madagascar (2)
Society Islands (1)
New Caledonia (2)

Indochina (7)
French Polynesia (8)

German colonies:
Samoa (1)
Nauru (3) (8)
New Guinea (1)

Dutch colonies:
Dutch Guiana (Surinam) (1) (2)
Dutch East Indies (especially
Sumatra, Banka, Bilitung) (6)

Danish colonies:
St Croix (1) (2)

Spanish colonies:
Cuba (3) (4)

Portuguese colonies:
Mozambique (2)

Belgian colonies:
Congo (1)

Others:
USA (California) (4)
Hawaii (1)
Panama (4)
Peru (4)
Chile (4)
Philippines (1)
Thailand (7)

Sources: (1) Sartorius, 1925; (2) Tinker, 1974; (3) Campbell, 1923; (4) Kung, 1962; (5) Roberts and Byrne, 1966; (6) Pelzer, 1935; (7) Weggel, 1983; (8) Graves, 1984.

permitted the recruitment of workers by other colonial powers. These colonial powers recruited workers from other areas too. During the 19th century and the first few decades of the 20th century, workers from India, China, Japan and Java were despatched to every continent with the exception of Europe.

The following page contains a table showing the regions into which coolies were imported. Though the list is undoubtedly incomplete, it nevertheless contains the names of more than 40 different countries which imported coolie labour. Coolies were despatched not only to the British colonies in various parts of the world, but also to colonial territories owned by France, Germany, Denmark, Spain, Portugal, The Netherlands and Belgium, as well as to the USA and her non-self-governing territories. The complexity of the migration process becomes apparent when one considers the fact that there were five major suppliers of coolie labour, that some territories imported workers from more than one country and that there was also a certain amount of migration between the host countries.

It must be said that the coolie system has been totally neglected in the more recent German literature in this general field. Indeed, there have been few treatises written on the subject in German at all. There has, on the other hand, been a great deal written on the subject in the English language, including in the recent past (see Saunders, 1984; Marks and Richardson, 1984, and so on). As a rule, however, such works deal with one particular country of origin or host country. There is, to my knowledge, no comprehensive account of the coolie migrations and coolie labour in the 19th and 20th centuries.

The scale of coolie migration

The statistics available on the subject of coolie migration are fragmentary and complex. They were compiled in the various regions affected and during the various phases of coolie migration with different considerations in mind and using different methods. A great many were compiled illegally. In addition, the privateers kept no records of the number of workers ensnared. The fact that to some extent coolie migrations were also of a seasonal nature makes a total estimate of the numbers involved more difficult still.

The following selection of basic data[2] is intended to give the reader a rough idea of the scale of the phenomenon as it affected India.

– Between 1834 and 1867, 366,000 Indian indentured labourers were exported to Mauritius, although in subsequent years the number of arrivals fell. In 1924, 255,000 Indians were living on the island, of whom 23,000 were still indentured.
– Between 1838 and 1918, 430,000 Indian workers were imported into seven British colonies in the Caribbean, including British Guiana. The majority were indentured workers.
– Between 1879 and 1916, 60,965 Indian coolies were imported to work on the plantations of Fiji.
– Between 1870 and 1900, 700,000 to 750,000 Indian workers arrived on the tea plantations of Assam.

The following figures, which take in men, women and children, relate specifically to Assam:

1865	100,000 coolies
1880	187,000 coolies
1885	291,000 coolies
1890	408,000 coolies
1900	662,500 coolies
1910	763,000 coolies
1920	1,011,000 coolies
1930	1,065,000 coolies

The tea-producing districts of India, most of them situated in Assam, were British India's leading plantation regions. Here migrant workers toiled and lived under the same conditions as those in overseas territories.

– The following data give an idea of the scale of coolie migration from India and Burma. Between 1913 and 1929, 4,580,730 Indians, including 311,400 women and 201,944 children, arrived in Rangoon. During the same period 3,456,985 Indians sailed from Burmese ports. The difference between the two figures is 1,123,745 people. In 1921 there were 887,000 Indians registered in Burma.

– By 1877 there were already 380,000 Indians working the plantations of Ceylon. By 1901 the number of Indians living on the island's plantations had risen to 404,000, and by 1931 to 693,000. During the period between 1843 and 1877, 1,954,000 men, 367,000 women and 120,000 children arrived in Ceylon. During the subsequent decades the following numbers were registered in the colony:

1871–1880	1,025,000 people
1881–1890	578,000 people
1891–1900	1,210,000 people
1901–1910	953,000 people
1911–1920	873,000 people
1921–1930	1,065,000 people

The extent of both migration to and remigration from the various colonies was determined by the state of that colony's plantation economy.

– In 1931 there were 624,000 Indians living in Malaya. Between 1921 and 1930, 622,772 Indian workers were imported into Malaya through the Immigration Fund.

It is possible to calculate from these figures, which do not take into account the emigration of Indians to the French colonies, that at least 5 million Indian workers left their country of origin as coolies. Table 3 gives an estimate of the total number of emigrants and remigrants affected during the period between 1834 and 1937 and includes:

– workers who left the country as indentured labourers, the signing of indentures being legal until 1916;
– workers who migrated, generally for short periods, under the *kangany* system (mainly between 1890 and 1920);
– free workers who went abroad as seasonal workers in the 1920s and 1930s;
– the so-called 'trader migration' which accompanied the coolie migrations. Those involved in this form of migration were retailers,

businessmen, pedlars, moneylenders and so on and were few in number.

Table 3
Estimated total migration to and from India, 1834–1937[a] (1000s)

Year	Emigrants	Returned migrants	Net[b]
1834–35	62	52	10
1836–40	188	142	46
1841–45	240	167	72
1846–50	247	189	58
1851–55	357	249	108
1856–60	618	431	187
1861–65	793	594	199
1866–70	976	778	197
1871–75	1,235	958	277
1876–80	1,505	1,233	272
1881–85	1,545	1,208	337
1886–90	1,461	1,204	256
1891–95	2,326	1,536	790
1896–1900	1,962	1,268	694
1901–05	1,428	957	471
1906–10	1,864	1,482	383
1911–15	2,483	1,868	615
1916–20	2,087	1,867	220
1921–25	2,762	2,216	547
1926–30	3,298	2,857	441
1931–35	1,940	2,093	−162
1936–37	815	755	59
Total	**30,192**	**24,104**	**6,077**

[a] These estimates, prepared by the writer on the basis of migration data and census statistics in India and in the countries of destination, are extremely rough and should not be taken literally, particularly for the earlier years.
[b] Net migration refers to *net emigration*. The figures do not always correspond to the exact difference between the first two columns because of rounding.

Source: Davis, 1951, p. 99

Table 3 reveals that more than 30 million people left India as coolies within the space of a century. The majority went to work on plantations established by the Europeans and under conditions almost identical to those of slavery. The table also records just under 24 million returns. To some extent this is a function of the seasonal nature of the later migrations in particular, but may also include the children and grandchildren of the original emigrants. Either way, the table shows a net outflow of 6 million workers, though this may be regarded as the minimum number of Indian coolies actually affected. The figures do not take into account the number of coolie migrations that took place within British India and in particular to Assam.

In attempting to determine the approximate total number of people involved in coolie migrations it is also necessary to take into consideration the other countries that supplied coolie labour.[3]

- Between 1840 and 1915 around 420,000 Melanesians and Micronesians were forced into indentured labour.
- Between 1847 and 1874 half a million Chinese coolies left China to work abroad.
- Between 1904 and 1907, 63,000 Chinese workers were imported into the Transvaal.
- In 1925 Sartorius von Waltershausen stated that 180,000 Chinese coolies emigrated annually to the Straits Settlements and the Malay States alone, of whom only 140,000 returned.
- Between 1928 and 1937, 2.8 million Chinese contract labourers emigrated to Malaya and 2.4 million returned to China.
- Between 1888 and 1931, 305,000 Chinese workers were imported to work on the plantations of eastern Sumatra. During the same period 117,800 returned to China.
- Chinese contract labourers were also employed in Siam. Some 154,000 arrived in the peak year of 1927/8 alone.
- The following figures show the number of Javanese contract labourers in eastern Sumatra during the late 19th and early 20th centuries:

1883	1,771
1893	180,000
1898	22,256
1906	33,802
1913	118,517
1920	209,459
1930	234,554

In 1931 there were 399,868 Javanese workers employed in overseas territories owned by the Dutch.
- On average around three quarters of a million people were involved in labour migrations within Southeast Asia each year. Map 4 gives an overall impression of the process. The majority of the migrations were seasonal, and though the migrants often travelled great distances, they did not generally pass beyond the borders of the Asian continent.
- In addition, there were also somewhere in the region of 200,000 Japanese coolies, most of whom were employed in America.

As well as Indian coolies, then, there were another 5 or 6 million workers at least from other parts of Asia employed under the coolie system to build infrastructure and to produce goods for the world market either on the plantations or in the mines. The total number of men, women and children sent abroad as coolies cannot have been less than 12 million, and an

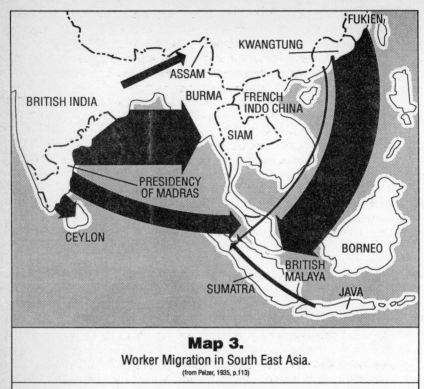

Map 3.
Worker Migration in South East Asia.
(from Pelzer, 1935, p.113)

Principal trends and average annual volume during the period from 1920 to 1930

An arrow thickness of 0.5mm represents the migration of 10,000 people.

← ——— 10,000 people   100,000 people

estimate of 37 million or more would not be entirely without foundation. Davis (1951, p. 102) attempts to assess the significance of the system, though he restricts his comments to Indian coolies: ' . . . the movement from India,' he writes, 'made up the major share of migration to the British colonies. It eclipsed in magnitude, if not in its permanent effects, the slave migration that preceded it.' Thus both the scale and significance of the coolie system were at least comparable to those of slavery. What is more, the newer system also surpassed the older in its intensity, for unlike African slavery, which was spread over several centuries, many millions of Asian coolies were recruited and exploited within the space of only a hundred years.

In the following sections, which are organized by country of origin, we will look at the basic features of those structures which characterize this stage in the development of the world market for labour power. When considering the export of coolies from India, I will also endeavour to outline what the coolie system meant for women.

Indian coolies

India's export of coolies, which began in the 1830s, had been preceded during the second half of the 18th century by the sale of Indians from the south of the country as slaves. Demand for these slaves had been great, not only in the British colonies, but also in those belonging to the French and the Dutch – and it was met. By 1800 there were some 6,000 Indian slaves working on the plantations of Mauritius, and thousands of enslaved Indians were held in the French colony of Réunión.

The abolition of slavery in India in 1833 (cf. Chattopadhyay, 1959, p. 60) ushered in the great age of coolie exportation, and Mauritius was among the first colonies to recruit Indian workers as coolies. The first shipments left in 1834. Once again it was not only the British who availed themselves of India's reservoir of labour power: the colonial authorities also permitted the recruitment of coolies in India for other colonies, primarily those owned by the French and Dutch. Whereas the French colonies were forbidden to recruit between 1878 and 1884, the Dutch colony of Surinam did not even begin to import Indian coolies until 1873, the year in which former slaves ended their 'apprenticeships'. Although shipments were interrupted for two years between 1875 and 1877, they then continued until 1916.[4] It has been estimated that in 1921 there were 2.5 million Indians living abroad, of whom 2 million came originally from the Presidency of Madras.

The port of Madras was the principal port of shipment for workers recruited in the Presidency; other ports of embarcation included Pondicherry, Karikal, Negapattam and Mandapam. In addition, many coolies came from northern India, for which Calcutta served as the port of shipment. Numerous others came from a district in the Presidency of

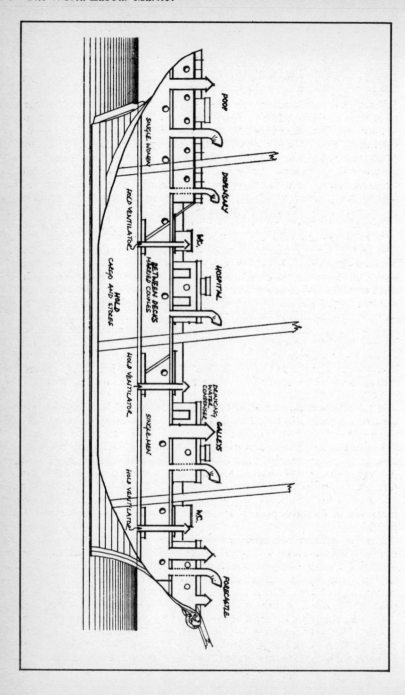

Notes to Illustration 3

This longitudinal section of a coolie ship dates from around 1880 and is therefore a hundred years more recent than the plans of slave ships.

Before the introduction of steam ships it took considerably longer to transport a coolie from India to his future place of employment than it had taken to transport slaves across the Atlantic, a journey for which four to six weeks had been usual. According to Tinker (1974, p. 154), optimum travelling times for the 1870s included 26 weeks for the journey from Calcutta to Jamaica, 25 weeks from Bombay or Madras to Jamaica, 12 weeks from Calcutta to Natal, and 8 to 10 weeks from Calcutta to Mauritius or Réunión. For the 9,000-mile-long journey from Macao to Callao in Peru, Chinese coolies could expect to be at sea for an average of 120 days (Kung, 1962, p. 17). These travelling times were shortened considerably when steam ships were introduced, since these were not only faster, but could also take different routes, yet even at the beginning of the 20th century some journeys still took two months. Coolies were transported, as the slaves had been, on the 'tween deck. They were generally allowed on deck during the day, but during storms the hatches, from which makeshift steps led to the 'tween deck, were closed and made water-and air-tight. Schmidt (1938, p. 213) maintains that after two days in which 400 people were locked up in this way on a sailing ship seven or eight deaths were certain.

What is more, coolies were transported by sailing ships long after these had been replaced on most other passenger routes by steam ships. The demand for coolies was relatively constant, as was their price, and as a result the use of sailing ships continued to be worthwhile for as long as their freight charges for human cargoes were even a little lower than those of steam ships (Tinker, 1974, p. 145).

After a while the British colonial government in India laid down the conditions under which Indian workers could be transported as part of a programme of controlled emigration. In order to reduce the high mortality rates it was ruled that 72 cubic feet should be available for each adult coolie on the ship. From this it can be calculated that ships were permitted to carry 1.4 coolies per register ton. In the slave trade it had long been the practice to load two or three slaves per register ton. The law of 1788, on the basis of which the plan for accommodating slaves on the *Brookes* had been prepared, laid down a maximum of 1.8 slaves per register ton for the British slave trade (Wirz, 1984, p. 37).

The bigger ships that came into service after 1850 transported coolies and freight at the same time. The biggest ship to sail to Mauritius during the second half of 1854 was the 815-ton *Kent*. It had 309 coolies on board. The smallest ship (330 tons) carried 195 coolies and some additional freight (Tinker, 1974, p. 146). According to Barth (1964, p. 61), one 350-ton ship generally transported more than 500 Chinese coolies to the USA on each journey and took $37,000 in fares.

Only gradually did the conditions under which coolies were transported begin to differ from those under which slaves had been shipped abroad – especially if one regards the somewhat greater amount of space available to them on the ship as being offset by the longer journey. The major difference was that unlike slaves many coolies paid their own fares.

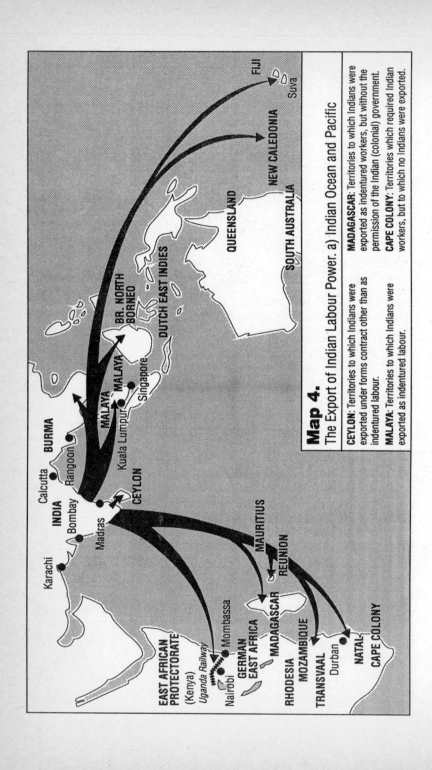

Map 4.
The Export of Indian Labour Power. a) Indian Ocean and Pacific

CEYLON: Territories to which Indians were exported under forms contract other than as indentured labour.

MALAYA: Territories to which Indians were exported as indentured labour.

MADAGASCAR: Territories to which Indians were exported as indentured workers, but without the permission of the Indian (colonial) government.

CAPE COLONY: Territories which required Indian workers, but to which no Indians were exported.

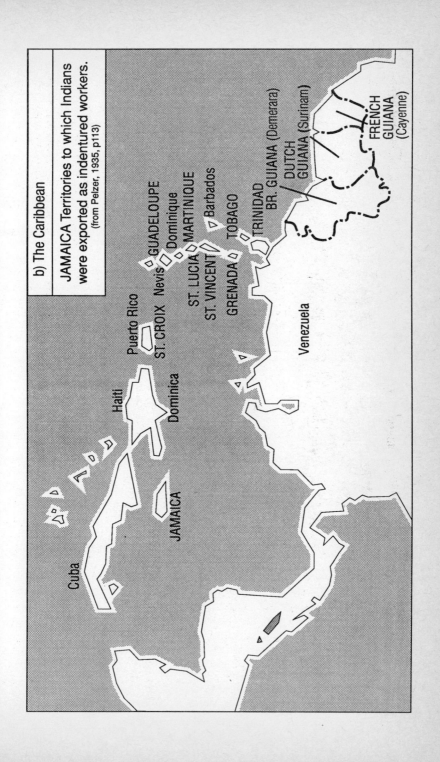

b) The Caribbean

JAMAICA Territories to which Indians were exported as indentured workers.
(from Pelzer, 1935, p113)

Cuba

Haiti

Puerto Rico

JAMAICA

Dominica

ST. CROIX   Nevis

GUADELOUPE

Dominique

MARTINIQUE

ST. LUCIA

Barbados

ST. VINCENT

TOBAGO

GRENADA

TRINIDAD

BR. GUIANA (Demerara)

DUTCH
GUIANA (Surinam)

FRENCH
GUIANA
(Cayenne)

Venezuela

Bombay and departed from the port of Bombay. In some of the ports, including Delhi, Lucknow, Allahabad and Benares, there were assembly camps for coolies waiting to continue their journeys.

The conditions which coolies were forced to endure during their voyages to the numerous distant host countries hardly differed at all from those on the early slave ships. In 1856/7 the average death rate for coolies *en route* from India to the Caribbean was 17 per cent. On one voyage it reached 31 per cent, and on another 28 per cent. When considering the total number of deaths which occurred during transportation it is worth remembering that the individual and average rates quoted here refer only to ships which actually arrived at their port of destination. Thousands of coolies perished when ships were lost at sea, since lifeboats were provided only for the crew. One observer writing in 1938 tells of three ships which sank for different reasons and which carried more than 1,300 coolies to the bottom of the sea with them. Tinker (1974, pp. 166f) quotes four more such cases, in which almost 900 Indians lost their lives, and stresses that conditions on coolie transportations from China were far worse again and death rates even higher.

The number of those who did not survive the crossing fell in subsequent decades, but even when they reached the colony of their destination coolies could not consider the danger past.

Millions of Indian workers were exported to numerous islands in the Caribbean, to French, British and Dutch Guiana, to various parts of Africa, to Madagascar, Mauritius and Réunión, Fiji and New Caledonia, Borneo, Malaya and Burma. They worked on rubber and sugar cane plantations, in mines, rice mills and ports. They built numerous railways, including several in Burma and Mozambique and the Uganda Railway in what was then Kenya.

The conditions under which Indian coolies lived and worked barely differed from those which the former slaves had had to endure: they received extremely low wages, regularly reduced by the numerous fines to which they were liable, were not often permitted to leave the plantation and were not entitled to marry and have a family.

Before the introduction of indentured labour newly arrived coolies, many of whom had been in bad physical shape even before setting out on their journeys and who would certainly not have recovered during the voyage, were broken in gently by their employers. For several months at least they were not required to meet their full quota of work, since they not only had to grow accustomed to their new surroundings, but also to their new jobs. Many had never done agricultural work, which often meant cutting sugar canes, in their lives before.

Once indentured labour was introduced, however, the planters and mine owners were concerned to receive their full quota of work from the very first day of the coolie's five-year contract. Since any time which a coolie spent in hospital resulted in a corresponding extension of his contract, the fact that a coolie might occasionally be unfit for work did not in any way damage the plantation owner's interests.

Thus a great many coolies died during the first year of their contracts as a result of the extreme working and living conditions to which they were subjected. One report compiled in Jamaica in 1871 revealed that 8.5 per cent of all the Indians who had arrived there in 1869 had died within a year, as had more than 12 per cent of those who had arrived in February and March 1870.

There were three main forms of coolieism: indentured labour, the *kangany* system and the *maistry* or contract system.

Indentured labour was the form for which the majority of the host nations, especially those outside Asia, recruited and employed Indian workers. Indentured labourers were shipped to a variety of countries including Mauritius (from 1839), the Caribbean (from 1838), Natal (from 1860) and Fiji (cf. Kondapi, 1951, pp. 8–28).

Under this system a worker was typically committed to work for a period of five years and during this time was not entitled to change employer or place of work. Employers recruited labour units, not families. They bore the costs of recruitment and of the crossing, and paid a fixed wage. The coolie received free accommodation and medical care, but was not entitled to a wage increase either during periods of inflation or when profits were high (cf. Kondapi, 1951, p. 8).

In addition to these common regulations, each colony had many of its own. In Jamaica between 1845 and 1847, for example, Indian workers without a contract were fined for each month in which they were unemployed. In Mauritius it was usual for Indians arrested for the first time for vagrancy to be sentenced to 28 days in prison and additional hard labour, and a second or subsequent conviction within two years led to the imposition of a prison sentence of six to nine months' duration. If at the end of this period the Indian's employer could not be found the former was required to work for three months in the service of the public and then to sign a new contract of employment (cf. Kondapi, 1951, p. 14).

Employers in Ceylon and Malaya used the *kangany* system to recruit their workers. A *kangany* was a foreman in charge of a gang of 25 to 30 coolies. He was an Indian and himself under the control of the plantation's head *kangany*. Each *kangany* acted as a middleman between the plantation management and the coolies, on all money matters as well. Part of his job was to travel to India with the plantation owner's money to recruit new workers. Unlike its Malayan counterpart, the *kangany* system practised in Ceylon was orientated towards extended family structures: each *kangany* led a group of related coolies, and even recruitment was organized on a family basis (cf. Kondapi, 1951, pp. 45f).

In principle the *maistry* system, which Kondapi also refers to as the 'contract system', was very similar to the *kangany* system. It too used advances to bind the indebted worker, but in addition its extensive hierarchy – from head *maistry*, through charge *maistry*, to gang *maistry* and a labour contractor – meant regular wage cuts for the workers and numerous other repressive measures. The *maistry* system was used chiefly to recruit Indian workers in Burma (cf. Kondapi, 1951, pp. 46ff).

Some employers relied on force and trickery to recruit workers, but eventually the Indian authorities took steps to counter this by questioning emigrating coolies as to whether their departure was voluntary.

A more likely motive for migration was the bad harvests and famine in India. Often people on the brink of starvation were picked up by the recruitment teams, given food and persuaded to sign contracts with their thumbprints. On the other hand, in years when the harvest had been good in India there were few people willing to emigrate. According to a report compiled by the Emigration Commissioner for Fiji this was the case, for example, in 1904, whereas in 1905 it was reported from Calcutta that many workers were willing to emigrate on account of the bad harvest and rising food prices (cf. Tinker, 1974, p. 119).

Indian women under the coolie system

Whilst there has at least been some debate within the social sciences on the situation of female slaves in America, accounts of how women were affected by the coolie system have, as far as I am aware, been restricted to observations scattered throughout the literature on the coolie system in general. These are, however, sufficiently detailed on the subject of Indian women to give us a rough idea of the conditions under which women on the plantations lived.

It is important to remember that women formed a minority of the contract labourers, and indeed of the entire Indian population, in societies centred on the plantation economy. European plantation owners were primarily interested in the labour power of healthy young men, and it was not profitable for them to attempt to reproduce labour power on their plantations themselves, since there were reservoirs of labour in Asia sufficiently large to meet their needs. For this reason they constantly sought to keep the number of women among their contract labourers to a minimum.

The British colonial authorities in India, on the other hand, were anxious to encourage a greater number of women to emigrate. This they justified in terms of the improvement in the social situation of Indians working abroad, but it is possible that the Indian authorities were also influenced by the idea that in this way they could export the social issues raised by colonization.

Ultimately, of course, all this is of secondary significance, since throughout the entire period the practice of exporting coolies was orientated towards meeting the needs of the plantation owners and characterized by its under-representation of women. Eventually the Indian authorities ruled that every shipment should contain 40 women for every 100 men (cf. Tinker, 1984, p. 79 and others), a quota of less than 30 per cent, and additional regulations were issued in the various host countries. The following are just a few examples of the relative size of the female coolie population in the colonies.

In 1844, 17 per cent of the Indian population of Mauritius was female, an increase on previous years. In 1861 a census revealed that the Indian population of the island was still 75 per cent male (Tinker, 1974, pp. 88f). Other territories in which the Indian population was predominantly male include Malaya, Ceylon and Burma. According to the regulations issued by the British-Indian migration authorities, the ratio of men to women in Malaya should have been 1,000:666. According to the census of 1925, however, there were only 468 women to every 1,000 men.

The situation in Ceylon was even worse. Between 1843 and 1850 only 27 women arrived in Ceylon for every 1,000 men. Although in the two decades which followed the figure rose first to 129, then to 276, it fell again in the period between 1871 and 1880 to a ratio of 253 women for every 1,000 men. The Indian population on the plantations, however, contained a greater proportion of women: 52 women to every 100 men in 1871, and 84 to 100 by 1911 (Kondapi, 1951, pp. 91f).

The most extreme shortage of women was in Burma, where the ratio of men to women was 8.2:1. In certain castes the disproportion was so great that there was only one woman to every 250 men (Kondapi, 1951, p. 92).

In 1911, relatively late in the lifetime of the coolie system and when the ratio of men to women had already levelled out somewhat as a result of natural reproduction, the Indian populations of Trinidad, Fiji, Jamaica and British Guiana were quoted as being 30 to 41 per cent female.

Table 4 shows the ratio of men to women and also the suicide rates for these colonies. As a rule the incidence of suicide among Indians, even those living there but not employed as contract labour, was far greater than in their native regions of India. The United Provinces recorded 63 suicides per million inhabitants each year. Of the plantation colonies named, Guiana's rate was lower than this at 52, but Trinidad's and Fiji's were considerably higher at 134 and 147. Among indentured labourers Guiana was once again the colony with the lowest suicide rate at 100, but the rate in the Caribbean colonies was around 400 and in Fiji 900. From these figures Kondapi deduces a correlation between the frequency of suicide and the proportion of women in a population: the fewer Indian women living in a colony, the higher that colony's suicide rate.

So what did coolieism mean for women? For one thing it meant wage discrimination, since women received only around one third of the already extremely low wages paid to men. In 1912, Indian men in British Guiana earned 26 cents a day, women 18 cents. In addition, women lost more working days than men, although neither men nor women were permanently employed (cf. Williams, 1962, p. 107).

Kondapi (1951, pp. 54f, 61f) produces evidence of similar wage disparity in Ceylon and Malaya. In 1929 Ceylon set an average minimum wage for Indian workers of 52 cents for men, 42 cents for women and 31 cents for

Table 4
The Indian population in selected colonies, 1911

Colony	Adults by gender		
	Men	Women	Proportion of women
Trinidad	31,989	17,169	34.9
British Guiana	53,083	34,799	39.6
Jamaica	7,137	4,775	40.1
Fiji	20,062	8,785	30.5

Suicides by section of the population			Suicide rate per million people	
Colony	Under indenture	Other Indians	Indentured	Other
Trinidad	12,747	13,306	406	134
British Guiana	9,114	57,336	100	52
Jamaica	407	–	396	–
Fiji	15,961	35,644	926	147

Source: Kondapi, 1951, p. 27

children. In future years these wage rates were forced down, and the disparity between men's, women's and children's wages increased by several percentage points. Not until 1941 did every worker's wages once again reach the level set in 1929.

Wage discrimination, though undoubtedly significant, was not the only form of sexist exploitation and oppression to which female Indian coolies were subjected. For many of them it was by far the least important. The fact that female workers were in the minority gave rise to all kinds of sexism, and female coolies had to endure far greater exploitation, misery and injustice than their male counterparts.

In addition to working on the plantation, women also had to take care of the children and in particular the men. This meant that women were responsible for household chores, but more important that they were exposed to the most extreme forms of sexual exploitation. The circumstances under which all this took place were essentially determined by the social isolation of coolies in societies centred on the plantation economy and by the conditions in which they lived. Indian and the other Asian contract labourers generally formed a new lower class among the working population in former slave colonies. Former slaves, who unlike the Asians were not bound by contract and who now enjoyed a relatively high degree of social and economic freedom, distanced themselves from the immigrants, whom they regarded as inferior. The immigrants took over responsibility for the work which the slaves had once done and hated, were often housed in what had once been slave accommodation, and were only permitted to leave the plantations under special circumstances. The plantation owners encouraged competitiveness and tension between the two groups. Whenever one of the groups made demands upon them the planters would use the other to smash the resistance of the first. In some colonies almost every lower-ranking police officer was a Creole (cf. Tinker, 1984, p. 181). These men were accomplices in the act of sustaining the coolie system, since penal sanctions were the disciplinary method which it most commonly used.

The divisions between the blacks and the coolies secured the livelihood and privileged status of the white minority in the colonies. In its report on British Guiana in 1870 a Royal Commission stated:

> The coolie despises the negro, for he considers him . . . to be less civilised than himself, whilst the negro despises the coolie for being so terribly inferior to him in terms of physical strength. There will never be much danger of rebellious disorder among the East Indian immigrants . . . as long as large numbers of negroes are employed alongside them. (Cited in Adamson, 1984, p. 49)

For an Asian woman the segregation of the coolies from the rest of the population meant that a much larger group of men from her own society than usual regarded her as the only attainable sexual object. The type of accommodation in which the coolies lived on the plantations also ensured that the few women among them would be, and could not avoid being, available to a large number of men: the quarters which they were allocated forced them to live in cramped conditions, without any sanitary facilities and exposed to heat and cold. Women were often accommodated in tiny rooms with several men and were not able to escape them.

The 'coolie lines', as the long barracks on the plantations were known, were subdivided inside only by medium-high walls and normally consisted of 30 to 40 rooms whose rear walls bordered on a row of identical rooms. Most were shared by single men.

For women, then, coolieism meant being raped by fellow workers, by foremen and by plantation owners, from whom even marriage did not protect them to any great extent. Coolies who became ill were forced to go into hospital, and under these circumstances, at least, married women who might otherwise have been protected were delivered helplessly into the hands of the other men in the barracks. Neither a woman nor her husband could offer resistance against a rape by the foreman, since the latter would then make use of his punitive prerogatives. An Indian worker in Fiji who hit a foreman in order to prevent his wife from being raped was thrown into prison along with the fleeing woman, and at the end of their sentences both had to return to work for the same foreman (Williams, 1962, pp. 107f).

Some colonial authorities even went so far as to regard marriages between Indian couples as non-existent, acknowledging only Christian marriages as valid (Tinker, 1974, p. 202; Gandhi, 1983, pp. 149f). Acting in the interests of the plantation owners, they thus replaced the patriarchal norm with a racist norm of the type which had prevailed during the slave age and which released plantation owners from their obligation not to split families. It was, of course, women who bore the brunt of this policy.

Even the plantation owners used their power over the coolie women for sexual gain. In British Guiana at the end of the 19th century they restored the feudal 'right of the first night', to which the daughters of coolies henceforth had to subject themselves (Tinker, 1974, pp. 221f).

Although women were widely traded and prostitution was rife, the form of exploitation to which women were most commonly exposed under the coolie system must surely have been polyandry, into which women were forced in Mauritius, Réunión and Fiji at least (Kondapi, 1951, p. 26; Tinker, 1974, p. 204). The practice consisted of the husband taking a number of 'lodgers' into the couple's room and demanding of the woman that she cook for them and be available to fulfil their sexual needs. A report compiled by the British Consul in Réunión in 1874 states:

> It is customary for four or five men to lie together in order to have sexual relations with one woman who has taken on the job of being a wife or lover to them all. This is an arrangement which frequently leads to arguments, violence and sometimes to bloodshed.

He continues:

> The disproportionately small number of women also leads to other acts of depravity which are of such an abominable nature that they cannot be described here.

Polyandry frequently resulted in women being murdered. Beween 1885 and 1920, 235 murders were recorded among the Indian population of Fiji. The majority of the victims were women, and the most common motive officially described as 'sexual jealousy'. In the period between 1890 and 1919 victims were recorded separately by sex. Of the 96 indentured labourers murdered between these years 68 were female and 28 male. This means that in a society where women made up less than one third of the population, more than two thirds of the murder victims were of the female sex (cf. Lal, 1984, p. 148).

The literature on coolieism does not, as a rule, deal with the extreme forms of over-exploitation and oppression to which women were subjected as such, but couches them in terms of moral decline, temptation or conjugal infidelity (see especially Lal, 1984, p. 148 and Kondapi, 1951, p. 26). Public authority reports on the subject stress, in particular the 'base nature' of female migrants (see Tinker, 1974, p. 205).

Women were the people most seriously exploited and oppressed by the coolie system, for they were exploited and oppressed not only by the plantation owners but also by their fellow slaves: in addition to doing the household chores, they also had to guarantee the sexual reproduction of their men. Women were also the people who offered the most resistance to coolieism. Like the men, they resorted to suicide, but in addition they denied themselves by refusing to bear children. The Indian birth rate in many colonies was extremely low, and abortions commonplace (cf. Tinker, 1974, p. 206). Women took part in large numbers and in leading roles in various strike movements. In 1920, for example, a woman by the name of Jayunkvar led a strike by the Suva-Rewa sugar workers in Fiji (Tinker, 1984, p. 83). Indian women also took part in huge numbers in the protest movement organized by Gandhi in South Africa. They fought against the invalidity of their marriages and the Three-Pound Tax payable by those Indians who did not wish to sign new contracts upon the expiry of their old ones. It was the women, in fact, who first mobilized the men (see Gandhi, 1983, pp. 149ff).

Despite huge variations in the forms of exploitation to which they were subjected, the lot of female workers from other parts of Asia and under the control of countries other than Britain was very similar to that of female Indian migrants. The Dutch pamphlet reproduced below demonstrates clearly that this was the case.

Chinese coolies

Chinese workers were being exported to various parts of Southeast Asia long before the Europeans began to employ Chinese coolies to any great extent for colonial production. Chinese businessmen ran the gold-mining industry in Borneo, for example, and had coolies sent from their homeland to work for them. At the beginning of the 19th century there were 30,000 Chinese working in the goldmines of the District of Sanbas, and others emigrated to Malaya, Indonesia, the Philippines and other parts of Southeast Asia in waves of migration controlled by Chinese businessmen and traders (cf. Barth, 1964, p. 54).

During the colonization of Southeast Asia in general, and in connection with the exportation of Chinese workers to the European colonies and the USA in the second half of the 19th century in particular, Chinese traders and businessmen acted as middlemen. They served both as intermediaries between the colonial rulers and the native populations and as labour recruiting agents – and they did well out of it. The Chinese coolies involved in each of the two phases of emigration, both that controlled exclusively by the Chinese as well as that regulated by the European colonies, came mainly from the southern provinces of Kwantung and Fukhien and the town of Canton. Macao, Hong Kong, Shantou (Swatow), Xiamen (Amoy) and the more northerly Shanghai were the ports from which they sailed.

The workers were recruited in brutal fashion indeed. Chen (1981, p. 21) refers to the fact that the term 'shanghaied', which has also entered the German language as *schanghaien* (to shanghai), dates back to the capture

A Dutch pamphlet published in 1902 denounced the abuses of the coolie system in Dutch India. The author of this pamphlet, J. van den Brand, described the plight of young Javanese women committed to working in Sumatra as follows:

How does a Javanese Woman Earn her Sarong?

Before I answer this complex question, I should like to put before the reader a model contract of the type signed by Javanese women, a contract drawn up under the watchful eye of the Governor-General...

'We, the undersigned, a Javanese woman, Sarina, aged 16, height 143cm, born in Serang, belonging to the Sundanese people, and Jan Tabak, administrator for the Tanah Kringet Company, acting as lawful agent for Pieter Voetblad, owner of the Tanah Kringet Company, situated in the Medan area of the district of Deli, do hereby declare that we are agreed on the following:

I   The first party shall be obliged to work in the service of the Tanah Kringet Company sorting and bundling up tobacco and to undertake any other work which may reasonably be required of her.

II   The first party shall work ten hours per day in the service of the Tanah Kringet Company.

III   The second party shall be obliged to pay the first party one dollarcent for roughly bundling up 10 bales of tobacco, 3 dollarcents for finely sorting and bundling 10 bales of good leaves, three dollarcents for 10 bales of broken leaves or, if paid by the day, a wage of 15 dollarcents per day.

IV   The first party confirms that she has received from the second party an advance in the sum of the amount stated after her name. This is to be repaid by means of monthly deductions from the wages due to her in amounts of less than one dollar and at an exchange rate of two guilders per dollar. The first party shall receive no wages for any day on which she misses work, whether through illness, imprisonment, or unruliness.

V   The first party may not be required to work on the following days: on the first and sixteenth of every month and on generally accepted Moslem holy days.

VI   The second party shall provide at his own expense accommodation and free medical care for the first party and her family.

VII   The second party shall not separate the first party from her family against her will.

VIII   The first party shall present herself on the first day of the month of July in the year 1900 at the offices of the company and register with the administrator.

IX   This agreement shall run for a period of three consecutive years from the date of this document.

Agreed in Medan this day, the 27th day in the month of June in the year 1900 and two.'

There then follow the signatures, particulars of the advance received, normally 15 dollars, and the wage rate, which is usually less but never more than 4.5 dollars.

... Let us assume that the planter takes the same view on such matters as this illustrious author and therefore pays the Javanese contract worker 4.5 dollars per month. From this, one dollar then goes towards repaying the advance. Now let us suppose (in view of her gender) that this woman is ill for an average of two days each month and therefore has to forgo 30 cents. She is then left with 3.2 dollars, in words three dollars and twenty cents, less than eleven cents a day!

Yet this is still above average. I know for a fact that one of the larger companies regularly pays Javanese women an average of 2.2 dollars per month – 7 cents a day!

Investigations which I have conducted have proved to me that a Javanese woman in Medan needs 13 cents a day in order to feed herself – and that does not include titbits or betel. Since everything is expensive on the plantations, it is fair to assume that the minimum which a woman there must earn in order to feed herself is at least 15 dollarcents.

It is, therefore, as plain as day that as she does not have enough to eat, the Javanese woman cannot put any money aside to buy clothes. Hence the question at the beginning of this passage: 'How does a Javanese woman earn her sarong?' (a kind of dress, the most essential piece of clothing for a Javanese woman, which costs at least a dollar and without which she cannot do.)

The short answer to this terrible question is that the Javanese woman earns, must earn, the money for her sarong through whoring. Five cents is what she receives each time she surrenders herself to a Chinaman. Thus in order to raise enough to buy that indispensable item of clothing, she must at least twenty times...

Oh God! It is abominable.

But there is more, worse.

Each year hundreds of Javanese girls are kidnapped and thrown to the Chinese like Christians to the lions. Hoards of young girls are bought and sacrificed to the Chinese.

Everyone knows that they do not earn enough – the girls, I mean – to feed themselves. The planters better than anyone. As the administrator of one of the larger companies led me around his plantation and allowed me to see the houses occupied by the Chinese and Javanese, I asked him where the unmarried Javanese women lived. It finally emerged that they do not have homes of their own, but have to find shelter wherever they can.'

(Source: van den Brand, 1902, pp. 66ff)

of Chinese peasants who had come to the town to sell vegetables or other goods. Sailors were only one of a whole range of groups whose members were 'recruited' in this way. Nor was it exclusively in Shanghai that Chinese were forcibly abducted by ship and press-ganged into working as coolies, but also in Swatow, Nan'ao (Namao), Canton and Macao. Kidnapping as a means of obtaining workers for territories outside China took on such dimensions that, according to a report on Amoy by the British Consul, no man could leave his home without the threat of being taken aboard a ship by force.

The cynicism with which labour power was exported from China found expression in the term most commonly used to describe the process. The trade in Chinese coolies was known as 'the buying and selling of pigs', in all probability by analogy with the European name for the plaits ('pigtails') worn by the Chinese men. The camps in which the workers were assembled before transportation were known as 'pig-pens' (see Campbell, 1923, pp. 95ff). The term very accurately describes the conditions under which the Chinese were forced to eke out their miserable existence in such camps. Nor were conditions on the ships, which often transported them to the other side of the world, any better. In China the transport vessels were known as 'floating hells' (Gernet, 1979, p. 518).

The European colonial powers not only recruited Chinese coolies for Southeast Asia, their traditional host region, but also for many other parts of the world. In addition to Java, Borneo and British Malaya, other host regions included Canada, New Zealand, Nauru, Western Samoa, Queensland, South Africa, Cuba, British Guiana, Peru and the USA (see Map 5). The working conditions and social situation of Chinese workers throughout the world were characterized by a total lack of rights, and absence of rights was experienced not only by those who had been abducted against their will, but also by those who had been inveigled into signing a contract or had signed because they had no alternative.

As is illustrated by the excerpt below from a coolie's contract, coolies who signed such a document lost every opportunity of defending themselves against over-exploitation. It is still uncertain whether coolies were actually able to return home when their contracts expired. Many, of course, did not survive that long, and often when one contract expired a new one was concluded under the same inhuman conditions.

In all, 40,413 Chinese coolies were exported to Cuba. Some 80 per cent of them had been kidnapped or deceived, and 10 per cent died during the crossing (Campbell, 1923, p. 135). The remainder were sold in the marketplace and treated like slaves. The contracts which they had signed back in China emphasized that they were now not only *de facto* but also *de jure* in a position which barely differed from slavery.

Chinese coolies were despatched not only to Cuba, but also to other parts of the Caribbean, yet measured against the number of Indian coolies in that region their number remained relatively small. This was because Chinese workers were more expensive than Indian coolies. This was due in

---

Excerpt from a coolie's contract

I, the undersigned... do... agree to the following conditions:

1. I pledge that on a day following this I shall embark for Havana on the island of Cuba, and moreover on any ship specified by the master named.
2. I shall both commit myself and submit myself to work in the named country for a period of *eight years* and undertake any work commonly carried out there in the fields, in the settlements, or wherever else I may be assigned on the orders of the colonizing society or any person to whom this contract shall pass.
4. The hours which I am obliged to work shall depend upon the type of work to which I am assigned and on the attention which this requires as determined freely (arbitrio) by the master under whose command I am placed, provided that I am guaranteed several consecutive hours for rest every 24 hours and time for breakfast and lunch, as are the other paid workers in that country.
5. In addition to being guaranteed these hours of rest during the working day, I shall also not be obliged to do any more work on any Sunday than that which my employer considers necessary on that particular day.
6. I shall submit myself to the *Disciplinary Code*... in force within the organization to which I am assigned and also to the *Penal Code* in force... in the same.

I furthermore declare that I am in complete agreement with the wage stipulated, although I know and understand that the free wage workers and slaves on the island of Cuba earn far higher wages. (Cited in Kautsky, 1883, pp. 396f)

---

part to higher transportation costs, but also to the fact that a considerably higher proportion of Chinese than Indians returned home. A planter who had committed himself in the contract to paying a worker's return fare after the expiry of that contract would have been presented with the following bill:

	£
Passage of 100 coolies from India at £16 per head	1,600
Return of 15 per cent to India at £13 per head	195
Total	**1,795**

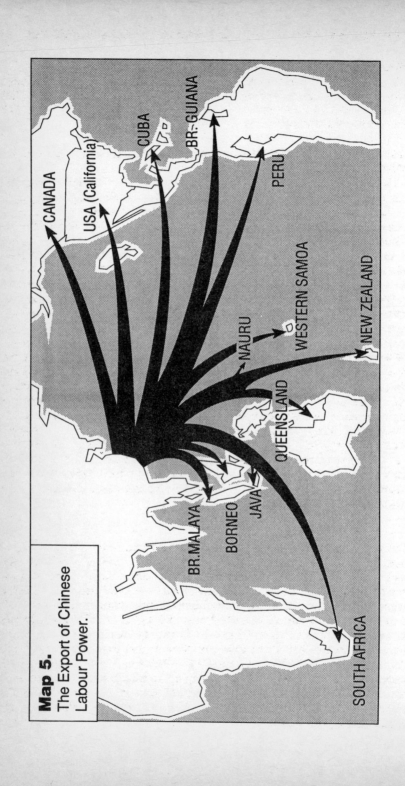

Map 5.
The Export of Chinese Labour Power.

CANADA

USA (California)

CUBA

BR. GUIANA

PERU

NAURU

WESTERN SAMOA

NEW ZEALAND

QUEENSLAND

BR. MALAYA

BORNEO

JAVA

SOUTH AFRICA

Under the conditions of the Convention:

Passage of 100 coolies from China at £25 per head	2,500
Return of 80 per cent (20 per cent mortality) at £15 per head	1,200
Total	**3,700**

(Campbell, 1923, p. 142)

Thus Chinese coolies cost the planters in the Caribbean more than double what they spent on Indian coolies.

The proportion of women among the coolies was typically far lower for Chinese than for Indian coolie migrations. To give but one example, in 1907 there were 2,515 Chinese men in New Zealand, but only 55 women. A medical report on the state of health of the Chinese in Canadian British Columbia estimated that as a result of the colony having such a large ratio of male to female Chinese inhabitants practically all of them were infected with a virulent strain of syphilis. Another report on the Chinese population of the same colony maintains that out of 144 women half were prostitutes and many of the remainder concubines. In California steps were taken in 1873 to counteract the sale of Chinese women and children, which was widely known to take place in the state (Campbell, 1923, p. 157). Male prostitution and homosexual rape were also widespread.

Cargoes of Chinese coolies being imported into Cuba had to contain a set proportion of women. This regulation led in one case to 44 young girls, of whom the eldest was eight years old, being bought in China for export to Cuba. The girls were locked up together in a room on the 'tween deck of a ship. The room had a floor space of around 25 square metres and was 1.7 metres high. After they had spent three weeks in the room, the children were freed by the authorities with the ship still in China. The only reason that they were discovered was that several members of the ship's crew had been taken ill and someone had noticed the stink coming from the children's cabin. The girls had not been permitted to leave it for the whole period (Campbell, 1923, p. 111).

The Chinese in the USA

The import into the USA of Chinese workers began in 1849, when gold deposits were discovered in California (cf. Barth, 1964, p. 63). At the beginning of the 1850s the transportation of coolies was big business for ship owners: instead of the commodities which they had transported in the bygone days of the boom, they now shipped Chinese workers. Barth (1964, p. 61) quotes the example of a 450-ton ship bought in 1853 for $5,000 and on which an additional $10,000 worth of repairs were carried out. Just one journey, on which just such a ship could carry more than 500 coolies from China to the USA, yielded takings of $37,000 in fares. In the first six months of 1852 there were 82 ships carrying such cargoes off the American west coast. The total tonnage ran to 42,724 tons. In the same six months 28,000 Chinese workers landed in the USA. Between them they had paid $2,329,580 for the journey.

Each worker who spent the two-month journey below deck had previously taken out a loan in China in order to be able to pay the fare. Chinese businessmen and traders whose businesses operated both in China and in the USA would generally advance $70, $50 for the passage and $20 for other expenses, and immigrants would commit themselves to repaying $200. Their aim was to save up $200 to $300 with which to return to China (cf. Barth, 1964, p. 68). Few succeeded, and even those who did ran the risk of arriving home as poor as they had been when they left, for often the cooks on the ships would organize games of chance. Eckstein reports that the stake in these games was never less than $1, and one captain estimated that his ship's cook would take on average $1,000 per cargo of 1,200 coolies per journey in such games. The ship's crew would also make money out of the coolies by placing their cabins at the disposal of a group of them for $60 to $80 or more. The sailors would then be allocated a passenger cabin by the captain.

Chinese coolies in the USA worked primarily in the mines and in the railway construction industry, but also as fishermen, agricultural labourers and in factories. Of the 36,557 Chinese workers on the Pacific coast in 1855, some 20,000 were employed in the Californian goldmines. In 1862 Chinese traders in San Francisco estimated that 30,000 Chinese coolies out of a total of 48,391 were employed as miners. In 1873 there were more Chinese working the mines in the USA than members of any other ethnic or national grouping, including Americans themselves (cf. Barth, 1964, p. 113).

Furthermore, the Chinese played a leading role in the construction of the American railway system. During the final stage in the construction of the Central Pacific Railroad they made up 90 per cent of the project's 10,000 strong workforce. They helped to build the Alabama and Chattanooga Railroad, the Houston and Texas Railroad, and a railway near New Orleans (Tung, 1974, pp. 12f). Chinese workers also took part in the construction of the Panama Railroad, which was completed in 1885.

Living and working conditions for all those in the railway construction industry were extreme. In his 1916 account of the construction of the Panama Railroad, Bishop writes, 'There is a folk legend which will be told and believed for as long as the Chagres flows into the ocean and according to which the construction of the Panama Railroad has claimed a human life for every sleeper.' In his view the 'myth' was implausible since 'there were some 150,000 sleepers in every 50-mile stretch, and there have not been that many inhabitants on the isthmus since the time when Pedrarius the Terrible killed all the Indians' (cited in Schubert, 1978, pp. 44f).

The lives of Chinese coolies in the USA were shaped not only by the physically hard and dangerous jobs which they did, but also by two further factors. The first was the Chinese coolie's dependence on Chinese businessmen, who had established a perfect system for controlling the workers through secret syndicates. Under the credit-ticket system described earlier, every Chinese coolie who entered the USA did so with debts. The businessmen acted as creditors. They also controlled access to job opportunities and therefore wages. These were always high enough to ensure that the businessmen's 'investment' paid off, and that workers subjugated themselves and continued to dream their dreams of success, but so low that it was virtually impossible for coolies to extricate themselves from their state of dependence, a dependence into which they had been forced by the sums advanced to them for the sea crossing. Through their syndicates Chinese businessmen controlled every, or almost every, Chinese man in the USA. The approximately 2,000 Chinese women in the USA were not recognized by the syndicates at all.[5]

The list in Table 5 was compiled by Barth (1964, p. 90) and is based for the most part on figures published in 1855. It is reproduced here in a slightly shortened form and shows the distribution of workers over the various syndicates, each of which controlled a demarcated district.

Table 5
The Chinese in California (c. 1855)

Name of syndicate	Arrivals	Returns	Deaths	Members
Sam Yap	8,400	1,300	300	6,800
Sze Yap	13,200	3,700	300	9,200
Yeong Wo	16,900	2,500	400	14,000
Yan Wo	2,100	160	160	1,780
Ning Yeong	8,349	1,269	173	6,907
Total	**48,949**	**8,929**	**1,333**	**38,687**

Source: Barth, 1964, p. 90

The syndicates were fully operational for around a decade, and the control they exerted extended to job opportunities, wages and medical care. They supplied Chinese cooks, delivered foodstuffs and organized Chinese New Year celebrations, games of chance and prostitution in the Chinatowns. The *coup de grâce* was that the businessmen's syndicates also had offshoots in the workers' home towns and villages and therefore had access to their families in China. The workers had no opportunity of escaping their creditors' spheres of influence.

The second factor, other than working conditions, that shaped the lives of the Chinese in America was white America's racism. This manifested itself in many ways. In 1863, for example, the Californian legislature passed a law forbidding any Indian, any person with more than 50 per cent Indian blood, any Chinese and any Mongol from testifying for or against a white person. In 1868, 40,000 Chinese mineworkers were driven out of California, and in 1871 Chinese workers were massacred in Los Angeles. Even the trade unions supported and adopted anti-Chinese measures. Finally, in 1882 the Chinese Exclusion Act was passed, making it impossible for Chinese workers in particular to enter the USA in the future.

In the decades that followed, an assortment of measures caused the working and living conditions of Chinese living in the USA to worsen still further (see Tung, 1974, pp. 12ff).

Further recruitment zones

From the 19th century onwards India and China were no longer the only reservoirs of labour power for the European-owned plantations and for the mines and the building of infrastructure throughout the world. Countless islands in Asia and Oceania also supplied labour power on a large scale: Java was of particular importance to the remaining Dutch colonies in Asia, the Japanese went to work in America, and extensive manhunts took place in the South Seas.

The Pacific Islands did not merely export labour for colonial production, some also imported it. It is as a result of the recruitment of coolies that Indians are the dominant grouping within the population of Fiji today. Indians account for 49 per cent of the population, Melanesians for 45 per cent (cf. Röben, 1985, p. 13).

Oceania

Scientific expeditions to the South Seas openly pursued the objective of supplying the colonial territories with workers. According to Georg Thilenius, Director of the Hamburger Museum für Völkerkunde (Hamburg Museum of Ethnology) and organizer of the 1908 Hamburg South Seas expedition:

> On the practical side, the object of the expedition was not to find exploitable minerals, animals, and plants, but human beings themselves. In the Tropics the native is the white man's worker and will always be cheaper than imported labour. These people live under very different conditions than those to which we are accustomed, and have always been few in number. Now, however, European property is under direct threat as a result of the decline in their numbers and the extinction which they face, and science has been charged with finding ways of obviating this decimation.

It was during the first half of the 19th century that Europeans began to show an interest in the Oceanian archipelago, in particular in whaling and fishing, sandalwood and copra for extracting coconut oil (cf. Graves, 1984, pp. 118f). After 1860 the plantation economy expanded into new territories, including Fiji and Queensland in Australia; these grew and exported cotton, sugar, coffee and flax. The colonial rulers regarded the islands of the Pacific first and foremost as a rich reservoir of labour power.

The American Civil War, during which Oceania's importance to the world market grew, gave the plantations a vital boost. Now highly profitable, they had to import large numbers of workers from abroad. In the early days in particular direct compulsion and deception were the main methods of recruitment. The demographic effects of colonial penetration and the abduction of large sections of the population proved just as devastating in South Seas societies as they had in America and Africa.

In the 1870s around 50 ships, mostly of British or German origin, took part in 'blackbirding' in Oceania. Their aim was to hunt down labour that they could sell to the plantation owners. Closely linked with 'blackbirding' was the operation of a 'sexual market economy' which had emerged in the previous decades, when European whalers had first headed for the islands. According to Vinke (1984, p. 32):

> The seamen, who arrived on the islands in a wretched condition, exhausted, dirty, and half-starved after their long journey, regarded it as a natural right that the women should be placed at their disposal, and the island women often made it all too easy for them.

What shines through clearly here is that Vinke has more interest in and understanding for the European seamen than for the female inhabitants of the Pacific islands. Despite the anti-colonialist intention of his book, he fails to break with the sexist tradition of colonial literature, according to which subdued, ravished, and exploited women are themselves to blame for their plight – whether for succumbing to the sex appeal which radiated from the Europeans, or whether for merely making it 'all too easy for them', as Vinke assumes. Yet all this is inconsistent with what he then proceeds to report, namely that the women did not make contact with the ship's crews themselves, but were sold to the seamen by their brothers or fathers: sexual services in exchange for nails.

Between 1840 and 1915, 280,000 Melanesians and Micronesians were exported to Queensland, Fiji, Samoa, Hawaii, New Caledonia, French Polynesia, Nauru and Peru as contract labour. A further 140,000 or so went as migrant workers to New Guinea or moved between the islands (Graves, 1984, p. 112).

The majority of these coolies were taken by Queensland in Australia. Apart from cattle breeding, the colony's main industry was the cultivation of sugar cane. At the beginning of colonization the workforce had been made up of European convicts, who had worked under conditions very similar to those of slavery, and although it became legal to import Chinese and Indian contract labour in 1809, it was not until 1837 that a small group of 40 Indians with five-year contracts entered the territory. Asian workers only became essential after 1849–50, when the last convoys of prisoners arrived. In 1859 Queensland seceded from the mother colony, New South Wales, and between 1863 and 1906 imported 64,000 coolies from the islands of the Pacific. In addition, the territory registered 11,000 Chinese coolies in 1881 and also imported Malayan and Javanese workers. As is evident from the following computation – a Queensland plantation owner's figures concerning a Kanaka whom he had employed for three years – they were all exposed to a high degree of exploitation.

£20 paid to the agents who supplied the work slaves
 £3 paid to the government of Queensland for 'supervising' importation
 £5 to be put aside for the return fare
£25 to be paid to the worker in the form of wages and clothing over a period of three years
 £7 for the worker's food

Total expenditure, then, was £60 or $100, of which almost half was shared by Europeans (Twain, 1976, p. 81) – the Kanaka received a 'wage' of 5 to 7 cents per day.

Whether this particular worker survived long enough to make the return journey for which the plantation owner had put aside £5 is uncertain. In comparing mortality rates, Twain comes to the conclusion that contract labour carried a risk of death that was 12 times higher for Kanakas than a traditional war (Twain, 1976, p. 86).

Conditions in other colonies were similar. At the beginning of the 1870s the Hamburg firm Goddefroy paid a premium of a hundred dollars on every worker which it imported into Samoa (Vinke, 1984, p. 28).

As far as Queensland is concerned, it is important to realize that in addition to convicts and coolies there was a third group of workers that was subjected to extreme exploitation: the Aborigines. The original inhabitants of Australia, men, women and children, were hunted down and forced to work for the whites under conditions which Evans maintains might easily be described as slavery, even allowing for academic precision and rigidity (Evans, 1984, p. 203). The Aborigines were regarded by the whites as little more than animals, sub-human and more or less impervious to pain. They were said to repay every act of 'friendship' which they were shown with 'ingratitude' and 'betrayal'. Violence was constantly employed to force them to work, and so many were exterminated that according to a report published in 1892 the settlers' cattle were herded by native women, since there were no men left (Saunders, 1984, p. 195).

Enslavement also brought with it the systematic psychological ruination of the Aborigines. Ultimately many were proud to accept the crescent-shaped brass discs awarded to them by the settlers for 'really good behaviour'. These discs were tied around their necks with leather bands and engraved with sardonic titles such as 'King Billy' (cf. Saunders, 1984, p. 194).

Japan

Japan served as a reservoir of labour power for a time; Japanese coolies migrated mainly to the USA and Hawaii. To some extent they replaced the excluded Chinese in the railway construction industry, but they were also employed as agricultural labourers and domestic servants. Japanese sugar workers in Hawaii were forbidden by law from entering the USA. The 100,000 Japanese living in the United States in 1910 all entered before 1907, the year in which the so-called Gentlemen's Agreement banning Japanese immigration was concluded. In Hawaii at this time there were some 70,000 Japanese sugar workers (cf. Katayama, 1910).

Java

For a long time the colonization of the Dutch Indies, begun in the 17th century, was founded on the state-controlled forced cultivation of the land by Asian peasants. This led to a fall in production and the outbreak of famine, yet not until 1871 did the Dutch abandon the 'culture system' and replace it with privately owned plantations. In the following year they abolished debt bondage, slavery having already been outlawed in 1860. The colonial rulers now considered it necessary to regulate the supply of labour anew, and this they did via the Coolie Ordinance, which came into force in 1880. The ordinance granted plantation owners extensive rights and imposed penal sanctions on the coolies. They were already punished every time they left the plantations.

On their plantations in eastern Java the Dutch primarily employed coolies from Madura, and for Sumatra they recruited Chinese (cf. Albertini, 1976, pp. 202, 210). As a result, the mass exportation of Javanese coolies to the Buitengewesten, as the other islands were known, did not begin until relatively late in the day.

After 1911, however, a great many Javanese coolies migrated to Sumatra, the major host country under Dutch rule. According to Dutch statistics, almost 400,000 of the nearly 500,000 coolies employed in Dutch colonies in 1931 were Javanese; this figure includes the 30,905 Javanese coolies imported into Surinam, a Dutch territory in America, between 1890 and 1929 (Kloosterboer, 1975, p. 33). Like coolies elsewhere, coolies employed by the Dutch were regarded as little more than slaves.

The abolition of the coolie system

The coolie system was not abolished simultaneously in every country of origin and host country, but in different ways and at different times. I have already mentioned the 1882 ban on Chinese workers entering the USA; relatively early too, the British colonial authorities halted the migration of Indians to non-English colonies. Indentured labour, the form of coolieism that most closely resembled slavery, was abolished in 1878 in Malaya, in 1911 in Trinidad and Natal, in 1915 in Mauritius, two years later in British Guiana and in 1920 in Fiji. After 1878 the *kangany* or *maistry* systems were the dominant forms of coolieism in Burma, Ceylon and Malaya (Spear, 1979, p. 259).

Indentured labour was not outlawed in India (a territory in which many indentured labourers had been recruited) until relatively late in the day, despite the fact that it met with growing resistance from the population.

> In 1917, after numerous investigations, all new indenture was suspended for the duration of World War I. In 1920 the system was completely abolished and the event was hailed as a red-letter day throughout India, where it was regarded as an event paralleling the abolition of slavery nearly a century before. It was natural that it should be followed by a system that had already developed, a system freer but not quite free, the *kangani* system. (Davis, 1951, p. 104)

The *kangany* system did not reach its peak until after the abolition of indentured labour. Gradually it was transformed into a system of free migrant labour with seasonal characteristics and from which a high proportion of workers returned home. Whereas 88 per cent of the Indian workers entering Malaya in 1920 had been recruited in India, by the mid 1930s this had fallen to less than 9 per cent. Restrictions on rubber extraction, the large number of immigrant Indians and Chinese already living in Malaya and the growing supply of local labour all led to a fall in demand. In 1936 recruitment for Malayan plantations under the *kangany* labour system was officially outlawed, although the system remained in use for a time in the palm oil industry and in newly acquired territories. In 1934–5 the Indian government imposed quotas for emigration to Malaya, and in 1938 a wage cut was ordered for Indian workers there. The result was ultimately a ban on all subsidized emigration of Indian workers to Malaya (Davis, 1951, pp. 104ff).

Indentured labour survived longest in the Dutch colonies. Even as late as the 1930s these colonies had only a graduated plan to reduce the proportion of indentured labourers which they employed – the abolition of the system was not on the agenda. The plan stipulated that from 1 January 1934 the ratio of free workers to contract labourers was to be 40:60, and that this was to reach 50:50 within another two years. The view of the colonial authorities was, 'It is not possible for us even to think of making changes in the labour law until the populations of the overseas territories are much larger and a sufficient number of people are willing to work on the plantations' (Pelzer, 1935, p. 108). So the Coolie Ordinance remained in force – it was not revoked until 1941, after the onslaught of World War Two, when the Japanese offensive against the Dutch East Indies, which ended in occupation in 1942, was already imminent.

Within the overall framework of the world market for labour power the coolie system served as a link between the slave era and that of labour migration and wage labour. In conjunction with the destructive effects of the colonial penetration of India, China and the Asian and Oceanian islands, it led to a large-scale mobilization of labour power in those parts of the world. As a result of this mobilization the abolition of certain particularly repressive forms of coolieism in no way posed a threat to the supply of labour power the colonial rulers desired.

Overview: coolie labour as a stage in the world market for labour power

1.	Scale	at least 12 million, but possibly more than 37 million Asian people
2.	Chronology	1830–1930
3.	Countries of origin	India, China, Java, Japan, Oceania
4.	Host countries	America and the Caribbean, Australia, South Africa, Mauritius, and other colonized territories
5.	Recruitment	through force, cunning, deception; in the later decades economic pressure also sometimes sufficed
6.	Selection criteria	1. health: examined by doctors, some of whom received bonuses for low mortality rates during the crossing 2. age: between 20 and 30 3. sex: predominantly male
7.	Means of transport	coolie ship
8.	Distribution	various: sometimes via slave-style markets, sometimes through conclusion of a contract or as the result of debt in country of origin, sometimes through middlemen, always with the possibility of being resold
9.	Nature of work	on plantations, in mines, in railway construction; physically tiring, often dangerous jobs, extension of the working day to the physical limits by force
10.	Reproduction	direct (daily): some distribution of foodstuffs, otherwise through wages replacement of the labour force: new imports
11.	Legal status/ political rights	coolies were generally bound by contract under penal sanctions, the low wages which they received were rarely adequate to enable them to settle their debts; plantation owners or other employers and creditors had extensive rights, coolies had no freedom of movement
12.	Social organization	'coolie lines' were communal barracks, often slave quarters; the majority of coolies had no opportunity to start a family or to live with their families
13.	Ideological justification	labour shortage, especially in regions in which whites could not work, opportunity to make savings to make possible a better life after return home

Coolieism, in which physical violence and punitive sanctions both played an important part, significantly aided the establishment of structures which both guaranteed an adequate supply of labour power for colonial production, and were able to dispense with a great many coercive measures other than economic pressure. In many territories, including those where in the past it had only been possible to recruit labour by force, migrant labour and labour migration now appeared to offer a prospect, an alternative to hunger and poverty. However, the abolition of indentured labour and the *kangany* and *maistry* systems, in other words the end of coolie labour as a stage in the world market for labour power, did not bring fundamental improvements in the lives of those workers concerned. Of course, migration did not occur on such a large scale, but then there was hardly a labour shortage any longer. An analysis of the living and working conditions of Indians employed in the sugar industry in the period between 1833 and 1970 concluded, 'The worker in the field is still the man who wields the hoe or machete. The major difference between the work today and the work during the days of slavery and indentured labour is that today the employment is seasonal not permanent.'

The labour movement and the coolie system

In Europe and the USA opposition to slavery, an important factor in its abolition, was voiced primarily by humanistically orientated people and organizations such as the British Anti-Slavery Society.

These same people and organizations were also active in the campaign against coolieism. Yet the fact that the system first emerged in the 19th century and was not abolished until the 20th century begs the question as to what stance was taken on this issue by the trade union and labour movements, both of which became important social and political forces during this period.

The coolie system was apparently not regarded as an important issue in such circles, for not until they perceived a threat to their own interests did they even begin to grapple with the problem. The first volume of *Die Neue Zeit*, the theoretical organ of the Social Democratic Party of Germany, tackled the question of the competition between German workers and Indian coolies thus:

> For years it has been the pet idea of European capitalists to replace the resistant workers of Europe with the submissive and incredibly cheap Indians and Chinese. In America the attempt has already been made and has led to the implementation of a law which restricts the importation of Chinese workers. In Europe this is not yet necessary. Instead, the worker here is faced with a threat of a different kind: *the coolie is in competition with him in China and India themselves*. India in particular is developing industries which, with the help of low wages and cheap raw materials,

are already successfully limiting Europe's exports. It will not be too long before the American and even European markets will also be flooded with its cheap products.

This excerpt clearly expresses the view that it would be detrimental to the interests of German workers if markets in the colonies were to be lost, that the revitalization of India's craft and industrial production, destroyed by British colonialism, would not be in their interests, and that these could be better served through alignment with British and German capital rather than with the workers of India or other colonies.

Another article published in the same journal and entitled *Die Verwendung von Kuli als Lohnarbeiter in der deutschen Seefahrt* ('The use of coolies as wage workers in German seafaring') aims to explain the threats facing German workers as a result of the use of coolies in the German shipping industry: hostility to German culture, the forcing down of wages, strike-breaking, lack of cleanliness, disease, and the possibility that the lives of the whole crew might be endangered as a consequence of one man's inability to speak the language in an accident. The author does not suggest redressing such actual or imagined grievances by encouraging coolies to agitate for change or by arranging their incorporation into the trade union or labour movements. Instead, he writes:

> ... it is inconceivable that coolies could adapt to trade unions or could be won for the German workers' endeavours, especially those of the organised seamen, to promote a civilized way of life ... even if they were to be granted full social, economic and political equality with German workers. The disparity between our languages and customs not only makes such fraternization more difficult, it makes it downright impossible. (Fischer, 1906–7, p. 793)

The author demands the promulgation of laws and regulations covering minimum wages, accommodation, food etc., thereby suggesting that finding a solution to the problem is the responsibility of the state and not of the labour and trade union movements.

Although *Die Neue Zeit* also contained several quite different angles on the coolie issue, including those expressed in articles by Eckstein which reported on a strike conducted under extremely difficult conditions by 11,000 'pullers' (rickshaw coolies) in Shanghai, it nevertheless failed to discuss the possible consequences of coolie labour, to make demands of any kind on behalf of coolies, or even to qualify the view that coolies were not organizable.

At its conference in Chicago in 1885 the Socialist Party of the United States debated the coolie issue, and a majority of the delegates passed a resolution demanding a ban on 'yellows' – in particular the Japanese and Chinese – immigrating to the USA, although they agreed that the country should remain open to European immigrants. The delegates, many adopting openly racist stances, argued that coolie labour forced down wages and that coolies were employed as strike-breakers, although Japanese workers employed for the fruit harvest in California, for example, received wages considerably higher than those earned by 'the clergymen of the Methodist community'. Elsewhere too coolies' wages were no lower than those of many white workers (cf. Eckstein, 1910, pp. 787ff).

According to a report published in 1910, a strike involving the 70,000 Japanese sugar workers in Hawaii was broken after three months by the planters with the assistance of the American and Japanese governments – neither the American unions nor the Socialist Party took any action to prevent the use of strike-breakers. Instead they remained silent (cf. Katayama, 1910, pp. 734f).

The conduct of the American political parties and unions has been criticized by German observers. Kautsky, for example, is in no doubt that agitation 'by individual comrades, not in England, but in America... is intended to replace the class struggle with racial conflict' (Kautsky, 1910, p. 777). Yet even the German labour movement's attitude towards coolies and other foreign workers was not free of racist overtones. There was a great deal of discussion of backward races, of their cultural poverty, and of the shameful nature (by European standards) of their lives, highly dangerous to public morality (cf. Eckstein, 1906–7, p. 549). Bauer (1906–7) maintained that such proletarian migrations would have consequences for international solidarity. Writing on behalf of the Western European labour movement, he explained:

> Hence the workers of every nation seek to support the social struggles of their class comrades in other countries. On the other hand, the proletariat feels threatened when workers of foreign extraction and from alien civilizations enter the international labour market as competitors, and the workers therefore seek to exclude the foreign proletariat from their labour markets. (Bauer, 1906–7, p. 489)

Rather than explain the contradictions of the international market for goods and capital, the function of the colonies as markets for goods and for capital exports on the one hand, and the national labour market on the other, Bauer expounds instead the niceties of proletarian international solidarity in a section on proletarian immigration policy. In doing so his *Lietmotiv* is the view, 'Above all the working class must take into account the fact that the lower the cultural level of the immigrants, the more dangerous such immigration will prove to be!' (p. 492). He demands the creation of a strictly defined alien law. The guiding principles for proletarian immigration should, according to Bauer, be as follows:

> Complete freedom of movement for emigrants from industrialized, capitalist countries; an energetic struggle against the import of workers by capitalists for the purposes of forcing down wages; freedom of

movement for those emigrating from countries with agrarian household economies, supplemented by a system of effective social and political protective measures. (Bauer, 1906–7, p. 494)

The above contains an undoubtedly legitimate and necessary rejection of contract labour, but also a call for a two-tier system of immigration ('freedom of movement' for one, 'complete freedom of movement' for the other) and a cry for assistance from the state – all basic elements of the policy which the Federal Republic of Germany has since pursued.

On the whole, the labour and trade union movements' attitudes towards coolieism demonstrate that they were, to a large extent, incapable of conceiving of Indian, Chinese and Javanese workers exploited by European or American capital as class comrades. What stood in the way were racist notions and stances, but also a partial identification of their interests with those of the capitalist system.

Notes

1. This is typical of the content of the numerous laws, decrees, etc. which governments promulgated for the purposes of regulating the recruitment and deployment of Asian labour. Their declared intention was generally to reform and humanize this system of exploitation, but the measures they adopted had little effect on the actual plight of the workers. For this reason, I do not intend to look in any detail at the debate surrounding such laws etc. or their consequences.

2. Taken from Ferenczi and Willcox, 1929; Lal, 1984; North-Coombes, 1984; Roberts and Byrne, 1966; Pelzer, 1935; and Tinker, 1974.

3. The following figures were taken from: Graves, 1984; Hertzmann, 1980; Katayama, 1910; Kung, 1962; Pelzer, 1935; Richardson, 1984, and Weggel, 1983.

4. Between 1873 and 1917, 34,000 Indians arrived in Surinam as contract labourers. Around one third of them returned home. The Indians who emigrated to Surinam represented only a small proportion of the total number of coolies who emigrated from India, yet today their ancestors form the largest grouping within the population of Surinam (cf. Goslinga, 1979, p. 159).

5. This probably means that they were regarded as the personal property of various men. The literature on the subject contains no further information on the matter.

4. Africa since 1880: From Colonial Forced Labour and Migrant Labour to Labour Migration and the Homelands System

The third stage in the development of the world market for labour power, following slavery and coolieism, was colonial forced labour and migrant labour, both of which were used first and foremost in Africa south of the Sahara. Not until decades after the first coolie migrations did colonialists begin to develop numerous new methods of acquiring African labour. Whereas in Asia the migration of unfree labour gradually came to an end during the first half of the 20th century, in Africa it lasted well into the second half of the 20th century. It still exists in some parts today.

Common to the two main labour systems used during the second and third stages in the world market for labour power was that they were both a mixture of and intermediate between slavery and forced labour on the one hand and wage labour on the other. Common to the first and third stages of the world market for labour power was that they both involved the exploitation of the African peoples. It was peculiar to the societies of this continent that their incorporation into the capitalist market for goods and capital did not precede their incorporation into the world market for labour power. In fact, it did not even occur at roughly the same time. Instead, Africa, unlike America and Asia, for a long time served exclusively as a supplier of labour (slaves) for colonial production. For the most part it was centuries before capitalist societies also began to buy large quantities of agricultural produce and raw materials there. By 1850 the imperialist powers had still only conquered 7.5 per cent of the entire surface area of the continent (Nzula et al., 1979, p. 20).

Not until the real colonial penetration of the continent in the second half of the 19th century did the European capitalists begin to doubt the expediency of exporting African labour to America: it was time for Africa itself to become the scene of colonial production. Since Africa was the last continent to be colonized, the labour power which such a move required could not be imported on a large scale from elsewhere, yet the population of Africa had been decimated by centuries of forced migration. In addition, the producers' free access to the soil, which characterized the traditional

African economy, made it difficult for the colonial powers to recruit workers to meet their needs, as bearers, gatherers, miners, plantation workers, ranch hands and domestic servants.

How then were the colonial powers to obtain the labour power which they required? The answer is simple: through various forms of forced and migrant labour. These represented the second form of or stage in the African peoples' incorporation into the world market for labour power. The first had been slavery. Thus the Age of Imperialism, which saw the division of Africa between the European colonial powers emerge as one of the most important questions of European policy, also witnessed the development of numerous strategies, which would guarantee the colonial rulers and settlers a supply of black labour until well into the 20th century.

From the beginning numerous foreign powers competed for the right to plunder Africa, as they had plundered Latin America and to some extent Asia. As each new territory was occupied the power responsible attempted to oust those who had been there before and to extend its jurisdiction and sphere of influence as far as possible. There were numerous different methods for recruiting labour: every colony proceeded differently, and even colonies owned by the same European country developed different methods depending both on the commodity which that colony or a particular region of it was intended to produce and on its political or social circumstances and objectives. A multitude of strategies, forms and methods emerged by means of which the African labour force could be incorporated into production for the capitalist world market, so many that they cannot each be examined in detail.

A basic feature of all these systems, however, was that they relied on the use of direct or indirect force. Nor did the colonial powers which employed them differ to any great extent from each other in their objectives: they all insisted that production be export-orientated and that the colonial rulers or settlers should be able to earn a living in the colonies. It was not uncommon in any colony for migrant workers to have to travel huge distances and to stay away from home for long periods.

The first section of this chapter gives an overview and various examples, especially from German colonial history, of forced and migrant labour in colonial Africa between 1880 and 1962.

Naturally the structures created as a result of colonial penetration did not disappear overnight in 1962. In fact, they still shape economic, social and political conditions in African societies today and are particularly apparent on the labour market. The problem nowadays, however, is no longer one of labour shortages, a great cause for complaint among European colonists everywhere, especially at the beginning of the colonial age when traditional modes of production were still largely intact. Instead the situation has been totally reversed. Nowadays free labour without access to the means of production can be found almost everywhere in Africa, for the destruction of traditional modes of production was one of the major consequences of colonial rule.

As a result of this change the physical violence and direct compulsion that once characterized the recruitment of workers in the colonies has been replaced for the most part by economic pressure. The supply of labour power to capitalist plantations, ranches, mines etc. is now guaranteed on a more continuous and rational basis than was previously the case.

Nevertheless, migrant labour is still one of the most important forms of labour in Africa, all the more so since most of today's African states are the result of imperialist rivalries from the end of the 19th century. The 'national' frontiers are the old colonial, artificially drawn frontiers and bear no relation to the continent's ethnic, geographical or economic structures. For migrant workers these frontiers often – not merely in times of crisis – mean increased lack of rights, since they can easily become 'foreigners' amongst members of their own people or in the territories they traditionally inhabit.

For the purposes of examining Africa's present-day structures we will look in detail at two examples. The second section of this chapter deals with the labour policy pursued by the Republic of South Africa, which continues to employ the tactics of a colony of white settlers and to take these to extremes. The third and final section looks at labour migration in West Africa. This came under close scrutiny when Nigeria expelled millions of migrant workers in 1983, and it is for this reason the section concentrates on these events.

Due to their membership of the Arab world and their geographic location near Europe, the states of North Africa enjoy closer ties with these regions than with black Africa, at least as far as the world market for labour power is concerned. Accordingly they will not be considered in detail in this chapter.

Forced labour and migrant labour systems in colonized Africa

'It is not an exaggeration to say that 20 per cent of the workers end up as agricultural fertilizer each year...'
Deutsche Reichs-Post, 1900, issue 93 on the working conditions of African plantation workers in the German colony of Cameroon
(cited in Mandeng, 1973, p. 93)

The colonial division of Africa between the European powers, which was agreed at the Berlin West Africa Conference in 1884, served as a prelude to the so-called Age of Imperialism. In Africa recruiting the labour required to exploit the continent's natural resources was a huge problem for each of the colonial powers. A *Deutsches Koloniallexikon* (German colonial encyclopedia) compiled in 1914 declared the procurement of workers to be 'one of the major tasks facing the colonial economy, since these are the basis of all colonial exploitation... The number of workers available in a colony is the measure of that colony's potential' (Schnee, 1920, p. 71).

By this time the colonizers had already developed numerous systems to procure the workers they required, whether by violence, by force, or through other methods. Rarely did they need to resort to importing workers from abroad; the majority of those who were imported came from India or China. The principal source of labour, however, was the Africans themselves.

Great Britain and France became great rivals very early on in the imperialist contest for the African continent, although Germany, Portugal, Spain, Italy and Belgium also conquered some areas. Table 6 gives a breakdown, according to surface area, of the territory controlled by the imperialist powers in 1928. According to this table, France and Great Britain were by far the leading colonial powers, and whilst Belgium and Portugal owned the third and fourth largest colonial empires in Africa, they had only been able to bring under their control an area a third or a quarter the size of that governed by the French or British.

Table 6
The territorial division of Africa under the imperialist powers (1928)

Great Britain	9,000,000 sq km
France	8,000,000 sq km
Belgium	2,410,000 sq km
Portugal	2,100,000 sq km
Italy	1,590,000 sq km
Spain	310,000 sq km
USA	100,000 sq km

Source: Nzula et al., 1979, p. 20

By 1928 the German Empire had already lost its colonies. With South west Africa, East Africa, Cameroon and Togo these had once covered a total of 2.7 million square kilometres (cf. Mamozai, 1982, p. 29).

When one considers the length of Africa's colonial history, the loss of the German colonies was premature, yet this did not mean that forced labour was any less important here. During the decades of German rule strategies for exploiting the native workforce in the African colonies were developed and employed systematically.

Speaking at the German Colonial Congress in 1910, government doctor and colonial official Dr Külz affirmed the need for a colonial health policy. His remarks clearly demonstrate the value which both the Germans and the other colonial powers placed on the Africans:

> The native is the most valuable economic capital in our colonies ... If it were possible for better hygiene to achieve a lasting increase in the population then the outlook for all colonial economic problems would obviously be much brighter as a direct result ... Let me give an example from a negative point of view: let us assume that a smallpox epidemic

spreads throughout a tract of land and claims – shall we say – 5,000 human lives. If one fixes the capital value, in terms of taxable capacity, productive capacity, purchasing and labour power, or even as a father or mother, of each deceased worker at a minimum annual rate of 10 Marks, then on the assumption that that worker would have lived on average another ten years we have suffered a direct loss of half a million as a result of a single limited epidemic ... (Cited in Bald et al., 1978, p. 107)

This notion of the African shaped colonial policy – luckily one might say, since in Africa itself the idea that the population and therefore the workforce had economic value still had to find practical acceptance.

Using the southern regions of Cameroon as a model, Mandeng (1973) examines the exploitation of African labour power under German colonial rule and demonstrates clearly that bearers were of vital importance in the early stages of colonial penetration. As the leading sectors of the colonial economy, the gathering of wild rubber under rubber farming and the extraction of palm kernels and palm oil initially formed the basis of colonial trade in this region. In 1902 the 'trade-back' system was introduced, whereby caravans carried various commodities (e.g. salt, soap, tobacco, alcohol, and later also cotton clothing and other textiles) into the hinterland, distributed them amongst the population there, and took wild rubber extracted on the way back in return.

The caravans required a large number of bearers, and from 1901 onwards recruiting them was a constant problem, which could only be solved by the use of force. The conditions under which bearers had to work (and about which they were often deceived) were extreme. They were required to travel huge distances, and until 1907 their wages consisted almost exclusively of spirits, tobacco and cheap wares. Food was often acquired through raids on African villages organized by the caravaneers. Mortality rates were high. Not only men but also women and children were forced to work as bearers, and in some areas they constituted more than one third of this particular workforce (Mandeng, 1973, p. 60).

According to Müller (1962, p. 36), the number of bearers employed in the German colonies actually exceeded

... the total number of workers employed on the plantations throughout the entire German colonial era. It is believed that in 1914 southern Cameroon alone had 80,000 bearers of both sexes carrying loads for colonial trade ... It was not uncommon for 30,000 bearers to be staying in each of the East African caravan centres of Tabora and Bagamayo at any one time.

The first traces of a plantation economy in southern Cameroon date back at least to 1884. During the first few years migrant workers from other colonies were of great importance to the plantations, but after a while private and official recruitment drives were conducted in Cameroon itself.

Once again compulsion and deception were widely used to recruit workers, and women and children as well as men were press-ganged into signing up. Numerous German ranches on Kilimanjaro relied exclusively on child labour (cf. Bald et al., 1978, p. 95; see also Müller, 1962, p. 31).

The third large sector for which labour was recruited was the building of infrastructure, which in southern Cameroon primarily meant the construction of railways. As was the case elsewhere, the physically tiring and dangerous work this involved was carried out first and foremost by forced labour supplied under duress by the chieftains. If a worker ran away, the chieftain who had sent him or her was responsible for finding a replacement (Mandeng, 1973, p. 170). In East Africa even children and adolescents were used in road construction. Often they worked in neck and foot irons.

Like others, the German colonies eventually suffered a decrease in population as a result of this excessive exploitation of the labour force. A letter mentioned in the Reichstag on 7 March 1914 states:

... that in the district of Yaunde, which we had all regarded as an inexhaustible reservoir of human beings, the population is actually falling in absolute terms. Out of 100,000 able-bodied men 92,000 are employed as bearers, or as railway or plantation workers, with the result that only 8,000 remain to tend the fields, reclaim land and clear the bush...

In the same year another report examined the situation in German East Africa and described the conditions thus:

At one time the population of the district of Tabora, actually Unyamwezi, was officially estimated at around half a million. Now it is 405,000. At one time there were an average of five inhabitants to each hut. Now there are only three. Children under the age of four are conspicuously rare. (Cited in Müller, 1962, p. 37)

At the end of World War One the German Empire lost its African colonies. For Africa and its inhabitants the war had meant not only the loss of lives and destruction, but also a large-scale mobilization of labour power. Not only did the imperialist powers conscript soldiers, they also recruited a large number of civilian workers for the war economy. Between 1914 and 1918 Great Britain recruited 55,000 bearers in West Africa alone. The number recruited in East Africa was higher still. 'Nevertheless, the recruitment of tens of thousands of British West Africans during World War One represented a mobilization of its labour force the likes of which West Africa had never seen before' (Killingray and Matthews, 1979, p. 7).

The bearers, who despised this 'donkey work', were generally forced into it and were employed not solely in their home regions, but also in distant territories and overseas. There were, for example, some 10,000 West Africans at work in East Africa, and around 15,000 bearers from

Cameroon and 10,000 East Africans carried loads overseas for the British. The conditions under which they lived and worked were extreme. A report compiled on bearers working in Cameroon during World War One recorded more than half of the 14,184 people concerned as invalids. Their disabilities included foot and leg ulcers, malaria, 'debility' (weakness) and 'wasting' (a lingering illness). The annual mortality rate for British bearers in southern Nigeria was 394 per 1,000. On average only 37 per cent of those recruited were still able to perform their duties after nine months.

'Coloured helpers' (cf. Fonck, 1917) were not of military importance for Great Britain alone. During the war Germany also recruited a large number of bearers in Cameroon and elsewhere.

> In 1919 one high-ranking German colonial official estimated that Germany had lost 100,000 to 120,000 bearers in East Africa and that in the same theatre of war the Allies had lost 250,000. He conjectured that during World War One an additional 300,000 or so people had perished in East Africa as a result of hunger, privation, and illness. According to this estimate, more than half a million Africans paid for Lettow-Vorbeck's diehard strategy with their lives. (Cited in Bald et al., 1978, p. 172)

During the war France used its North African and Asian colonies first and foremost as reservoirs of labour power; 1916 saw the creation of the Service des Travailleurs Coloniaux, a body answerable to the Ministry of War. In creating this body the government took over direct responsibility for the recruitment, importation, distribution and supervision of the colonial labour force. By the end of the war 130,000 to 150,000 colonial workers – as they were appropriately known – from the Maghreb alone had been forced to emigrate to France (cf. Talha, 1976, p. 244). They travelled each with a sign around their neck on which was written the name of the 'addressee', e.g. 'M. Lehoux, à Authon (Gare), Eure et Loire'. In addition, France imported some 49,000 workers from Indochina (Alouane, 1979, p. 23) and 140,000 from China (Gernet, 1979, p. 520).

The colonies also had to supply the European powers with large numbers of soldiers. France recruited 175,000 men for this purpose in Algeria alone, 51,000 in Tunisia and 34,000 in Morocco (Meinicke-Kleint, 1961, p. 108).

Assessing the significance of World War One to the mobilization of labour power in the Maghreb, Talha writes:

> The war was an excellent testing ground on which to carry out the required conversion of dispossessed peasants into an industrial proletariat. The operation had not long begun, but as a result of its proven effectiveness it was soon adopted as a practical method of recruitment. (Talha, 1976, p. 245)

In terms of French labour policy this meant the mobilization of workers not merely for exportation to other colonized territories, but also directly to Europe. For Africa it meant an enormous forced mobilization of labour power organized from outside within the space of a few years.

What these few figures indicate about the nature and scale of recruitment during World War One also applies to colonial rule before and after the war. Forced labour in various forms was the principle universally applied to the exploitation of Africa by every European power. It reached a relatively early and extreme peak in Congo Free State during the programme of plunder embarked upon by the Belgians under the rule of Leopold II in 1885. Leopold regarded this country, 60 times the size of Belgium, as his own personal property. Its inhabitants existed, he believed, above all to supply rubber. Within the space of 25 years his bloody programme of plunder cost 8 million human lives (cf. Morel, cited in Bodley, 1983; see also Morel, 1904, pp. 237ff).

A multitude of methods were used to force the population into handing over large quantities of rubber. Armed men were stationed in the villages, and hostages, mostly women and children, were taken in order to force the men into submission. Many of the hostages died, since they received no attention at all in the purpose-built huts. Further examples of methods used to press-gang the population into work included high monetary fines and military punitive expeditions including the destruction of villages and the mutilation of their inhabitants (see among others Kloosterboer, 1976, pp. 122f). The severing of hands was a common punishment. In some places soldiers had to present a hand for every cartridge which they had used, and men, women and children were also tortured in this way for delivering rubber late or in insufficient quantities.

The following extract from King Leopold's *Bulletin officiel* gives an idea of the profits realized by such means:

> The results were unprecedented. In 1895 the district produced more than 650 tons of rubber, which were bought for a few pence per kilo [sic!] and sold in Antwerp at thirty times their cost ... (Conan Doyle, 1985, p. 67)

This was a profit margin of 3,000 per cent. Although what happened in the Congo is the most extreme illustration of the nature, scale and effects of forced labour in Africa, this form of labour was also used in the colonies belonging to other powers. The consequences were always the same. In 1910, for example, the French colony of Equatorial Guinea had a population of 7.5 million. By 1924 only 2.5 million inhabitants were left (cf. Padmore, 1931, p. 242).

After World War One the extent to which forced labour was used in Africa diminished considerably, yet decades later it was still common throughout the continent. Table 7 gives, among other things, an overview of the extent to which compulsory labour was used in various colonies according to official figures published by each of the colonial powers. In the French, Spanish, Belgian and Portuguese colonies, which the table covers, there was often not only forced and compulsory labour, but also forced planting and punitive labour.

Table 7
Africa: the pattern of labour regulation (compiled in October 1939)

+ = exists
- = does not exist
empty = no data

	Belgian Congo	Rwanda-Urundi	French Equatorial Africa	Madagascar	French West Africa	French Mandate Cameroon	French Mandate Togo	Angola	Mozambique	Spanish colonies
1. Special native authorities	+		-	-	-					+
2. Forced and compulsory labour	+	+	+	+	+	+	+	+	+	+
3. Forced planting	+	+	+		+	+		+	+	
4. Statutory contract of employment	+	+	+	+	+	exceptional	almost extinct	+	+	+
5. Worker's pass or similar (in use)	+	+	+	+	+	+	+	+	+	+
6. Length of contract of employment (years)	1–3	1–3	max. 2	max. 2	max. 2	max. 2	max. 2	1–4	1–4	1
7. Contractual duty to send home	+	+	+	+	+	-	-	+	+	+
8. Contractual monetary advance	-	-	+	+	+	+		+	+	+
9. Medical examination before contract	+	+	+	+	+	+	+	-	-	
10. Feeding scheme regulated by contract	+				+				+	+
11. Accommodation included in contract	+	+	+	+	+			+	+	+

Table 7
Africa: the pattern of labour regulation (compiled in October 1939)

+ = exists
- = does not exist
empty = no data

	Belgian Congo	Rwanda-Urundi	French Equatorial Africa	Madagascar	French West Africa	French Mandate Cameroon	French Mandate Togo	Angola	Mozambique	Spanish colonies
12. Punitive labour	+	+	-	-	-	-	-	+	+	+
13. Female and child labour (in use)	+		+	+	+	+	+	+	+	+
14. Type of recruitment	a	a	b	b	b	a	c	a	a	d
15. Advertised maximum rate (for suitable men)	-26(31)%	-20%	-33.3%	(50%?)	-20%	-12%				
16. Number employed	1930: 409,665 1938: 528,200	1933: 20,062 1937: 54,638 (+49,257)				1935: 53,604	1937: 1,539 in private concerns			
17. Public health officers	1:34,000	1:130,000	1:40,000	1:65,000	1:81,000	1:52,000	1:76,000	1:43,000	1:52,000	
18. Taxes (for natives)	Poll tax Polygamy tax	Poll tax Polygamy sub. tax	Co-op sub. Poll tax		Co-op sub. Poll tax Cattle tax	Co-op sub. Poll tax Cattle tax Health tax	Co-op sub. Poll tax	Poll tax	Poll tax	

a: semi-official and private b: semi-official c: private d: official and private
NB For the sake of clarity the table can only give an approximate overview.

The only way in which the natives could raise enough money to pay the taxes levied almost everywhere was by working for the colonial rulers, and these taxes must therefore be regarded as an indirect form of forced labour. Table 7 makes it clear that the colonial powers used female and child labour as a matter of course.

One further feature common to all of the African colonies was that they each recruited labour power on a large scale for the building of infrastructure, above all roads and railways. These traffic routes helped to make the exploitation of the colonies more effective, to facilitate the transportation of goods and to guarantee military control.

Although some Indian coolies were imported, for example to build the Uganda Railway, the majority of the labour power needed for such projects was generally supplied by the Africans themselves, and these were procured without exception among the colonial powers by forced recruitment. Countless people died in the process.

A report in the Paris *Quotidien* of 26 February 1929 claimed that 25,000 negroes had perished 'so far' whilst building the stretch of railway between Brazzaville and Pointe Noire in the French Congo, and the report of an English missionary from the Belgian 'mandated territory' of Rwanda-Urundi (which he calls the 'land of skeletons'), maintained that as a result of forced labour 60,000 workers in the last year and 30,000 in the year before had met a horrible fate. (Furtwängler, 1929)

In the British colonies, which have not yet been discussed, the regime was equally harsh. In southern Nigeria the British used forced labour in order to complete planned railway lines by 1926 and a road network adequate for their purposes by 1930. Later they replaced forced labour with indirect taxes (cf. Pogarell, 1984, p. 70).

According to Padmore (1931, p. 240), forced labour was more common in the English colony of Kenya than anywhere else in Africa. All natives between the ages of 15 and 50 had to register. Their fingerprints were taken and they had to wear signs, so-called *kipandi*s, around their necks. In 1927 a third of the people registered in this way were called up for work; an order issued to the chieftains in 1919 by the colonial government resulted in 70,000 women and 150,000 children being sent to work on European ranches within the space of a few months (Padmore, 1931, p. 241).

Under colonial conditions there was no difference between forced labour and wage labour. In some cases wages were paid for forced labour and in some cases wage labour carried out by dispossessed peasants or in order to pay taxes was nothing short of indirect forced labour. 'In most African colonies a breach of a contract of employment on the part of a native is an offence under criminal law and may thus be punished by the colonial authorities' (Karstedt, 1941, p. 5). Illustration 8 shows a Bill of Indictment specially drafted for use in the event of a worker leaving his job without permission. The bill is of the sort in use in Kenya in 1922.

The Chief Registrar of Natives,   N.A.D Form No. 54/ .
        NAIROBI.
        COMPLAINT OF DESERTION OF REGISTERED NATIVE.

Native's Certificate No.............................Name...................... ....,

The above native deserted from my employ ....
                                                        (date)
He was engaged on........................... .on.................... .days verbal contract
            (date)   ....months written contract

    at..   ....
            (place)   (Called upon to produce evidence
        I wish to prosecute him for this offence and hereby agree to appear to give evidence
if and when called upon

                            ....
                                    Signature of Employer.

Address ....

        ....
Date...................................

The Chief Registrar of Natives,   N.A.D Form No. 54/ .....
        NAIROBI.
        COMPLAINT OF DESERTION OF REGISTERED NATIVE.

Native's Certificate No..........................Name...,

The above native deserted from my employ...
                                                        (date)
He was engaged on..................................on...................days verbal contract
            (date)   ....months written contract

    at..   ....
            (place)   (Called upon to produce evidence
        I wish to prosecute him for this offence and hereby agree to appear to give evidence
if and when called upon.

                            ....
                                    Signature of Employer

Address ....

        ....
Date...................................

A Bill of Indictment for use when a worker deserts his job, Kenya, 1922
(Source: McGregor Ross, 1927, pp. 196f)

*In Kenya in 1922 the natives were taught 'the value of work'. A native
committed a criminal offence if he left his job without permission. The
above tear-off slip would be supplied free of charge by the government,
and if the employer filled it in then the government would hunt down and
arrest the deserter. Any employer summoned as a witness in the resulting
trial was entitled to claim witness expenses.*

The terms 'forced labour' and 'wage labour' were often interchangeable under colonial rule, and the two forms of labour regularly overlapped. Time and time again both they and their countless blends were combined with migrant labour, itself another common solution to the colonial labour question in Africa.

Africa's intercontinental labour migrations were composed of a multitude of large-scale and small-scale movements, and though most of these movements took place within the borders of just one European colonial empire, workers often had to negotiate distances of up to several thousand kilometres. The trend was for workers to head for the coast, since this was where the majority of the European plantations and ranches that required workers were located.

In Africa forced and migrant labour continued throughout the 19th and early 20th centuries. Müller (1962) refers to a recent case:

> In the summer of 1960 a colonial slave trader sent hectographed advertisements to England in which he offered 'strong and healthy [African] workers aged between 20 and 30' to English farmers as 'temporary workers'. The 'natives' concerned were to be 'consigned' to the nearest railway station and could be met there. The slave trader was asking £150 as his 'agent's commission'.

It was not only in those parts of Africa that remained English or Portuguese colonies until the 1960s or 1970s that forms of forced labour continued to exist. The solution to the labour question in the Republic of South Africa still relies on it today.

It is true to say that colonial forced and migrant labour in Africa was comparable in character and scale with both African slavery and coolieism, the system which had tossed the Asian peoples onto the world market for labour power. It took on similar dimensions, and the levels of exploitation and destruction for which it was responsible were of no less significance. Yet colonial forced and migrant labour retained its importance well into the second half of the 20th century.

The homeland system as a 'solution' to the labour question in the Republic of South Africa

White settlers began to colonize southern Africa as early as the 17th century, considerably earlier than they did the interior of the continent or North Africa. It was not long before large numbers of the region's original inhabitants had been exterminated (cf. Ripken, 1978, p. 155).

Initially most of the settlers were engaged in agriculture, for which they recruited Africans as forced labour and slaves. For a long time the territory settled by the whites expanded slowly, but in the 19th century the pace of advance quickened. In 1806 the Cape region became a British colony, and in 1834 the British banned the ownership of slaves. During the years which followed the Boers, the descendants of Dutchmen who had settled in South Africa after 1652, headed northeast on the Great Trek and founded two republics: the Orange Free State and the Transvaal. The emergence of Natal added another name to the list of British colonies. In 1880–81 a second Boer War broke out. Although the English won the war, they allowed the Boers to keep their republics, and the founding of the Union of South Africa in 1910 finally signified the victory of the Boer line on the African population and above all on labour policy. One manifestation of this victory was the fact that numerous laws were passed in the following decades, the aim of which was to exclude all non-whites from the economic, political and social life of South Africa to such an extent that their only role was as 'cheap' labour for ranches, mines and the nascent industrial sector.

The mines were particularly important. At the end of the 19th century diamonds were found in Kimberley and huge gold deposits were discovered in the Transvaal. These events triggered off a programme of economic restructuring and caused growing demand for labour. The South African economy's centre of gravity shifted from agriculture to mining and consequent industrialization. Today mining is still the economy's leading sector. South Africa commands a 59 per cent share of the world's gold production, a 55 per cent share of the world's platinum production, a 46 per cent share of the world's vanadium production, a 30 per cent share of the world's chrome ore production, and has also reached double figures for antimony, manganese, diamonds, uranium and asbestos (Ripken, 1978, p. 148).

This crucial branch of industry relies on the exploitation of Africans: 90 per cent of the workers, whether South African or from other states, are black.

Table 8
South Africa: proportion of black workers in the various economic sectors (1970)

Mining	90%
South African workers	38%
foreign workers	52%
Agriculture	89%
Service industries	67%
Manufacturing industry	49%

Bantus make up 71.2 per cent of the total population (1975)

Source: Hübner-Dick and Seidelmann, 1978, p. 162

The transformation of African societies into a ready, flexible source of labour power for the settlers' economy began in the 18th and 19th centuries. The first pass laws were introduced as early as 1760, more than 200 years ago (Callinicos, 1980, p. 47). Poll, hut and in particular labour taxes forced black Africans to work in the white sector. Labour tax, for example, was payable at the rate of one rand per annum by anyone who could not prove that he had worked for three months of the year as a wage worker (Callinicos, 1980, p. 30). Nevertheless, it has always proved difficult for the South Africans to recruit sufficient numbers of workers (cf. Olivier, 1906, pp. 88ff), especially since the dramatic growth in the demand for labour when mining began at the end of the 19th century. Between 1887 and 1899 the number of Africans employed as mineworkers in the region of Witwatersrand rose from 3,000 to 10,000 (*Zwangsumsiedlungen in Südafrika*, 1984, p. 43). What is more, the labour force had suffered serious erosion: in 1903, for example, 5,022 black workers died in the mines (Callinicos, 1980, p. 57).

It was under these circumstances that the white settlers in the Union of South Africa, founded in 1910, arrived at a systematic solution to the region's labour question. In essence their strategy, which still forms the basis of the South African economy, consisted of three interlinked elements:

1. 'White territories: almost all the nation's territory (87 per cent) was reserved for the white settler minority. Today there are 4.8 million whites, 4.8 million privileged people out of a total population of 31 million. Black people living in the 'white' areas were deprived of all their rights and most were removed. Only those required as workers were permitted to remain, and then under extremely restrictive conditions.
2. Reservoirs of labour power in the form of 'homelands' or 'Bantustans': these were formed out of the old reservations and were gradually granted so-called independence. However, the homelands have consistently lacked the basic elements necessary to life. Their essential function was and is to serve as reservoirs of labour power for the South African economy and to supply it with migrant labour.
3. Satellite states: a series of satellite states served as additional reservoirs of labour power and also as markets, met additional demand for migrant labour, and intensified competition between workers.

These three elements will now be considered in greater detail.

1. 'White' territories

Soon after the founding of the Union of South Africa in 1910, numerous laws were passed, the purposes of which were to permit black workers to reside in the towns and white territories only if they were really needed there and to keep wages as low as possible. In 1911 it was decreed that Africans should not be awarded skilled workers' qualifications and that a breach of contract on their part was a criminal offence. In 1913 Africans were forbidden from acquiring land outside the reservations scattered around the country, although initially these reservations covered only 7.3 per cent of the country's entire surface area. Between 1923 and 1930 the government introduced segregation by race in residential areas, and municipal authorities were granted the right to expel from their districts blacks who were 'surplus to requirements'. Other measures adopted included the 1925 requirement for all Africans to present a valid receipt for their taxes following a request from any government official, including a policeman; the imposition in 1927 of a curfew for blacks; the establishment in 1950 of a government department to deal with racial classification, the resettlement in 1951-2 of thousands of black families, and the 1952 extension to women of the pass laws. Four years later the passes were replaced by workers' books, which all Africans over the age of 16 had to carry on them at all times. In 1953 it became illegal to protest against any law in force in the country, and in 1956 the government introduced 'job reservation', whereby certain jobs were reserved for certain racial groups (cf. Weiss, 1980, pp. 142ff, and Ripken, 1978, pp. 155ff).

The above list is by no means complete, but it demonstrates that every measure adopted by the government pursued the same goal: to supply the settlers' economy with disenfranchised and exploitable workers.

Following the founding of the Republic of South Africa and its secession from the Commonwealth in 1961, the government continued to pursue the same policies. From 1968, Africans living in the towns were only permitted to inhabit rented accommodation, from 1975 onwards, the government was able to punish violations of the pass laws by sentencing offenders to time in labour camps, and in 1978 the government granted itself extensive powers to deport unemployed black workers to the homelands.

The above measures were all accompanied by the forcible resettlement to the homelands of millions of black Africans. As early as the 1950s it was decreed that every black belonged to a homeland, regardless of whether he or she was born there (cf. Weiss, 1980, p. 150). Between 1960 and 1980, 3,372,900 Africans were resettled, and another 1,740,500 are currently threatened with the same fate (*Zwangsumsiedlungen in Südafrika*, 1984, p. 15).

2. Reservoirs of labour in the form of homelands or Bantustans

By means of such flexible resettlement, the South African government has created a total of ten homelands, all of which are surrounded by the national territory of South Africa and most of which are composed of various separate sections of territory. The KwaZulu homeland, for example, consists of 40 separate territories. Between 1976 and 1981 the Transkei, Bophuthatswana, Venda and Ciskei homelands were all declared 'republics'. Although these 'republics' have been denied international recognition, their creation has resulted in the inhabitants of these territories, a total of 9 million people, being granted alien status in South Africa. 'The Africans are forced to live on reservations, but it is virtually impossible for them to survive there. The Bantustans are incapable of guaranteeing even a few of their *de jure* citizens a living' (Gervasi, 1972, p. 47). The white government has scattered the dismembered and overpopulated homelands throughout the national territory in such a way as to allocate them to various white ranches, mines and industrial and residential areas. The black workers living in these giant camps are then exploited as commuters and migrant workers. All those who are surplus to requirements, those not yet or no longer fit for work, children, the elderly, the infirm, and sick workers, remain in the homelands and must seek to secure their survival by cultivating tiny patches of often barren land.

In this way the white settlers' capitalist economy is able to reproduce black labour power in the homelands at no cost to itself. The homelands are also instruments of political oppression. Strikers, for example, are often deported to them.

The situation in the homelands is continually worsening.

> The reservations' share of South Africa's Gross Domestic Product is continually on the decline: whereas it amounted to 7 per cent in 1936, it had fallen to 3.7 per cent by 1950 and 2 per cent by 1970. In 1970 some 30 per cent of the total population of South Africa lived in the so-called homelands... yet only 10 to 15 per cent of their per capita income is generated in the homelands themselves. The remainder is earned in the white territories by migrant workers.' (Ripken and Wellmer, 1978, pp. 196f)

Due to growing unemployment in the white territories migrant workers are now finding it increasingly difficult to get work. In 1985 some 3 million blacks outside the 'independent' homelands were unemployed, and 58 per cent of the population of Soweto live below the poverty line (cf. Brückner and Hättig, 1985, p. 20).

In order to maintain this system for the benefit of the white settlers the government has successfully adopted a racist variant of the old 'divide and rule' strategy. The labour force is first classified according to race (black, white, coloured or Indian), and the black majority then subdivided. The homelands are established and settled by tribe, and this and other measures adopted by the government serve to promote tribal divisions. Moreover, the rivalry between black workers feeds the antagonisms that already exist between the permanently settled urban proletariat with its higher paid jobs as semi-skilled workers on the one hand, and the migrant and ranch proletariat on the other. The latter has, to all intents and purposes, been deprived by migration control legislation of every opportunity to enter the higher-paid professions. A third group is made up of the blacks who serve the white government, as policemen for example, and who act as buffers to the opposition to white rule.

The particular form of migrant labour in South Africa, which feeds off the homelands and black bedroom townships on the outskirts of the white industrial towns, is quite blatantly based on force – although the ruling classes in South Africa naturally see it somewhat differently. A recent

Homeland	No. of people living in homeland (1983)	No. of people classed as belonging to homeland (1980)	Area, sq. km (1983)	'Republic' since	No. of larger sections (1983)
Transkei	2,502,317	4,157,269	42,000	26 Oct. 1976	3
Bophuthatswana	1,425,066	2,082,741	40,000	6 Dec. 1977	7
Venda	339,808	522,446	6,870	13 Sept. 1979	1
Ciskei	780,807	1,071,515	6,500	4 Dec. 1981	1
KwaNdebele	169,262	679,237	920		1
KaNgwane	173,963	736,853	3,720		2
KwaZulu	3,691,785	5,495,294	31,000		40
Lebowa	1,884,194	2,350,303	22,000		11
Qwaqwa	169,500	1,937,826	480		1
Gazankulu	554,602	985,070	6,750		4

South Africa: Population

23,000,000 blacks
4,800,000 whites
2,800,000 coloureds
900,000 Indians

Examples of townships

Soweto	c. 2,000,000 blacks
Lenasia	c. 60,000 Indians
Sharpeville	c. 100,000 blacks
KwaMashu	c. 200,000 blacks
Umlazi	c. 200,000 blacks
Mitchells Plain	c. 250,000 coloureds
Kayelitsha	c. 200,000 blacks

Raw materials in South Africa

Compared with:

	Deposits as % of world deposits (1978)	Extraction as % of world extraction (1981)	USSR extraction as % of world extraction (1981)
Platinum	73.4	44.0	49.1
Chrome	72.0	30.9	25.9
Vanadium	19.0	33.9	25.1
Gold	48.0	51.8	20.7
Iron	n.a.	3.5**	35.1**
Phosphate	46.0	2.4	19.2*
Manganese	44.0	21.4	39.9
Uranium†	15.1	15.3	n.a
Diamonds	7.0	27.6*	35.1*
Hard coal	n.a	4.8**	17.1**

* 1980   ** 1982   † Figures only for the Western World

government report stated, 'The fact is that the tribal natives now regard migrant labour as a tradition and a custom.'

3. Satellite states

The South African economy is not serviced only by black workers from South Africa. It also employs migrant workers from a whole series of black African states. Table 8 shows that 52 per cent of those employed in the mining industry come from black African countries; Table 9 gives a more detailed breakdown by geographical origin of all black workers employed in the mines. According to these figures, three quarters of the 401,000 blacks employed by the Chamber of Mines in the gold- and coalmines of South Africa are of foreign extraction. This can be explained first by the extreme working and living conditions in the mines: for example, only 3 per cent of the black workers employed in the mines are allocated family accommodation. Almost all are forced to live in massive compounds nothing short of labour camps, which afford the employer almost total control over the workforce.

Employment in the mines is based on the principle of rotation, with contracts of employment generally lasting between 12 and 18 months. The average depth of a mine shaft is 2,300m, the average temperature is 40°C, and humidity is relatively high at between 85 and 90 per cent. When workers are exposed to such conditions for long periods it is absolutely vital that they are then able to rest for several weeks. When they reapply, those who are no longer useful are weeded out and rejected (Weyl, 1976, pp. 193f).

The second factor that accounts for the large number of foreign workers willing to take on South Africa's most dangerous and physically exhausting jobs is the social and economic position in which the citizens of South Africa's satellite states find themselves as a consequence of their colonial past. Labour migration from Mozambique, for example, is directly linked with colonial policy. Between 1935 and 1960 the Portuguese used forced labour in Mozambique. The women worked in the cotton fields and the men on the sugar cane plantations. The mass migration which took place at the beginning of the Salazar era was partly caused by South Africa intensifying its recruitment campaigns in Mozambique, but also by the fact that migration was seen as a means of escape from colonial oppression and exploitation.

Botswana, Swaziland and Lesotho are all former British protectorates that have been kept in an extremely underdeveloped state. Botswana shares a border with South Africa, and the other two are surrounded by South African national territory. All three countries are heavily dependent on South Africa. Botswana, for example, has 50,000 wage workers employed within its own borders as opposed to around 46,000 migrant workers employed in South Africa. Out of a total population of less than one million it was expected that Botswana would have 35,000 migrant workers and 46,000 workers permanently unemployed during the period covered by the economic plan for the late 1970s.

The situation in Lesotho is similar. Here 45 per cent of the men and 7 per cent of the women who are economically active work in South Africa, and earnings from migrant labour amount to more than the country's gross national product. In Swaziland the economically active population numbers 72,000, of whom 35,000 work abroad (cf. Ripken, 1978, pp. 250f).

Table 9
South Africa: geographical origins of black workers engaged by the Chamber of Mines (1970)

Transvaal	3.1%
Natal and Zululand	1.5%
Swaziland	1.3%
Cape Province	17.9%
Lesotho	17.7%
Orange Free State	1.7%
Botswana	4.1%
Mozambique	28.2%
North of the 22nd Parallel	24.5%

Source: Randall, 1973, p. 97

Malawi is another leading reservoir of labour power, and not only for South Africa. Almost every Malawi man has worked abroad at least once in his life. In 1973 45 per cent of Malawi's migrant workers were employed in South Africa. In Table 9 they are included in the category 'North of the 22nd Parallel'.

One further feature of South Africa's use of migrant labour from its satellite states is that wages are negotiated directly between the governments. The workers receive part of their wages only when they return home. Such an arrangement strengthens the governments' economic commitment to this form of labour migration, for it supplies them directly with foreign currency. Nevertheless, South Africa's persistent economic crisis and the growth in the supply of labour from the homelands have led South Africa to record a decline in the number of workers employed from Mozambique and Malawi (cf. Stahl, 1981, pp. 38f).

At least in periods of low demand for black labour power, the South African government is generally able to rely on its own black population for the labour power it needs. The workers who supply that labour power are excluded from all social and economic participation in South African life, and their labour power is reproduced outside the settlers' capitalist economy.

It is no longer possible to ignore the growing opposition of those whom South Africa exploits. It is anybody's guess just how long the system can survive in its present form.

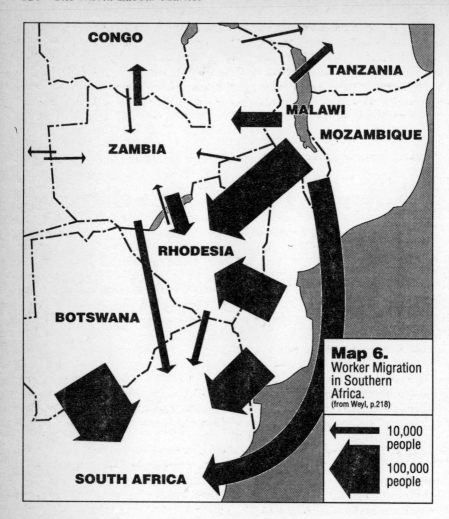

Map 6.
Worker Migration in Southern Africa.
(from Weyl, p.218)

10,000 people

100,000 people

Labour migration in Africa today

Though migration is still common today in Black Africa, statistical surveys on the subject are few and far between. Some of the migrants may almost certainly be described as migrant workers, but there are also large numbers of expellees and refugees on the move. UN estimates for 1981 suggest that

Africa is accommodating around five million of the eight million refugees currently being catered for worldwide; data compiled by the Organization of African Unity (OAU) talks in terms of 12.6 million refugees worldwide, of whom half are in Africa (*World Labour Report 1*, 1984, p. 103).

Refugees and migrant workers are not always easily distinguished, especially on the African continent. Table 10 gives an estimate of the number of migrant workers in West Africa in 1975.

Table 10
Estimated number of migrant workers in West Africa (1975) (1,000s)

Country of origin	Host country				
	Gambia	Ivory Coast	Liberia	Sierra Leone	Total
Ghana	–	24	2	3	29
Ivory Coast	–	–	8	–	8
Liberia	–	2	–	6	8
Mali	3	200	–	–	203
Senegal	15	11	–	–	26
Sierra Leone	–	1	3	–	4
Togo	–	7	–	–	7
Upper Volta	–	418	4	–	422
Others	15	36	18	35	104
Total	33	699	35	44	811

Source: *World Labour Report 1*, 1984, p. 103

It can be assumed that the 1975 figure of 1.3 million migrant workers employed in the region applies equally to 1980, since no great changes took place between these two years. In addition to migration within West Africa, we should also consider migration to other countries: at the beginning of the 1980s there were, for example, around 100,000 black African workers employed in France (cf. Kamara, 1980; Samuel, 1978).

Migration began in West Africa in pre-colonial times, when there were no clearly definable territorial borders and many sections of the population were nomadic, but it was colonization which first led to the large-scale liberation and mobilization of the labour force. The various forms of forced and taxation-led labour previously described drove countless members of peasant families, and indeed entire families, to leave their land. It is estimated that the forced cultivation of cotton alone caused an exodus from Upper Volta of 100,000 peasants, who then sought work on the former Gold Coast.

Early on it became apparent that as a general trend the flow of migration led from the countries lying on the edge of the Sahara to the coastal states of Nigeria, Ghana, the Ivory Coast and Senegal (cf. James, 1983, p. 10). The drought in the West African Sahel in the early 1970s, which coincided with the beginning of the Nigerian oil boom, gave added impetus to huge waves of migration from that region. Most of these migrations are not included in Table 10.

The scale of these migrations, in which almost all of the nations of West Africa took part, did not become clear until January 1983, when the Nigerian government ordered the expulsion of all illegal immigrants. According to official Nigerian figures, 2.2 million people left the country within a very short space of time.[1]

Nigeria's action was not, of course, the African continent's first ever mass expulsion. In 1969, Ghana expelled some 100,000 foreigners, many of whom were Nigerians. Zaire, Uganda, Gabon, the Ivory Coast and Equatorial Guinea have also taken similar measures in the past.[2] It was, however, the scale of the Nigerian compulsory expulsion which made it unique in the history of labour migration. I will now look in more detail at the background to this measure and its implementation.

With an estimated population of 70 to 90 million, Nigeria is black Africa's most populous nation. It is also its biggest exporter of crude oil. At the beginning of the 1980s 90 per cent of the country's national income, 85 per cent of its government revenue and 90 per cent of its foreign-currency revenue was derived from the sale of crude oil (cf. among others Onoh, 1983, p. 66). These figures illustrate the total dependence of the Nigerian economy and state on oil revenues. The proportion of Nigeria's export revenues derived from the sale of crude oil increased from 2.7 per cent in 1960 to 57.6 per cent 10 years later. By 1980 it amounted to 96 per cent (Onoh, 1983, p. 70).

With the exception of 1977, Nigeria's income from oil exports increased throughout the entire decade. This financed the importation of consumer goods and basic foodstuffs, costly construction projects and improvements in the country's infrastructure. Numerous roads, dams, universities and other educational establishments, and ten international airports were built, and countless irrigation projects were funded. The government also undertook the construction of a new capital city inland.

All these measures created a considerable demand for labour, and as a result millions of people looking for work migrated from neighbouring countries during the 1970s, there being no particular formalities involved. The borders were poorly guarded, and in any case, under an agreement concluded by the Economic Community of the West African States (ECOWAS), every citizen of a member country had the right to remain in another member country for up to 90 days, although officially this did not include the right to work there (cf. James, 1983, pp. 12ff).

For as long as the oil boom lasted and there was continued demand for labour power, these migrations were of little concern to the Nigerian authorities. The immigrants were employed as construction workers and teachers, decorators, nurses, guards, cooks, waiters, hotel and domestic staff, textile workers and as self-employed retailers. The majority of them were young men between the ages of 20 and 30. Some of them were recruited directly by firms. Often Nigerians did not care to do the jobs on offer, or qualified local workers could not be found. In other cases the employers preferred to take on workers who had no family or tribal ties in the country.

When their 90 days expired the immigrants remained. Like the jobs themselves, this was illegal, but it was so difficult for foreign workers to obtain residence or work permits that even the time this process took exposed the worker to the risk of losing the job. It is estimated that 90 per cent of all foreigners in Nigeria were able to remain there illegally in this way.

At the beginning of the 1980s Nigeria's economic boom ended. Within the first few weeks of 1983 falling Nigerian oil prices and slack markets led observers to predict a fall in the national income over the year of at least 20 per cent (*The Times*, 27 January 1983). Oil production had not reached the level upon which national budget and investment calculations were based since 1981. Target production was 2 million barrels a day, yet in 1982 production was less than 1.5 million barrels a day, and for the first few months of 1983 forecasts ran at an average daily production of only 800,000 or 600,000 barrels (*Financial Times*, 4 February 1983). All this had drastic consequences for the labour market. Workers defended themselves against cuts in their real wages by striking. During the first half of 1982 the number of working days lost through strikes was three times higher than in the corresponding period of the previous year (*MTM – Marchés tropicaux et méditerranéens*, 31 December 1982, *Financial Times*, 29 and 30 November 1982).

Other forms of protest were also to be expected. Nigeria was one of the few oil-exporting countries in the world with a large native population; the majority of its nationals had neither profited from the oil revenues during the boom nor been liberated from their productive labour, as, for example, the Kuwaitis and Saudi Arabians had been. Until the onset of the crisis the native population's only privilege was that its wages were relatively high in comparison with those earned in other countries and by migrant workers employed in Nigeria.

At the end of the 1970s several religiously motivated social movements burgeoned in Nigeria and began to pose a threat to the economic and political system. The uprisings were cruelly suppressed, but the movement apparently was not crushed (cf. James, 1983, pp. 19ff). The fact that elections were planned for the second half of 1983 merely made the economic and political crisis more explosive.

By issuing the expulsion order and stirring up every possible form of xenophobia the government managed, at least in the short term, to divert attention from the real problems facing the country. On 17 January 1983 the Nigerian Minister of the Interior announced that all illegal immigrants must leave the country within 14 days. He gave notice that an inspection of all households and companies would follow. The announcement triggered off an exodus from Nigeria encompassing millions of people. The communication and transport systems collapsed. Many of the expellees, most of whom faced journeys of several hundred kilometres, made their way home on foot, others by lorry, by ship, or by air. Most of them lost their possessions in the process, and a decline in the Nigerian currency exchange rate and exorbitant fares also cost them their savings.

The explusion order was implemented rigorously, and no exceptions made either for the infirm or for pregnant women. There were numerous deaths. Those most seriously affected were the Ghanaians, of whom at least one million, possibly even two million, returned home within a short space of time. Another large group of illegal immigrants in Nigeria came from Niger. They numbered between 180,000 and 500,000. In addition, some 700,000 people had fled to Nigeria from Chad, and many of them now had to return. There were also large numbers from Togo, Benin and Cameroon, and several hundreds or thousands from Upper Volta, Mali, Senegal, Gambia, Guinea and the Ivory Coast. Like the Ghanaians, many of those who were unable to travel by air or by ship had to cross several countries.

The government received a great deal of support for its xenophobic campaigns from the Nigerian media. The home press published a letter from Nigerian beggars thanking the government for banishing their foreign competitors, and Lagos radio broadcast the following commentary:

Some of these aliens have constituted themselves into social liabilities to the country. There is no gainsaying that the incidence of robbery and other social vices has increased with the influx of illegal aliens. Many have been arraigned in the courts for perpetrating all kinds of economic crimes like trafficking in the Nigerian currency. They have also been involved in religious riots, which they masterminded. At a time when the nation is embarking on the Ethical Revolution we cannot afford to watch these illegal aliens pollute our much-cherished traditional values. All over the place there are brothels patronized by them. In fact, the security of the nation is no doubt threatened with such unregistered aliens in our midst. (Cited in *The Times*, 27 January 1983)

In this atmosphere the departing millions fell victim to all kinds of plunder and persecution. The outbursts were directed in particular against Ghanaians, with the result that even Ghanaian teachers, upon whom the Nigerian education system relied and who practised their profession quite within the law, chose to leave the country.

Despite the scale of the expulsion and the fact that it was implemented in such a short time, the process was nevertheless selective: qualified migrant workers who already had jobs were given a period of four weeks in which to place their residence on a legal footing.

There are two points to note with regard to the mass expulsion from Nigeria. The first relates to the nature of the African labour market: the reception accorded the returning workers in their countries of origin was a great surprise. In Ghana, a country with a population of only around 12 million, the one to two million workers who returned home were all absorbed into the villages and towns. They were not concentrated in camps. This indicates that African social structures were still largely intact, flexible enough to enable individual countries to supply capitalist sectors with labour power, but also to reabsorb liberated workers at short notice.

The second point worth noting is that the mass expulsion did not put an end to labour migration to Nigeria. Shortly after the expatriation, reports emerged of new influxes and in 1985 more mass expulsions were undertaken which affected an estimated 700,000 people (*International Herald Tribune*, 16 March 1983, *MTM*, 15 April 1983, *Le Monde*, 26 November 1983, and *Frankfurter Rundschau*, 19 June 1985).

Notes

1. Cf. among others the *Neue Zürcher Zeitung* of 28 March 1983. My account of the expulsion and return home of Nigeria's migrant workers was gleaned for the most part from international press coverage of the episode.

2. *MTM (Marchés tropicaux et méditerranéens*, Paris) 28 January 1983 and 11 February 1983, *NE (Le Nouvel Economiste*, Paris), 7 February 1983.

5. The Capitalist Metropole and the World Market for Labour Power

So far in this study I have considered those workings of the world market for labour power initiated in and directed from Europe which profited the capitalist metropole or its forerunners, but which were not immediately in evidence in the metropolitan societies of Europe themselves.

Until the 19th century the geographical relocation of workers throughout the world and their incorporation into the capitalist productive process via slavery, coolieism or colonial forced and migrant labour excluded the possibility that such people might be brought directly to Europe. Indeed, this was the very essence of primitive accumulation in European society: exploitation at home appeared to be quite distinct from exploitation abroad, for the latter was based on colonialism and imperialism.

In the USA there was no such clear-cut distinction. The over-exploitation of imported workers living on American soil, for example slaves working on the plantations of the Southern states or Chinese coolies, had taken place inside the country all along and was perfectly in evidence there. In Europe, however, it was a relatively late development: in fact, when Europe embarked upon industrialization the continent actually witnessed the first large-scale transfers of *European* labour power. During the 19th century many millions of people migrated either to the USA or within Europe. Early in the 20th century the colonial powers also began to transfer labour power from the colonized territories to Europe. I have already mentioned the *travailleurs coloniaux*, who migrated to France during World War One.

This chapter will attempt to outline the basic characteristics of the workings of the world market for labour power in the metropole. A great deal has been written on the subject of emigration and labour migration, and the theme has also been the subject of a great deal of debate – detailed consideration of the subject would go beyond the scope of this study. Instead I will attempt a) to supplement the reader's picture of the processes dealt with in the previous chapters by outlining the basic characteristics of transfers of labour power within the capitalist metropole, b) to place these in the context of the present-day world market for labour power, and c) to consider to what extent the present-day world market for labour power is a continuation of previous stages in the world market.

Significant transfers of European labour power

Industrialization, emigration and labour migration

The 19th century was a period of industrialization for Europe, and this process was closely linked with huge transfers of labour power, of which there were two main forms. The first, which reached its peak earlier than the second, was emigration, above all to the USA, and the second, which in principle still plays an important part in the world market for labour power, was European labour migration.

During the 19th century considerably more people emigrated to the USA than took part in labour migration within Europe. Within the space of less than 100 years, between 1820 and 1914, 25.5 million people emigrated from Great Britain, France, Germany, Russia, Austria-Hungary, Italy and many other European countries to the United States of America (Lewis, 1982, p. 35). The population of the USA stood at only 5.3 million in 1800, but by 1820 it had reached 9.2 million. In the next 20 years or so it doubled several times over, and at the beginning of the 20th century it passed the 100 million mark. By 1905 there were already 105.7 million people living in the USA (cf. Sternberg, 1971, p. 544).

The scale and nature of this wave of emigration are closely connected with the course of the industrialization process in the countries involved and the unequal development of capitalism in Europe. A comparison of these countries (Table 12) reveals that in every case the major waves of emigration took place before industrialization had been fully achieved.

According to the figures in Table 12, emigration from Great Britain and France reached its peak some 30 years before emigration from Germany, Holland, Switzerland and Scandinavia. Emigration from a further group of countries, to which Austria-Hungary, Russia, the Balkans and Portugal belong, did not reach its peak until later still, in fact not until the 20th century. Whereas emigration from France, Great Britain, Germany and Holland began as early as the second quarter of the 19th century, emigration from this second group of countries did not begin until the end of the century.

Essentially, these peaks correspond with the timing of the industrialization process in the various countries under consideration, a process which initially liberated labour power on a massive scale in the agricultural and handicraft sectors everywhere, and created impoverishment and misery from which the only escape appeared to be emigration.

The immigrants' origins were of considerable significance in America, since they were used as the basis for hierarchization and differentiation. To give but one example, the majority (70 per cent) of agricultural labourers

Table 11
European emigration to the USA, 1880–1914: total

	Total (millions of people)
Great Britain	6.1
German Empire	4.3
Italy	3.2
Austria-Hungary	3.2
Russia	2.5
Sweden	1.0
Norway	0.7
France	0.5
The Balkans	0.4
Belgium, Netherlands, Luxembourg	0.3
Denmark	0.3
Switzerland	0.3
Iberian Peninsula	0.2
Other Europeans	0.8
Emigration via: Canada	1.2
Asia and Oceania	0.7
Central and South America	0.3

Source: Lewis, 1982, p. 35

Table 12
European emigration to the USA: cycles and peaks

Country	Cycles of emigration	Year of maximal	Amount emigration	No. of emigrations in 1909 (rounded)
France	1832–1892	1851	20,000	7,000
Great Britain	1842–1895	1851	270,000	72,000
Germany	1846–1894	1882	250,000	25,000
Holland	1847–1894	1882	10,000	4,700
Switzerland	1852–1894	1881	11,000	2,500
Scandinavian Peninsula	1869–1894	1882	105,000	32,000
Austria-Hungary	1881–1909	1907	338,000	170,000
Italy	1882–1909	1907	285,000	183,000
Russia	1887–1909	1907	259,000	120,000

Source: Ferenczi, 1913, p. 12

who emigrated to the United States from Southern and Eastern Europe became factory workers, whereas the greater number of opportunities open to immigrants from Northern and Western Europe meant that only a third of these sought this particular form of employment (cf. Ferenczi, 1913, p. 14).

The line between labour migration and emigration from Eastern and Southern Europe was not always sharply drawn, especially during the later stages. For example, four out of ten of the Italians and a quarter of the Slovakians who landed in New York in 1903 had been to the USA before (cf. Ferenczi, 1913, p. 37).

Between 1908 and 1914, 14 Britons left the USA for every 100 who arrived. For the Germans the ratio was 21:100, but for Croats, Slovenes, Italians, Hungarians, Slovakians, Spaniards and Turks it was at least 50:100. Between these years 777,911 people migrated to the USA from the above countries, and 451,752 returned home. The highest rate of remigration was found among the Turks: for the 4,261 people who migrated to the USA between 1908 and 1910, 3,010 returned home, a proportion of 72 per cent. The region that produced the greatest number of remigrants, however, was southern Italy: whereas 457,414 people from southern Italy arrived in the USA during this period, more than a quarter of a million returned (cf. Piore, 1980, p. 151, own calculation).

The significance of this inability to draw a distinction in every case between emigration and labour migration should not, however, be overestimated, for as a whole the process of emigration to the USA – or Canada or Australia for that matter – differed from every other stage in the world market for labour power so far discussed in many respects:

1. Emigration from the leading countries of origin was not caused by outside interference[1] (colonialism/imperialism), but resulted from those countries' own economic and social developments. It was basically a question of exporting social problems.
2. The host country applied no direct or indirect force for the purposes of encouraging migration.
3. Together the emigrants formed new societies that basically represented an extension (and modification) of the social system which had developed in Europe and that ultimately evolved into new capitalist centres of activity.

In view of these important differences, I have dispensed with a thorough discussion of the process of emigration from Europe.

I will now look instead at the contribution to the development of the world market for labour power made by labour migration within Europe. Like emigration from Europe, labour migration within Western Europe began in the 19th century as the result of industrialization, and although it also occurred in other centres of activity we shall take as our examples France and Germany. 'The rapid expansion of English industry could not have taken place if England had not had in the large and poor population of Ireland a reserve army of labour of which to avail itself,' wrote Engels in 1845. By 1851 there were already more than 700,000 Irish migrant workers in England (cf. Power, 1979, p. 13). In the same year there were 379,000 foreigners registered in France, around 1 per cent of the entire population.

During subsequent decades this number increased constantly: by 1886 there were 1,127,000 foreigners in France and if 1911 with its figure of 1,160,000 appears to indicate a period of stagnation, this is only because many immigrants had become naturalized citizens in the interim (cf. Lannes, 1953, p. 3)[2] and not, for example, because immigration had slackened off.

The majority of France's migrant workers came from neighbouring countries such as Belgium, Spain and Italy, as well as from Eastern Europe (cf., among others, Minces, 1973, pp. 26ff). Early in the 20th century France also began to import workers from the Maghreb. By 1912 there were some 4,000 to 5,000 workers from Algeria in France. They were employed either in the industrial sector in Marseille, in building the Paris Metro or in the mines in the north and Pas-de-Calais (cf. Simon and Noin, 1972, p. 244). This distribution of migrant workers over the various sectors of the economy did not differ greatly from year to year or from country to country. The mining industry, the industrial sector and the building of infrastructure were the areas in which they were most commonly employed.

By the eve of World War One the number of workers from the Maghreb employed in France had climbed to 30,000 (Simon and Noin, 1972, p. 245 and Minces, 1973, p. 46) and during the war it multiplied many times over. The year 1916 saw the creation of the Service des Travailleurs Coloniaux, which was answerable to the Ministry of War and whose job was to organize forced recruitment in the colonies. At the end of the war the colonial workers returned home, and by 1919 there were only 10,000 workers from the Maghreb left in France (Simon and Noin, 1972, p. 245).

Table 13
France: immigrants from the Maghreb, 1921–68

Year	Algerians	Moroccans	Tunisians
1921	36,277	–	–
1926	69,789	–	–
1931	85,568	–	–
1936	72,891	–	–
1946	22,114	16,458	1,916
1954	211,675	10,734	4,800
1962	350,484	33,320	26,589
1968	473,812	84,236	61,028

Source: Talha, 1974, p. 18

During the economic boom of the 1920s the North African French colonies once again assumed greater importance as reservoirs of labour power. Table 13 shows that between 1921 and 1926 the number of Algerians in France almost doubled. By 1931 it had increased again. According to other statistics, there were already 120,000 immigrants from the Maghreb in France by 1924, 10,000 of them from Morocco and a similar number from Tunisia.

France's total alien population fluctuated from year to year: in 1921, 1.5 million foreigners were registered in France. By 1931 this figure had increased to 2.7 million, and by 1936 it had fallen again to just under 2.2 million (cf. Lannes, 1953, p. 3 and Minces, 1973, p. 28). When the trend of France's economic activity was downward the number of workers from the Maghreb employed in France fell accordingly. During World War Two the number of migrant workers employed in France fell even further. Nevertheless, at the end of the war there were still around 1.7 million foreigners in the Republic (Lannes, 1953, p. 5), among them some 40,000 people from the Maghreb.

Germany's evolution into a host country of foreign workers looked a little different. Industrialization began later than in France, and accordingly the employment of foreigners did not become important to Germany until later. As Table 14 shows, the employment of foreign workers increased substantially shortly after the founding of the Empire in 1871.

Table 14
Foreigners in the German Empire, 1871–1910

1871	206,755
1880	276,057
1885	372,792
1890	433,254
1895	486,190
1900	778,737
1905	1,028,560
1910	1,259,873

Source: Statistics compiled by the German Empire, cited in Herbert, 1986, p. 25

For hard-coal mining in the Ruhr, a sector of the economy without which Germany's industrialization would have been unthinkable, migrant workers assumed great importance very early on. After 1890 this sector of the economy experienced a rapid growth, and the number of workers which it employed doubled within the space of 10 years. On 1 January 1900 'around 70,000 (33.9 per cent) of the 204,000 strong workforce of the regional Mines Inspectorate in Dortmund were workers drawn from the eastern provinces. Of these, 6,258 came from Upper Silesia, 24,667 from Poznán, 30,628 from East Prussia and 7,897 from West Prussia' (Köhne, 1901, p. 186).

The majority of the workers from Poznán, West Prussia and East Prussia were of Polish extraction and were thus imported labour.[3] In addition, 6,604 of the workers employed in hard-coal mining in this most important of regions came from Austria, Italy, The Netherlands or Belgium. As had been the case in England and France, the development of capitalism in Germany was closely linked with the recruitment of foreign workers, and these were exposed to extreme forms of exploitation. In the Ruhr the foreign miners were employed first and foremost in the particularly dangerous newly opened pits in the north. On 1 January 1900 more than half the entire workforce in the region's 19 pits were foreigners, and in the 'Ewald' pit near Herten foreigners made up 85 per cent of the workforce (Köhne, 1901, pp. 186f).

At the beginning of the 20th century every sector of the German economy employed large numbers of migrant workers of both sexes. Figures for 1907 reproduced in Table 15 reveal that whereas just under one third of all foreign workers were employed in the agricultural sector, more than half worked in industry (including the mining and construction industries). The majority of these workers came originally from Eastern and Southeastern Europe, and substantial contingents hailed from Italy (c. 15 per cent) and Holland (6.5 per cent).Even in those early days more than a quarter (27 per cent) of all foreign workers were women.

Table 15
Foreign workers in the German Empire on 12 June 1907

Sector of the economy	Total no. of foreign workers	Origins		
		Eastern and South-eastern Europe	Italy	Holland
Agriculture	279,940	246,827	864	11,912
Industry (incl. mining and construction)	440,800	250,249	120,945	31,351
Trade, transport and restaurants	45,205	24,550	2,760	4,639
Domestic service	33,918	19,972	951	4,137
Total	799,863	541,598	125,520	52,039
Women	219,539	178,252	7,164	10,550

Source: Katsoulis, 1978, p. 15

The Poles in the Ruhr ('Ruhr Poles') formed the largest group among the migrant workers in Germany; their number in 1914 was estimated at roughly 300,000, although some sources suggest that there were 450,000 Polish families in Germany by 1912. In some towns and administrative districts the Poles made up over 40 per cent of the entire population.

As is the case today, the migrant workers at the beginning of the century were subject to special legal provisions which enabled the authorities to prevent them from remaining in Germany during non-productive periods, to carry out expulsions at any time, and to ensure optimum exploitation of the labour force. One such measure was the so-called *Karenzzwang* (compulsory leave without pay):

In order to prevent their becoming resident and to counter possible swamping by the Poles [*Polnisierung*, 'Polandization'], the Poles were forced to leave Germany during the winter (at first from 1 December to 1 March, and from 1900 on from 20 December to 1 February). During World War One the *Karenzzeit* (waiting period) was abolished. Foreign workers were forbidden to leave the country and were not permitted to quit their jobs. (Katsoulis, 1978, p. 16)

Another such measure was the so-called *Inlandslegitimierung* (internal legitimation), which was introduced throughout the German Empire in 1908. Compulsory legitimation tied foreign workers to a particular place of work and effectively allowed the authorities to supervise and regulate them. The Deutsche Arbeiterzentrale (German Labour Office), a body established in 1905 as the Deutsche Feldarbeiterzentralstelle (German Agricultural Labour Office) was given authority to issue compulsory legitimation cards to all foreign migrant workers crossing into Germany from Prussia, and until World War Two this office was responsible for the procurement of foreign labour, in particular for the agricultural sector. From 1922 onwards it exercised a virtual monopoly in this field.

Although there were already 1.2 million foreign workers employed in the German Empire by 1910, the level of labour imports rose substantially during World War One. For the first time large quantities of forced labour were recruited abroad. Their over-exploitation usually led to physical ruination. After the defeat of the German Empire the majority of the surviving foreign workers returned to their countries of origin.

Although migrant workers continued to enter Germany during the Weimar Republic, the employment of foreign labour power did not return to its previous level. The introduction of new scientific and technical processes, especially of new forms of labour management (including Taylorism and Fordism), led to changes in policy on the employment of foreign labour. These new processes became generally accepted in the course of the 1920s and led to a restructuring of the working class, the major consequence of which was dequalification. They resulted directly in an increase in surplus product for the capitalist and although they also made migrant workers almost superfluous for a short time, these very techniques would later require and make possible the import of workers in considerably larger numbers than ever before. To begin with, however, they were not the decisive factor affecting the employment of foreign labour power: the world economic crisis that set in at the end of the 1920s drove the employment of foreigners down to a low level. In 1932 only 142,000 foreign workers were employed in the German Empire.

Forced labour during World War Two
As early as 1914–18 the imperialist powers developed and tested various methods of recruiting and deploying labour for the war economy both in Europe and in other continents, and often resorted to direct physical

compulsion. We have already discussed the importance of this process both
to the African population and to the French economy.

During World War Two the amount of forced labour deployed in
Europe increased many times over. The Third Reich played by far the
leading role and set a new record for the greatest number of human beings
exploited and exterminated within a short space of time.

In many respects it pursued the same objectives and employed the same
strategy as had Germany's wartime leaders during World War One:
occupied territories were transformed into reservoirs of labour power and
their populations were forced by means of more or less direct compulsion
to make themselves available for work either at home or in the Reich itself.
The following comments were made by the president of the German
Kriegsnährungsamt (Wartime Ministry of Food), von Batocki, and
indicate clearly just how smooth the transition from the recruitment of
labour power to compulsory deportation can be, especially in times of war.
In 1917 he recommended to the Großen Hauptquartier (German High
Command) that:

> In those districts which in peacetime supply a great many seasonal
> agricultural labourers, and which are still awash with people today,
> attempts should be made to requisition large numbers of dairy cows, as
> many potatoes and as much grain as possible. Then we should send
> recruiting officers into that district. They would certainly meet with
> success. (Cited in Elsner, 1974, p. 21)

The number of workers recruited and the brutality of the methods used
increased during the course of the war. During World War One Belgium
and Poland supplied the German Empire with the bulk of its forced labour:
in all probability the process involved at least 150,000 Belgians, and there
were still some 600,000 so-called Russo-Polish people working in Germany
in 1918. Elsner has carried out research which suggests that in 1918
Germany's big landowners employed some 700,000 foreign workers on
their estates, most of them of Polish nationality (Elsner, 1974, p. 24).

One of the German Empire's wartime objectives was to ensure that its
recruitment and exploitation of foreign workers in Germany in the post-
war period would not be hindered, and this objective played a considerable
part in negotiations conducted and treaties concluded with the Austrian,
Finnish and Russian governments, and the Ukrainian Rada. When a treaty
was concluded with the Ukrainians the large farmers protested that not all
of Germany's demands had been written in. The Director of the German
Labour Office commented, 'This treaty should have been a labour treaty as
well as a food treaty.'

During World War Two forced labour, and not only that of foreign
extraction, was used in a far more open and inhumane manner than it had
been between 1914 and 1918. Concentration camp detainees, mainly Jews
but also gypsies and Romanies, political prisoners, prisoners of war and

The value in terms of profitability of the direct economic "employment" of living concentration camp slaves, who could be procured without any capital expenditure, was as follows:

Daily rental between ....RM 6.00 and RM 8.00
On average ....RM 6.00
Less
1. Food..RM 0.60
2. Depreciation of clothing .... RM 0.10 RM 0.70
                                                     RM 5.30

Therefore, assuming an average life span of nine months
.... 270 × RM 5.30 = RM 1,431.00
This profit was increased through rational utilization of the detainees' corpses after nine months, i.e. by the proceeds of
1. .... gold fillings
2. .... personal clothing
some of which was supplied as clothing for detainees in other camps, thus saving the cost of purchasing new clothes, and some of which was used as textile fibres for SS uniforms.
3. ....valuables left
4. .... money left
Before and during the first years of the war valuables and money were only returned to their rightful owners if these were among the few detainees who were citizens of the German Reich.
The above profits were reduced by the cost of cremating each corpse, on average ....RM 2.00
so that a direct or indirect net profit was made on each corpse of at least ....RM 200.00
and often as much as thousands of Reichsmarks.
The total profits earned from the deployment of detainees over nine months was therefore at least .... RM 1,630.00
Some of the camps even guaranteed themselves extra income by making use of the bones or ashes.

You must not think that this calculation is of my doing. It was drawn up by the SS, for Pohl was obsessive in his attempts to ensure that no one should "meddle in his affairs". The SS-WVHA was constantly devising regulations that would counter the threat of slight or serious competition such as that, for example, attempted time and time again in the east by the German police in the form of "labour camps", "police detention camps" and suchlike.

Source: Kogon, 1948, pp. 349f

deportees from Poland, the Soviet Union and France, were the main source of labour power.

The initial function of the concentration camps was to perpetrate organized terrorism and industrial homicide (cf. Demps, 1974, p. 107), but after the blitzkrieg failed, the more than seven million people who were sent to the concentration camps under the Third Reich, of whom only around half a million lived to see the end of the war, were used mainly as a reservoir of labour power. Their exploitation was based on 'extermination through work'. This is borne out by the number of dead and immortalized in a peculiarly fascist variation on the calculation of profitability.

In the reorganization of SS Central Office in 1942, Oswold Pohl, mentioned by Kogon, became the director of the new Wirtschafts- und Verwaltungshauptamt or WVHA (Central Office for the Economy and Administration) and was placed in charge of the section responsible for managing the concentration camps. Soon after taking up his new post in April 1942 he announced that he had reorganized the existing concentration camps 'in order to mobilize all able-bodied detainees'. He told the camp commandants, 'This employment must be *exhaustive* in the true sense of the word if we are to achieve maximum levels of output' (cited in Ferencz, 1981, p. 43).

Even before the beginning of the war the concentration camps had been testing grounds on which the Germans had hoped to find that 'method of organizing the working and living conditions of foreign workers that would prove most favourable for capitalism' (cf. Demps, 1974, p. 109). Their findings were implemented after the onset of war.

For the first two years of the war the majority of Germany's slave labourers were Polish and French prisoners of war (Eichholtz, 1974, p. 79). However, the appointment in 1942 of Fritz Sauckel as General-bevollmächtigten für den Arbeitseinsatz – GBA (Chief Commissioner for the Utilization of Manpower) marked an important turning point for the recruitment of forced labour in the occupied territories, for Fritz Sauckel organized the recruitment of millions of workers and had them transported to Germany (see among others Eichholtz, 1974, p. 82). There they were forced to work as slaves in the agricultural sector and in industry, especially the munitions industry, or as otherwise required by the economy.

A broad overview of the number of foreign workers deployed in the German Reich reveals that whilst in 1939, directly before the outbreak of war, there had been 525,000 foreign workers in Germany, by 1942 this figure had risen to six million – an increase of more than 1,000 per cent within the space of three years.

> Some 1.6 million people were transported to Germany in the period between April and August 1942 alone. Most of this slave labour came from the USSR, and during this brief period the proportion of all foreign workers which Soviets represented rose from 4 per cent to 30 per cent. In the summer of 1942 the Germans also turned their attention to forced recruitment in France, Belgium and Holland in order to make good their shortage of qualified workers. At the close of Sauckel's second campaign in December 1942 there were almost six million slave labourers and prisoners of war working for the German war economy. (Roth, 1977, p. 141)

Recruitment was almost exclusively forced recruitment, and in 1944 Sauckel stated that 'of the five million workers who have come to

Germany, fewer than 200,000 came voluntarily'. Foreign workers were subjected to inhumane exploitation and died in their tens of thousands from exhaustion, overwork, disease, hunger, mistreatment and torture.

Towards the end of World War Two foreign civilian workers and prisoners of war made up roughly a quarter of the German Reich's entire labour force, 7 or 8 million people, including some 1.5 million Soviet and Polish women. Estimates of the total number of foreigners transported to Germany during the Nazi period range from 10 to 20 million. Data gathered at the Nuremburg trials sets the total number at 12 million, although no more than 8.1 million worked in Germany at any one time. This estimate does not include slave labourers exploited by the Germans on their own occupied territory (cf. Schupetta, 1981, p. 302).

Forced labour in fascist Germany and Germany's commitment to 'extermination through work' undoubtedly mark the Nazi period as one of the most extreme in the history of the world market for labour power. The situation was, admittedly, somewhat exceptional to the extent that Germany was operating a war economy, yet earlier forms of forced labour used during World War One are not the only factors which suggest a certain degree of continuity. I therefore cannot agree with Bade (1983, p. 52) when he writes that the episode was 'a clearly demarcated historical exception', for this view reveals a limited perspective on Germany's development between 1880 and 1980, and consideration of the workings of the world market for labour power since the beginning of colonization confirm that it is untenable.

Developments after World War Two

For a short while immediately after 1945, during the first stage in Germany's recovery, West Germany's native population, constantly supplemented as it was by a stream of refugees first from the then Soviet-occupied zone and then from the GDR, was sufficient to meet the country's demand for labour. This phase ended with the construction of the Berlin Wall in 1961. Before then between 150,000 and 200,000 workers annually had fled to West Germany.

Between 1960 and 1961 West Germany recorded a considerable increase in the number of migrant workers it employed. Their number virtually doubled within the space of a year and only four years later it passed the million mark (see Table 16). Agreements concluded on the subject of recruitment with Italy in 1955 and Spain in 1960 had already created the preconditions for a programme of controlled immigration planned from West Germany. These agreements were followed by similar agreements with Turkey in 1961, Morocco in 1963, Portugal in 1964, Tunisia in 1965 and Yugoslavia in 1968, although no workers entered West Germany until several years after each agreement had been signed – proof indeed that the agreements were intended to facilitate the longer-term planning of the labour market.

During the recession of 1966–7 it became clear that the function of migrant labour was to provide room for manoeuvre and to act as a reserve army: the number of foreigners employed in West Germany was abruptly reduced by one third, falling from 1.34 million in September 1966 to 903,000 at the end of January 1968 (cf. Bundesanstalt für Arbeit [Federal Institution for Labour], 1970, p. 94).

Table 16
Foreign workers in the Federal Republic of Germany, 1954–85 (in 1,000s)

Year	Total	Alien	Italy	Greece	Spain	Turkey	Portugal	Yugoslavia
1954[1]	72.9	0.4	6.5	0.5	0.4	–	–	1.8
1955[1]	79.6	0.4	7.5	0.6	0.5	–	–	2.1
1956[1]	98.8	0.5	18.6	1.0	0.7	–	–	2.3
1957[1]	108.2	0.6	19.1	1.8	1.0	–	–	2.8
1958[1]	127.1	0.6	25.6	2.8	1.5	–	–	4.8
1959[1]	166.8	0.8	48.8	4.1	2.2	–	–	7.3
1960[1]	279.4	0.3	121.7	13.0	9.5	2.5	0.3	8.8
1961[2]	507.4	2.5	218.0	43.9	51.0	–	–	–
1962[3]	629.0	3.1	239.0	70.4	83.9	–	–	–
1963[3]	773.2	3.7	264.9	106.3	112.2	–	–	–
1964[3]	902.5	4.3	267.9	143.2	138.4	67.8	–	–
1965[3]	1,118.6	5.3	328.6	179.2	171.5	118.8	10.8	–
1966[3]	1,244.0	5.8	362.1	191.5	175.2	149.9	18.9	92.1
1967[3]	1,013.9	4.7	266.8	150.1	127.0	133.1	18.4	94.3
1968[3]	1,018.9	4.9	275.9	139.8	112.6	141.2	18.9	106.4
1969[3]	1,365.6	6.5	327.0	177.9	135.0	215.8	26.9	222.7
1970[3]	1,806.8	8.5	363.7	229.8	162.9	323.1	40.2	373.6
1971[3]	128.4	9.8	393.6	260.9	179.7	418.5	54.3	452.2
1972[3]	2,284.5	10.5	411.8	268.1	181.1	488.7	63.1	462.9
1973[4]	2,595.0	11.9	450.0	250.0	190.0	605.0	85.0	535.0
1974[4]	2,286.6	10.9	331.5	229.2	149.7	606.8	78.5	466.7
1975[3]	2,060.5	10.2	292.9	203.0	129.1	550.5	70.2	416.6
1976[3]	1,924.8	9.6	274.0	178.4	110.8	523.5	63.5	387.7
1977[3]	1,872.2	9.3	277.3	160.6	99.6	512.9	60.0	374.4
1978[3]	1,857.4	9.3	284.3	146.3	92.4	510.8	58.7	366.8
1979[3]	1,924.4	9.3	297.0	139.1	89.6	535.8	58.9	364.4
1980[3]	2,018.3	9.6	304.5	132.2	86.1	578.2	58.5	353.7
1981[3]	1,911.9	9.2	286.5	123.3	81.5	577.9	54.8	336.7
1982[3]	1,783.9	8.8	258.6	115.5	76.6	553.9	50.8	312.6
1983[2]	1,713.6	8.5	238.9	108.8	72.3	540.5	46.4	305.9
1984[2]	1,592.6	7.9	214.0	98.0	67.3	499.9	39.6	288.7
1985[2]	1,584.0	7.8	202.0	103.0	67.0	499.0	35.0	294.0
1986[2]	1,591.5	7.7	193.3	101.5	65.9	513.0	35.1	294.8
1987[5]	1,557.1	7.5	177.1	110.1	64.2	511.6	35.4	284.2

[1] End of July
[2] End of June
[3] Annual averages
[4] End of September, 1973 computer forecast
[5] End of March

Source: Bundesanstalt für Arbeit (Federal Institution of Labour), various publications

In subsequent years the number began to rise again with the upturn in the West German economy. Within the space of a few years it had doubled. By the end of 1971 it had passed the 2 million mark, and when the employment of foreign workers in West Germany reached its peak in 1973 there were 2.6 million foreigners working in the country. At the end of that year the government called a halt to recruitment, and thereafter the employment of foreigners showed a downward trend. At present it stands at around 1.6 million.

As early as the 1960s West Germany began to switch its recruitment of migrant workers from Southern Europe to countries that had not been permitted to develop. This trend is illustrated in Table 17, although Tunisians and Moroccans are not included in the figures. The table demonstrates clearly that the Turks are rapidly becoming by far the largest group of foreign workers in Germany, even though they did not begin to enter the country until after 1963.

Table 17
Foreign workers according to selected nationalities
(each as a percentage of the total number of foreigners employed)*

	1963	1966	1969	1972	1979	1987
Turks	–	12.0	15.8	21.4	27.8	32.9
Yugoslavians	–	7.4	16.3	20.3	18.9	18.3
Italians	34.3	29.1	23.9	18.0	15.4	11.4
Greeks	13.7	15.4	13.0	11.7	7.2	7.1
Spaniards	14.5	14.1	9.9	7.9	4.7	4.1

* The corresponding absolute figures are contained in Table 16.

The employment of Europeans in West Germany, by contrast, is on the decline: in 1963 Spaniards were the second largest group of migrant workers in West Germany, now they are the smallest of the five nationalities for which figures are given. Particularly sharp, both in absolute and relative terms, has been the decline in the number of Italians working in West Germany: 450,000 in 1973, but only 288,000 in 1979. In 1963 Italians made up 34 per cent of the foreign workforce, but by 1979 this figure had fallen to 16 per cent. The proportion of foreign workers in West Germany who are of Greek or Yugoslavian extraction has remained more or less constant since 1969.

West German government policy on labour migration may be divided into three main phases. Initially governments pursued a policy of rotation, whereby only the workers themselves, whether male or female, were permitted to enter the country. They were then given fixed-term contracts of employment and accommodated in hostels. As the recession in 1966/67 demonstrated, this approach allowed governments a flexible response, even at short notice, to changing labour market conditions.

At the beginning of the crisis in 1973 the Government imposed an embargo on recruitment, and the number of foreigners employed in West Germany stabilized and even began to show a downward trend (see Table 16). The policy of reuniting families that the Government then adopted (as a result of which the foreign population increased as a percentage of the resident population) shifted responsibility for the reproduction of labour power from the hostel to the family and was aimed at the middle-term planning of the labour market: the highest figures for foreign school leavers were recorded in the years following those in which the number of German school leavers leaving compulsory education was particularly high. To a government anticipating a stable or expanding labour market these young people represented an important source of labour for those areas of employment which required few or no formal qualifications, in fact for those areas of unemployment upon which most foreign youths were forced to concentrate as a result of their academic qualifications. Unlike immigrants, who enter a country specifically to find work, these young people have the advantage of having learned to live with adaptive difficulties and language problems as children and at school.

During the third phase, in the 1980s, West German government policy on the employment of foreigners has been aimed at selectivity. The number of foreigners employed and permitted to live in West Germany has varied in line with labour market conditions, i.e. with growing unemployment, and the days when a worker's family could join him or her are past. A new policy designed to encourage unemployed foreign workers and those facing unemployment to return home with their families has been introduced and has had predictable social repercussions (the so-called *Ausländerfeindlichkeit*, 'hostility towards foreigners'). Workers who are no longer required are now sent back to their countries of origin – mainly Turkey. Not only have these countries supplied West Germany's metropolitan economy on request with ready-made workers, they are now also acting as catch basins for labour power which is no longer needed.

A comparative outline of the labour question in France since 1945

At the end of World War Two large-scale immigration was regarded by the French as a prerequisite for making good their country's war losses, and was therefore encouraged. For the first few years immigration was relatively low: by 1951 only 500,000 of the 1 million immigrants anticipated had entered France. During the 1950s, however, the number of immigrants rose steadily, and by 1962 immigration was running – even without Algerians – at more than 100,000 people annually. This trend continued until 1973 or 1974, when, as Table 18 reveals, immigration fell off dramatically. The table includes Algerians, but excludes most of the emigrants from France's former black African colonies. In 1973 the total number of actively employed foreigners in France was officially estimated at 1.8–1.9 million, but by 1975 it had fallen again to less than 1.6 million.

This overview demonstrates clearly that in France, as elsewhere, immigration and the employment of immigrant workers is directly linked to the course of economic activity.

Table 18
Immigrant workers entering France
(excluding seasonal workers)

Year	No. of people
1970	212,785
1971	177,377
1972	119,649
1973	152,419
1974	64,462
1975	25,591
1976	26,949
1977	22,756

Source: *L'immigration en France en 1977*, 1978, p. 3

The geographical shift in recruitment that took place in West Germany also occurred in France. Before World War One and during the inter-war period workers from the Maghreb had been hugely outnumbered in France by foreign workers from other countries, but after the Second World War the situation began to change and their number began to grow steadily. In 1946 only 1.3 per cent of all foreigners in France were Algerian, but by 1968 this figure had risen to 18.1 per cent; those from the Maghreb as a whole made up almost a quarter of France's foreign population (see Table 19). The proportion of France's migrant workers who were of Polish, Yugoslavian or Italian extraction fell appreciably, and this trend has continued since 1968. It is even more marked if one takes into account the fact that France also employs black Africans.

Table 19
Foreign peoples in France according to nationality 1921–68
(as % of the foreign population)

Year	Al- gerian	Moroc- can	Tun- isian	Total from the Maghreb	Portu- guese	Span- iard	Italian	Polish* and Yugoslav
1921	2.4	–	–	2.4	0.7	16.6	29.4	3.2
1926	2.9	–	–	2.9	1.2	13.4	31.5	13.5
1931	3.1	–	–	3.1	1.8	13.0	29.8	19.9
1936	3.3	–	–	3.3	1.3	11.5	32.8	20.3
1946	1.3	0.9	–	2.2	1.3	17.3	25.8	25.5
1954	12.0	0.6	0.3	12.9	1.1	16.3	28.7	16.2
1962	16.1	1.5	1.2	18.8	2.3	20.3	29.0	9.1
1968	18.1	3.2	2.3	23.6	1.1	23.2	21.8	6.8

* Since statistics for Poland and Yugoslavia are not shown separately, no statement can be made as to the size of either of these national groups. It may be assumed that the Poles represent a small, stagnant number of immigrants.

Source: compiled from census statistics quoted in Talha, 1974, p. 19

Labour migration in Western Europe after World War Two was not, of course, limited to West Germany and France. Table 20 demonstrates just how extensive and diverse the migrations have been. The employment of migrant workers in Western Europe reached its peak in the mid-1970s: in 1975 migrant workers represented 10 per cent of all those in employment in these countries.

Figures for Great Britain, which is not included in Table 20 and which after France and West Germany is the third largest importer of labour in Western Europe, put the number of migrant workers in that country at 1,773,000 for 1970 and 1,858,000 for 1981 (Castles, 1987, p. 121). The majority of Britain's migrant workers come from Ireland or from the countries of the New Commonwealth and Pakistan, that is to say, former British colonies whose populations are not of British extraction.

When considering labour migration from countries that have not been permitted to develop, it is interesting to note the congruency which exists between the imperialist power that dominated in each region and the host country to which that region's workers tend to migrate. The obvious example is migration from the Maghreb, in particular from Algeria, to France: Algeria is the Maghreb country with the highest number of emigrants in absolute terms and also has the highest number of emigrations as a proportion of its entire population. Official figures reveal that in 1975 5.5 per cent of the Algerian, 4.4 per cent of the Tunisian and 1.6 per cent of the Moroccan population emigrated (cf. Simon, 1977, p. 1). Algeria is the North African country most seriously and directly affected by French imperialism and was a so-called overseas territory and settlers' colony.

Whereas the Maghrebs are the largest group of foreign workers in France (31 per cent of all foreigners in 1973), the largest group of foreign workers in West Germany is the Turks (also 31 per cent), for Turkey is the country where German imperialism was at its strongest. In Great Britain workers from India and Pakistan head the list.

The close link between labour migration and a dominant imperialist power becomes still clearer if one examines the process from the point of view of the countries that supply migrant labour: 93 per cent of Turkish migrant workers are employed in West Germany; 98 per cent of all Algerian migrant workers, 70 per cent of all Tunisian migrant workers, and 58 per cent of all Moroccan migrant workers are employed in France. The comparatively small number of Moroccan migrant workers employed in France is explained by the fact that many workers from the former Spanish zone in Morocco have emigrated to other countries. In this respect the structure of emigration from former British colonies is thoroughly comparable with that of migration from North Africa and Turkey.

At this point it is worth mentioning another important process which links labour migration and imperialism: even the European countries from which workers typically migrate, i.e. Italy, Spain, Greece and Portugal, also import labour power. As the workers in these countries migrate to the most highly industrialized countries, they are, to some extent at least,

Table 20
Immigrant workers in eight Western European countries in 1973/4 and 1978 (1,000s, rounded)

Country of origin	Belgium		West Germany		France		Luxembourg		Netherlands		Austria		Sweden		Switzerland	
	1973	1978	1973	1978	1973	1978	1973	1978	1973	1978	1974	1978	1974	1978	1974	1978
Algeria	3.0	2.4	2.0	–	450.0	361.0	–	–	–	–	–	–	–	0.3	–	–
Finland	–	–	?	2.9	–	–	–	–	–	–	–	–	–	104.5	–	–
Greece	2.0	9.6	268.1	153.3	5.0	–	–	–	1.1	2.0	–	–	–	8.1	–	4.8
Italy	86.0	106.4	409.7	305.1	230.0	175.8	11.0	10.8	4.5	10.4	–	2.0	–	2.7	–	240.1
Yugoslavia	1.2	3.0	466.1	380.2	50.0	43.1	0.5	0.6	8.8	8.1	–	121.1	–	24.6	–	26.2
Morocco	16.5	22.2	15.3	–	120.0	181.4	–	–	14.2	31.0	–	–	–	0.6	–	–
Austria	?	3.7	?	76.0	–	–	–	–	–	–	–	–	–	2.0	–	19.5
Portugal	3.5	3.9	69.1	59.0	380.0	385.0	8.0	12.9	2.5	5.4	–	–	–	0.9	–	4.9
Spain	30.0	27.3	179.0	95.8	270.0	184.5	1.2	2.2	14.8	17.6	–	0.2	–	1.7	–	61.6
Tunisia	2.1	1.9	11.2	–	60.0	73.7	–	–	–	1.2	–	–	–	0.4	–	–
Turkey	12.0	17.0	528.2	540.5	18.0	36.3	–	–	20.9	46.1	–	26.2	–	4.5	–	16.7
Other EEC countries	40.0	87.7	156.0	131.6	69.0	66.2	17.0	20.7	40.0	52.6	–	12.7	–	32.0	–	83.7
Non-EEC countries	93.0	18.2	239.5	216.6	130.0	135.8	2.3	1.9	9.7	23.0	–	14.5	–	42.2	–	31.9
Total	289.3	303.3	2344.2	1961.0	1782.0	1642.8	40.0	49.1	116.5	197.4	218.0	176.7	200.0	224.5	593.0	489.4
Change 1973/4–1978	+4.8%		–16.3%		–7.8%		+22.8%		+69.4%		–18.9%		+12.3%		–17.5%	

Host country

Source: *OECD Observer* and other publications, Statistical Office of the EEC cited in 'Ausländische Arbeitnehmer in Westeuropa', 1980

replaced by workers from countries that have not been permitted to develop. Here, too, the rule is that recruitment is generally carried out in the importing country's former colonies.

Thus Italy, a classic example of a country from which workers migrate, employs workers from Tunisia, other Mediterranean countries and the Orient, most of whom are illegal immigrants. The trade unions estimate that there are roughly 1 million such people in Italy; according to a study carried out for the city and province of Rome, more than 90 per cent of the region's female workers are illegal immigrants (cf. *Frankfurter Rundschau*, 17 March 1984). Spain imports workers from Morocco and also Algeria, and in Portugal, the 'poorhouse of Europe' as it is so often known, there are even workers from the Cape Verde Islands (cf. Houdaille and Sauvy, 1974, p. 727). Greece, a country without a colonial past, is no exception, for although their numbers are small, there are workers here from Egypt, Sudan, Somalia, Turkey and Ethiopia (see ibid. and Nikolinakos, 1973, p. 149).

There would, then, appear to be some kind of hierachy pertaining to the migration of workers on an international scale: workers from the less industrialized regions of Europe migrate to the highly industrialized countries and are then replaced in their countries of origin by workers from those countries which have not been permitted to develop. This tendency is in addition to the process described earlier whereby the highly industrialized societies of Western Europe are switching their recruitment of migrant workers to the developing nations.

The import of labour power by the USA

Historically, the United States owed its very existence to the import of labour power. The fact that white immigration represented an influx of labour that cost nothing was of fundamental significance for the country's development and later for its industrialization.

From the very beginning the USA was only interested in white immigrants, and even then some took precedence over others: there were, for example, more opportunities open to Northern and Western Europeans than to Southern and Eastern Europeans. The exclusion from the USA of non-white immigrants, which was not embodied in law until relatively late in the day, did not prevent the importation of such people as workers. The first to enter the country were African slaves, upon whom the economy of the Southern States relied, followed some time later by the Chinese, Japanese and other Asiatics. When slavery was abolished, workers who had been imported from Africa and their descendants became citizens of the USA, yet even as citizens they were the subject of numerous discriminatory laws and measures designed to ensure that they would continue to provide cheap labour. Even today that is still the function of the black population of the USA. Blacks now account for 28.6 million people out of a total population of 236 million (1985).

In addition to the white immigration, slavery and coolie migrations of earlier centuries, there has also been labour migration to the USA during the 20th century. The majority of the USA's migrant workers come from Mexico, but Puerto Rico and other Caribbean islands such as Haiti and Jamaica also act as reservoirs of labour power for the United States. Puerto Rico is, in fact, a special case: migration from there has occurred mainly during the second half of this century. In 1910 there were only 1,513 Puerto Ricans in the USA, and these were scattered throughout 39 states. By 1940 their number had risen to 70,000 and by 1970 stood at 1.4 million. Although statistically speaking nine out of ten of the Puerto Ricans in the USA are white, this fact has had no bearing on their social and economic status. One million Puerto Ricans live in New York alone, most of them in slum areas (cf. Röhrbein and Schultz, 1978, pp. 89ff).

What is unusual about migration from Puerto Rico is that the island has now become part of the USA, with the result that Puerto Ricans are no longer foreign workers. Today the island has around 3 million inhabitants. An extremely brutal programme of sterilization and family planning has halted the growth of the population and safeguarded the US labour market from unwanted large-scale immigration.

Migrant workers are not shown separately in statistics compiled in the USA, and Table 21 can therefore only give a clue as to the scale of labour migration from Latin American countries, since it also includes immigrants, political refugees etc. The table suggests that some 2 million Latin Americans, around half of them from Mexico, entered the USA legally between 1960 and 1978. At the beginning of the 1980s the total number of migrant workers employed in the USA was calculated at 6 to 10 million. Estimates for the number of illegal immigrants range from 4 to 12 million. It is assumed that up to three quarters of all illegal immigrants come from Mexico and that the next largest groups are those from Haiti and the Dominican Republic, then Columbia, Southern Europe, and the Orient (cf. Piore, 1980, p. 164).

It is significant that the Mexicans are the largest group of migrant workers in the USA, since until the mid-19th century the present-day US states of Texas, California, New Mexico, Arizona, Nevada and Utah all belonged to Mexico. The border between the two countries was still open at the turn of the century, yet there was little Mexican immigration: no more than around 24,000 people between 1900 and 1909 (cf. Ehrke, 1981, p. 7). Migration increased as a result of the Mexican Revolution and the USA's demand for workers during World War One, and this trend, which continued even after the war was over, caused concern in Mexico over the number of qualified workers involved. The depression in 1928 led to a virtual ban on immigration which remained in force for at least part of the 1930s.

During the late 1940s the USA once again experienced a considerable demand for labour. This led to the ratification in 1942 of the so-called

Table 21
Latin Americans as a proportion of total immigration into the USA, 1960–78

	Total immigrations (absolute)	Latin America (%)	Mexico (%)	Cuba (%)	Central or South America (%)
1960	265,398	22.3	12.3	3.1	6.9
1961	271,344	29.1	15.3	5.3	8.5
1962	283,763	35.1	19.4	5.7	9.9
1963	306,260	34.8	18.0	3.5	13.3
1964	292,248	32.5	11.3	5.4	15.8
1965	296,697	35.8	12.8	6.7	16.4
1966	323,040	34.3	14.0	5.4	14.9
1967	361,972	30.1	11.7	9.2	9.2
1968	454,448	39.7	9.6	21.8	8.2
1969	358,579	27.6	12.4	3.8	11.3
1970	373,326	26.5	11.9	4.4	10.2
1971	370,478	29.6	13.5	5.8	10.2
1972	384,685	30.7	15.6	5.2	8.8
1973	400,063	33.2	17.5	6.0	9.6
1974	394,861	33.6	18.1	4.8	10.7
1975	386,194	33.7	16.1	6.7	10.9
1976	398,613	32.0	14.5	7.3	10.1
1977	462,315	36.1	9.5	15.1	11.5
1978	601,442	32.1	15.4	4.9	11.8
1960–9	3,213,749	32.5	13.4	7.7	11.3
1970–8	3,771,977	32.0	14.8	6.8	10.5
1960–78	6,985,726	32.3	14.1	7.2	10.9

Source: Massey and Schnabel, 1983, pp. 216f

Bracero Programme involving the USA and Mexico. 'For 22 years the Bracero Programme, originally designed as a wartime emergency measure, was dedicated to the procurement of cheap labour' (Ehrke, 1981, p. 10). Those who entered the country as part of this programme were given certain guarantees regarding permanent employment and working and living conditions which those working in the USA illegally could not expect.

Nevertheless, for every *bracero* who entered the country in the 1950s, there were another four immigrants who entered the country illegally. These illegal immigrants were known as 'wetbacks', for more often than not they entered the USA by swimming across the rivers which formed the border. During the Korean War the USA's demand for workers increased once more, but in 1954–55 2.9 million Mexicans were expelled under Operation Wetback, and measures were adopted later which also restricted legal immigration.

Yet illegal immigration to the USA still persists today. The majority of the Mexicans find work as domestics and agricultural labourers; more often than not they stay in the country for several months, return home, then enter the USA again at some future date.

In addition to the wetbacks, there are currently around three million *chicanos* in the USA. *Chicanos* are people of Mexican extraction, but with American citizenship and American passports. They make up approximately 15 per cent of the Californian population (cf. Michels, 1976, p. 12). Even the *chicanos* are affected by the discrimination that Mexicans generally encounter in the USA. They frequently work as seasonal and itinerant workers in the agricultural sector, where numerous migrant workers from other countries are also employed.

Around 2.5 million migrant ranch hands have entered the USA as part of the various waves of migration. They are supplied from the border regions of Mexico and via Florida, where migrant workers from the Caribbean enter the USA. From these two starting points the stream of migrant workers runs through the entire country like a network of arteries. The typical composition of this source of labour may be revealed by quoting the example of 280,000 people who applied for jobs as ranch hands in California:

> The majority of them, roughly 75 per cent, are Mexicans and *chicanos*, naturalized Mexicans with American passports. Another ten per cent are Filipinos, the rest blacks, Portuguese, Arabs and Anglo-Americans. In other states, especially Florida, the blacks are by far the largest section of the agricultural workforce. (Michels, 1976, p. 16)

Koreans and *Burakumin* in Japan

I will continue this look at present-day labour migration by examining the Japanese experience, which is characterized by relatively late, but rapid industrialization. Japan differs in several respects from the European and American experiences, yet it also exhibits some basic similarities. It is worth remembering that the workings of the world market for labour power were also at play here in a condensed and temporarily restricted form.

The first thing to note is that foreign, unqualified workers have so far been denied access to the Japanese labour market. In 1899 an imperial decree forbade foreigners, particularly the Chinese, from working in the agricultural sector and the fishing, mining, transport and construction industries except with special permission from the Japanese authorities (cf. Totsuka, 1980, p. 265).

Japanese imperialism, whose major conquests were Korea and China, reached its peak during the first few years of the 20th century. From 1910 on Korea was regarded as a component part of Japan, and workers began to travel from there to Japan. In 1930 the Japanese began to emigrate in droves to Manchuria and China: in 1933 there were 180,000 Japanese living

Table 22
Koreans in Japan, 1900–44

Year	No. of Koreans	Year	No. of Koreans
1900	193[a]	1929	387,901
:	:	1930	419,009
1915	5,046[b]	1931	437,519
1916	7,225	1932	504,176
1917	17,461	1933	573,896
1918	27,340	1934	689,651
1919	35,995	1935	720,818
1920	40,755	1936	780,528
1921	48,774	1937	822,214
1922	82,693	1938	881,347
1923	112,051	1939	1,081,394
1924	168,002	1940	1,241,315
1925	187,102	1941	1,469,230
1926	207,853	1942	1,625,054
1927	246,515	1943	1,768,180
1928	341,737	1944	1,911,307

Source: [a] Annual Statistics of Japanese Empire
[b] Estimates by Pak Jaeil, *Comprehensive Research on Korean Residents in Japan*, 1957, cited in Totsuka, 1980, pp. 266ff

in Manchuria, and by 1940 this figure had reached 820,000 (ibid.). Thus although emigration was certainly part of the Japanese experience, it did not occur on such a large scale as emigration from Europe. During World War One and in particular during World War Two a great many Koreans were imported into Japan as forced labour.

Before 1939 Korean migration to Japan was undoubtedly labour migration caused primarily by Japanese colonial policy in Korea, which consisted of the dispossession of the peasants and the pursuit of an anti-industrialization strategy. Japanese capitalists recruited workers in Korea, and from time to time the government endeavoured, for political reasons, to control or at least restrict migration. After 1939 the process became one of forced recruitment for the Japanese war economy, and as a result the number of Koreans in Japan rose from a few hundred thousand during the 1920s to more than half a million during the 1930s and almost two million in 1944.

After 1942 forced labour was recruited through a Government-financed public body and redirected to private firms. The total number of people involved in forced migration from Korea was somewhere in the region of 820,000 (cf. Totsuka, 1980, p. 272). Today there are still some 660,000 Koreans living in Japan, most of them the descendants of these forced labourers and a source of 'cheap labour' themselves. They are not permitted to join the state pension scheme, and the one third who profess loyalty to what is now North Korea have no permanent residence permits and cannot return to Japan once they travel outside her borders. Although two thirds of the Koreans living in Japan are unemployed or work part-time, Koreans receive no sickness or unemployment benefit. They are frequently sold by 'employment agencies' like slaves (cf. Dettloff and Kirchmann, 1981, pp. 122ff).

Koreans are the largest group of foreign workers in Japan, yet out of a total population of around 120 million people they represent a relatively small source of labour, especially if one compares Korean labour migration to Japan with the scale of labour migration in Western Europe and the USA.

At least one important section of the Japanese population itself supplies cheap labour largely reproduced outside the capitalist sector.[4] The workers who belong to this group are neither migrant workers, nor are they excluded for racial or ethnic reasons. Instead, in a move peculiar to the Japanese experience, Japanese capitalism has resorted as a criteria for exclusion to those antiquated structures of the estates of the realm which shaped pre-capitalist Japan.

The *burakumin*, also known as 'non-persons' or 'four-footers', were the most despised class in Japanese feudal society and contained the members of those professions which dealt with killing and the dead: shoemakers, tanners, furriers, slaughterers, knackers, morticians and so on (cf. Dettloff and Kirchmann, 1981, p. 126ff).

Today not only the descendants of these occupational groups belong to the *burakumin*, for 'It is not any continuous lineage, but the fact of having been born and/or living in a certain residential district, the *buraku*, which exposes the *burakumin* to discrimination' (Kaneko, 1979, p. 295). The traditional occupations have lost significance, and today the majority of the *burakumin* no longer have links with any kind of *buraku* industry (Kaneko, 1979, p. 296).

There are somewhere in the region of 6,000 *buraku*s in Japan, and all must be regarded as ghettos. They house some three million people. When engaging or dismissing staff companies are able to avail themselves of various devices for discovering a person's *buraku* descent. Since 1975 one firm has been selling a register of all *buraku*, and by 1978–79 eight different registers were known to exist. These are purchased mainly by big business and monopolies (Kaneko, 1979, p. 302), and effectively exclude the *burakumin* from Japan's economic and social life. Yet the discrimination they perpetuate is clearly not feudal class-based discrimination. 'Instead, the essence of the continued existence of discrimination against the *burakumin* lies in its reorganisation in the capitalist cause.' Unemployment is high among the *burakumin*, they are denied access to all but the most despised, least secure, and badly paid occupations, and are deprived of almost every opportunity to better themselves socially.

A study carried out in a Kyoto *buraku* at the beginning of the 1970s revealed that 90.7 per cent of the workers there were employed as labourers or blue-collar workers. The corresponding figure for Kyoto as a whole was 66.5 per cent. The study also revealed that 68 per cent of all *burakumin* workers were employed as unskilled labour, whereas the figure for Kyoto as a whole was only 14.3 per cent. In the *buraku* studied more than one quarter of the labour force was unemployed. In Kyoto as a whole the unemployment rate stood at only around 2 per cent.

Of the unskilled workers in the *buraku* almost two thirds were employed as *gengyō kōmuin*, public employees responsible, for example, for refuse collection, sewage removal, water purification, burial and catching stray dogs. Despite the violent contempt with which such occupations are regarded, many *burakumin* regard employment as a *gengyō kōmuin* as desirable, since it at least offers job security, to which they would have no access in other fields. In the town of Kyoto approximately 90 per cent of the *gengyō* workers employed as refuse collectors are *burakumin* (Kaneko, 1979, pp. 303ff).

A comparison of the position of Koreans and *burakumin* on the Japanese labour market with that of other groups in Western European countries and the USA proves the universality of the principles according to which the world market for labour power operates in capitalist societies. Moreover, the discrimination suffered by the *burakumin* suggests that the criteria according to which certain groups are excluded from society and which lead to those groups being particularly susceptible to exploitation are a relatively flexible feast. Where there are insufficiently large numbers available for exclusion and exploitation by dint of race or sex, or where the indigenous source of labour power is extensive enough, then recourse to certain elements of feudal society can also serve the same purpose: to force workers back into non-capitalist structures as far as the reproduction of their labour power is concerned, but also to incorporate them into the capitalist productive process at the lowest level and as required.

Overview: today's world market for labour power

To the extent that it is directly concerned with the transfer of living labour, i.e. the direct transfer of labour power, today's world market for labour power is essentially a mixture of the various forms of labour migration. In Western Europe the history of labour migration can be traced back to the 19th century, but it is and has also long been a feature of the labour markets in the USA and other metropolitan areas that evolved from settlers' colonies.[5]

Present-day labour migration shows three main trends: migration to Western Europe, migration to the USA and migration to the oil-exporting countries, above all those of the Near East. The import of labour power into the first two regions has already been discussed. With the exception of Nigeria, I have not yet considered the more recent transfers of labour power to the oil-producing countries, and will therefore examine them briefly now.

Though crude oil deposits were first discovered in the Arab countries in the 1930s, the region did not begin to export oil on a large scale until the 1940s, 1950s and 1960s, a period which also saw the founding of many of the region's present-day states. Since then a considerable proportion of world oil production has originated in the Arab countries – 31.5 per cent in 1980 (without Iran). The export of oil earned the region large amounts of foreign currency, and this income increased considerably after the rises in oil prices in 1973 and 1975. A large percentage of this income found its way into various state coffers and financed state budgets almost singlehanded: 90 per cent of Saudi Arabia's, 88 per cent of Kuwait's, and 98 per cent of Libya's.

This huge revenue was not spent exclusively on imported consumer goods, but also on private and public construction projects, in particular the building of infrastructure and production plants: strategically positioned roads, military and civilian airfields, luxurious airport buildings, ports, military bases, hospitals, schools, universities, other public establishments of all kinds and entire manufacturing plants. The Saudi Arabian economic plan for 1974 to 1979 provided that half of the nation's budget would be spent on construction projects.

Technical personnel, machinery, material and so on were purchased with foreign currency from the capitalist metropole, and in this way some of the funds the capitalist countries had spent on crude oil flowed back to them. However, the majority of the Arab oil-exporting countries lack the labour forces required to execute their projects. Their indigenous populations are small: roughly 4.6 million in Saudi Arabia (1975), 2.3 million in Libya (1975), around half a million in Kuwait (1975), less than 200,000 in Bahrain (1971) and only 45,000 in Qatar (1970). Of these small indigenous populations only about one in five people is listed as gainfully employed.

In order to invest their oil revenues the Arab countries are therefore forced to import large quantities of labour power: one 1975 survey estimated the number of migrant workers in nine of the Arab countries[6] at 1.6 million. By 1980 this figure had risen to 2.8 million (without Algeria, but including the Yemen) (see Table 23), and the nine had plans to further increase the figure to 4.3 million by 1985. The seven leading importers of labour power planned to increase the number of foreigners working within their borders from three to ten million in the decade from 1975 to 1985 (see Serageldin et al., 1983). It is estimated that at the end of the 1970s the population of the Arabian Peninsula stood at seven million natives and 4.5 million foreigners. In Kuwait, Qatar and the United Arab Emirates there were actually more foreigners than natives.

Since labour power is recruited from Africa and Asia, as well as from other Arab countries such as Egypt and Tunisia, the entire surrounding region is becoming a reservoir of labour power for the sparsely populated oil-exporting countries. The oil-exporting countries are also profiting from the colonial penetration of India, Pakistan, Egypt and various other

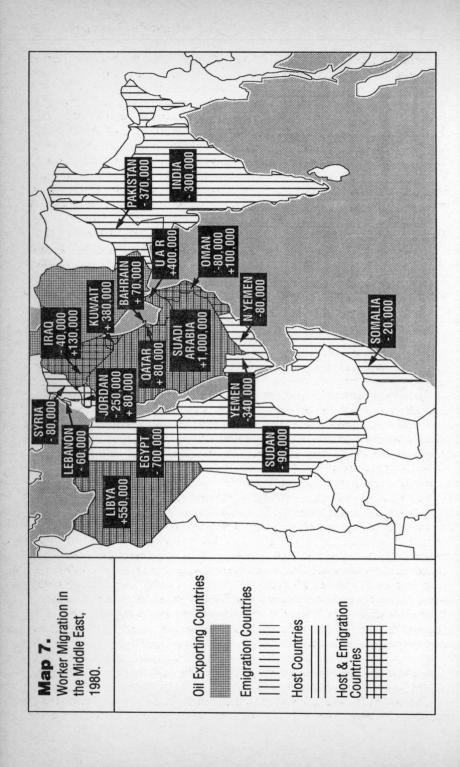

Map 7.
Worker Migration in the Middle East, 1980.

Oil Exporting Countries

Emigration Countries

Host Countries

Host & Emigration Countries

LIBYA +550,000

EGYPT -700,000

SUDAN -90,000

LEBANON -60,000

SYRIA -80,000

IRAQ -40,000 +130,000

JORDAN -250,000 +80,000

QATAR +80,000

KUWAIT +380,000

BAHRAIN +70,000

U A R +400,000

SUADI ARABIA +1,000,000

OMAN -80,000 +100,000

N. YEMEN -80,000

YEMEN -340,000

SOMALIA -20,000

PAKISTAN -370,000

INDIA -300,000

countries, for this has led to a large-scale liberation of labour power and the formation of a belt around their oil-rich territories (see Map 7).

The pattern of migration to the Arab states is extremely complex. It is not possible to match up countries of origin and host countries, since each host country's foreign workforce hails from a number of different states. For example, the region's leading importer of labour is Saudi Arabia, and though the largest group of foreign workers employed there comes from the Yemen, there are also a great many workers from Egypt, Jordan, Palestine and other countries. According to Table 23, the second largest importer of labour, after Saudi Arabia with its million-plus foreign workers, is Libya, which employs more than half a million, including a quarter of a million Egyptians. Libya is followed by the United Arab Emirates and Kuwait, each employing 400,000 migrant workers.

The country that supplies the region with the largest number of foreign workers is Egypt, which has 700,000 workers abroad; it is followed by Pakistan, South Yemen, India, Palestine and Jordan, each with around a quarter to a third of a million workers abroad. Some of the workers concerned have general and academic qualifications, for example teachers and administrative employees.

For migrants with few or no formal qualifications living conditions in the host countries are inconceivably bad. Not only is their work toilsome and dirty, but also their wages are insufficient for even their most basic needs. This is partly due to the high cost of living, but also to the fact that the privileges enjoyed by the native populations, such as free medical care, free schooling etc., are not granted to migrant workers. Often not even flats are available to them, and they are accommodated in tents or barracks. Since migrant workers make up such a large proportion of the total population in Arab countries, they are regarded by the ruling élite as a potential threat to the system, and are consequently subject to political repression and police supervision.

As a whole the process of labour migration to the oil-exporting countries is not, however, comparable with transfers of labour power to the capitalist metropole. In the latter, migrant workers are employed primarily in industrial production and are therefore direct producers, whilst in the oil-producing countries it is a question of spending foreign currency on construction projects and in the service sector, since industrial production does not exist. The employment of migrant workers neither lays the foundations for industrialization nor for any other form of production. Instead, it stimulates industrial development in the metropole, since it is companies from the countries of the metropole that supply materials and know-how, as well as the management for the projects.

We have now covered all large-scale transfers of labour power in the world today. In conclusion, they will be considered as a whole.

Like other official sources such as the report of the Brandt Commission, the *World Labour Report 1* concludes that there were around 20 million

Table 23
Migrant workers in Arab countries, 1980 (estimate)

Countries of origin	Host countries										Total
	Bahrain	Jordan	Iraq	Kuwait	Libya	Oman	Qatar	Saudi Arabia	UAE	Yemen	
Yemen	1,125	–	–	9,500	–	120	1,500	65,000	6,600	–	83,845
Egypt	2,800	68,500	100,000	85,000	250,000	6,300	5,750	155,100	18,200	4,000	695,650
India	12,300	500	2,000	45,000	32,000	35,600	11,850	29,700	109,500	2,000	280,450
Iraq & Jordan	310	–	–	40,000	–	–	–	3,250	1,200	–	44,760
Palestine	1,400	–	7,500	55,000	15,000	2,250	7,800	140,000	19,400	2,000	250,350
Lebanon	300	–	4,500	8,000	5,700	1,500	750	33,200	6,600	500	61,050
Oman	900	–	–	2,000	–	–	1,150	10,000	19,400	–	33,450
Pakistan	26,160	4,000	7,500	34,000	65,000	44,500	20,770	29,700	137,000	3,000	371,630
Somalia	–	–	–	500	5,000	400	–	8,300	5,000	500	19,700
Sudan	900	–	500	5,500	21,000	620	750	55,600	2,100	2,250	89,220
Syria	150	–	–	35,000	15,000	600	1,000	24,600	5,800	1,000	83,150
South Yemen	1,125	–	–	3,000	–	120	1,500	325,000	5,400	–	336,145
Other Arabs	–	–	–	300	65,600	120	–	500	–	–	66,520
Other Asians	10,000	1,000	1,500	10,000	27,000	–	4,500	93,500	20,700	300	168,500
Others	10,250	2,000	2,000	45,900	44,200	4,670	22,930	49,800	54,100	1,450	237,300
Total	**67,720**	**76,000**	**125,500**	**378,700**	**545,500**	**96,800**	**80,250**	**1,023,250**	**411,000**	**17,000**	**2,821,720**

Source: *World Labour Report*, 1984, p. 102

migrant workers worldwide in 1980 (*World Labour Report*, 1984, p. 99, *Das Uberleben sichern*, 1980, p. 139). On the one hand, it should be remembered that this figure reflects the fact that there has been a reduction in the employment of foreigners since 1973: at the beginning of the recession there were 15 million migrant workers in Western Europe alone (Newland, 1979, p. 9). On the other hand, it is undoubtedly a low estimate: the International Labour Organization postulates that there are actually some 25 to 30 million people who, in order to find waged work, have left their home countries and now live abroad. In addition to the migrant workers themselves we must add a roughly equal number of family members who likewise reside abroad (*World Labour Report*, 1984, p. 100).

Thus it must be assumed that between 50 and 60 million people are directly affected by labour migration today, and it has been suggested that even this figure is too low. The *World Labour Report*, for instance, estimates the number of illegal immigrants in the USA at 2.5 million, whilst the Worldwatch Institute maintained as far back as 1979 that the figure fluctuated between 2 and 12 million (Newland, 1979, p. 6). Europe too has vast numbers of illegal immigrants: we have already mentioned Italy, but the campaigns for the legalization of illegal immigrants that have been conducted in France at regular intervals, and that have also been called for in West Germany in recent years, likewise indicate the not inconsiderable size of this group in Europe.[7]

The figures published in the *World Labour Report* do not include such groups, nor do they take into account refugees, those expelled from their own countries, those seeking political asylum etc., most of whom come from Third World countries and who are often members of a mobile reserve labour force. The Worldwatch report stresses that it is often difficult to distinguish between these groups and migrant workers.

Although it is impossible to determine the precise scale of labour migration, available data indicate that the process is one of considerable significance worldwide, even during periods of economic crisis, embargoes on recruitment, rationalization and high unemployment in the capitalist world. In attempting to assess just how significant the process is, it is important to remember that *labour migration is closely linked with development and underdevelopment*. More than half of the world's migrant workers come from the developing nations (according to *Das Uberleben sichern*, 1980, p. 139, 12 out of 20 million), in the USA the figure is around two thirds, and in the oil-producing countries it could be as much as nine tenths (*World Labour Report*, 1984, p. 100).

In comparison with the number of unemployed in those countries that have not been permitted to develop – estimated at 54 million for 1973, with a further 250 million underemployed (cf. Mukherjee, 1981, p. 68) – the scale of labour migration from such countries may appear relatively small. However, in attempting to assess the significance of the process one must consider not only quantitative but also qualitative factors. These obviously assume greater importance in a negative sense for countries that have not been permitted to develop when, for example, one considers the selectivity which is applied to labour migration. The workers taken from such countries are often those with above average training and qualifications and they are generally recruited at the most productive time of their lives.

Consequently, it is more illuminating to compare the number of workers migrating from countries that have not been permitted to develop with the size of the 'modern proletariat' within these countries (see Table 24). According to the figures in Table 24, labour migration from developing nations now equals total employment in these countries' processing industries. Such figures indicate the fundamental significance of the world market for labour power to countries of this kind.

Table 24
The structure of the modern proletariat in the developing nations, 1970

	No. employed (millions)	%
Processing industries	17–18	27.6
of which: heavy industry	5– 6	8.7
light industry	12–13	19.7
Extractive industries	2	3.1
Transport and construction	11–12	18.1
Large-scale agricultural production	15–16	24.4
Total	**60–67**	**100**

Source: Ernst and Schilling, 1981, p. 260

The former colonies do not merely supply workers with few or no formal qualifications: since the mid-1950s the world has also witnessed the emergence of a 'brain drain', the emigration of academics from Asia, Africa and Latin America to Western Europe and the USA. In the period between 1956 and 1959 some 14,000 highly qualified workers migrated from Mexico, the Caribbean and Latin America to the USA (cf. Kidd, 1967, p. 6). In the years that followed the scale of migration increased substantially. In 1973 alone the US Immigration Service registered more than 41,000 academics and engineers from other countries (cf. Portes, 1976, p. 489).

The *Brandt Report* estimates that during the 1960s and 1970s some 400,000 people from developing nations migrated to Western Europe and the USA as part of the brain drain (*Das Überlebern sichern*, 1980, p. 140). This is without doubt a low estimate. Between 1961 and 1975/6 the USA, Canada and Great Britain alone imported 285,000 doctors, engineers, natural scientists and other academics from developing nations (*Lenins Imperialismustheorie und die Gegenwart*, 1980, p. 230).

The departure of such personnel represents a great loss to nations that have not been permitted to develop, since their training requires a high level of social expenditure which then generally becomes unrecoverable as a result of their emigration. The cost to the developing nations of migration to the USA in 1970 has been estimated at $3,660 million (Strahm, 1975, p. 34). Another estimate, this time for 1972, assesses the gain which accrued to the USA, Canada and Great Britain as a result of the brain drain from the developing nations to be more than $10,000 million. A third source calculates the total loss suffered by the developing nations as a result of the brain drain during the same year at $20,000 million (Faulwetter, 1977, p. 10).

The transfer of technology to the USA and Western Europe costs these regions nothing, yet at the same time the developing nations are faced with the huge cost of importing technology and technical and economic services from the capitalist metropole.

Nor do countries which have not been permitted to develop merely lose fully qualified academics through the brain drain: they also lose students. These students have already enjoyed an education which has cost their countries of origin a great deal and which is only available to a minority. Yet few students return home who conclude their studies abroad, since the host country generally has an interest in their remaining, and they have often become socially integrated (not least by marriage). Between 1960 and 1979, 52,613 students left Taiwan, whilst during the same period only 6,200 returned (Kwok and Leland, 1982, p. 91).

One cause of the brain drain is the fact that the education system in almost every country that has not been permitted to develop conforms to European or US structures, content, methods and objectives, and at higher levels is still often staffed by European or American personnel. It is rarely adapted to the country's own social structure or labour market. Medical training is an example. Highly qualified specialists are trained to deal with diseases of affluence. They are capable of using the most modern equipment and have ambitions to go into research. Since there are few opportunities to practise such medicine in their own countries, except in the capital city and perhaps a few other larger towns, and since the demand in their own countries is for doctors with a basic understanding of practical medicine to work in rural areas, where earning potential is low, well-qualified doctors in particular seize every opportunity to emigrate. According to a study carried out in Argentina, 84 per cent of all doctors asked and who had not yet emigrated expected that they would find it difficult to obtain the prerequisites for an adequate medical practice in Argentina (cf. Portes and Walton, 1981, pp. 40f).

Finally, socio-economic conditions in countries that have not been permitted to develop, for example, unemployment among academics, are also a major cause of the brain drain. In 1970 there were 140,000 graduates (9,300 of them engineers) and 655,000 high-school graduates (33,000 of them technicians) without work in India; 10 per cent of all Indian doctors were employed abroad, and 30 per cent of all medical school graduates were leaving the country (cf. Strahm, 1975, p. 35). In Nigeria less than one person in 200 who qualified in 1959/60 found work within six years (cf.

Yesufu, 1978, p. 345). Of 417 Nigerian people who emigrated to the USA between 1962 and 1967, 255 were qualified professionals, including 131 scientists and technicians, 31 engineers, 9 doctors and 34 nurses (Aderinto, 1978, p. 324).

In addition to unemployment, underemployment, variations in the standard of living, fewer promotion opportunities and lower earning potential, the political situation also has a considerable influence on the scale of brain drain from many of the countries that have not been permitted to develop. Schipulle (1973, p. 358) explained the matter thus: 'There is,' he wrote, 'an obvious link between emigration and unstable political conditions. Those affected include members of the political opposition, intellectuals in general and religious and/or ethnic minorities.'

Ultimately, however, the decisive factor affecting the brain drain is the host countries' interest in this labour resource. It is the capitalist metropole that makes the whole process possible, for it is the capitalist metropole that profits from it. Though academics from countries that have not been permitted to develop acquire a social and economic status that differentiates them clearly from other migrant workers, the experiences of foreign doctors in West Germany over the last few years demonstrate that their actual function is to provide the capitalist metropole with room for manoeuvre.[8] In the past few decades such doctors have been the foremost custodians of hospital health care in West Germany. In the meantime, however, the labour market for doctors has changed, and the expectation is that in future there will be more than enough German doctors, even for the less attractive posts. As a result, 'alarming shortcomings in the health care provided to broad sections of the population of the Third World, as well as the universally articulated and not inconsiderable burden placed on the German labour market by doctors and specialists from the developing nations' have heaved into view. They 'offer plenty of scope for future reintegration' (Gross et al., 1982, pp. 102f).

The brain drain, the most recent development on the world market for labour power, may be modified by such considerations, possibly even limited, but certainly not eradicated.

Notes

1. Until the mid-19th century nine out of every ten people who emigrated to the USA came from Great Britain, Ireland or Germany (Chiroux, 1979, p. 7). Migration from Britain and Germany was undoubtedly stimulated by developments within those countries themselves.

2. Here we see a major difference between French and German policy on the employment of foreign labour. In France migrant workers were often regarded as a means of achieving a politically and economically desirable increase in the native population, for population growth in France had virtually come to a standstill: between 1900 and 1939 the population of France grew by only 3 per cent, whereas the German population grew by 36 per cent (Minces, 1973, p. 27) and was roughly in line with the European average. Naturalization was easier and more common in France, and even the statistics relating to the foreign population were very different. Whereas in Germany their major consideration was the size of the labour force, in

France the statistics generally took account of the entire foreign population or the number of immigrants who entered the country each year.

3. At this time Poland did not exist as an independent state, but was divided between Russia, Prussia and Austria. Some Polish workers were therefore treated in statistics as Russians, others as Austrians and others again as Germans.

4. In addition to the Koreans and the *burakumin*, Ernst (1980, p. 216) identifies the elderly, the disabled, women, migrant workers (*dekasegi*) and the rehabilitated as 'groups exhibiting a high incidence of employment instability' on the Japanese labour market. The migrant workers come from the rural districts of Japan, where there are few job opportunities other than in the agricultural sector. In 1973, for example, 300,000 people left their homes for several months in order to take up waged employment in other parts of the country (ibid. p. 245). The other groups mentioned above typically make up the labour market's reserve army in all capitalist countries. To some extent at least discrimination against these workers in terms of the jobs they do, wages and social security is more extreme in Japan than anywhere else: in 1974, women's wages were only half of what a male worker earned (Dettloff and Kirchmann, 1981, p. 142 and Kaneko, 1979, p. 310).

5. It is often difficult to distinguish in such societies between labour migration and immigration, the latter being reserved mainly for Europeans. The following is an historical example of the phenomenon and relates to Australia. When the continent first became accessible the labour force consisted not only of white immigrants, but also of deportees, Aborigines and coolies. In the 1850s camel drivers were imported with their animals from Afghanistan and to a lesser extent also from Egypt, Persia and Turkey. Camel trains were important for the exploration of the interior of the country and for the building of infrastructure (railways and telegraph lines). During the 1920s, once the camel trains were no longer needed, the government passed a Camel Destruction Act. Having been refused Australian citizenship, most of the Asians returned to their countries of origin.

The second example also relates to Australia, but is more recent. After World War Two the country was opened up to European, especially British, immigrants. Estimates for the number of immigrants living in Australia during the mid-1960s were around the 2 million mark (cf. Martin, 1978, p. 27). At the end of the 1970s a recruitment treaty was concluded with Turkey, on the basis of which some 14,000 people entered the country. These people did not, however, acquire the status of immigrants. Although the number of workers affected was small, the process nevertheless points up just how universally race, nationality and so on are used as criteria for exclusion on the labour market.

6. Algeria, Bahrain, Iraq, Kuwait, Libya, Oman, Qatar, Saudi Arabia and the United Arab Emirates.

7. Meillassoux (1976, p. 140) and Portes and Walton (1981, pp. 25, 57) stress that illegal immigration is a component part of the system. Illegal immigrants are deprived of an even larger part of their wages than other workers, and their extreme lack of rights makes them a particularly flexible labour resource whose scale and composition is directly dependent on economic development in the metropole.

8. While the major host countries for academics from countries that have not been permitted to develop are the English-speaking regions of the metropole, West Germany also profits from the process. In 1981 21,519 academics from the developing nations were employed in West Germany (Gross et al., 1982, p. 82), including 7,056 doctors in salaried employment. The number of doctors from developing nations who have settled in Germany is estimated at 1,000, and there are another 20,000 qualified personnel from developing nations (including male and female nurses) working in the country's public health sector (ibid., p. 102). During the winter term of 1980–81 there were 35,872 students from developing nations studying in West Germany (ibid., p. 37), of whom 3,093 were studying medicine.

6. The World Market for Labour Power According to Theories of Imperialism and Development

The main purpose of this chapter is to ask in what context and with what results a theoretical analysis of those workings of the world market for labour power has so far been achieved. In doing so I will consider not only theories of imperialism and development and migration theory, but also labour market theory and economic history.

As is evident, for example, from Fischer and Heier's 1983 overview of the development of labour market theory, this discipline has so far been concerned almost exclusively with waged labour in the capitalist metropole. Accordingly it has only occasionally taken up the question of labour migration and emigration. Other processes of the world market for labour power, such as geographical shifts in production to countries that have not been permitted to develop, are a part of labour market theory only to the extent that they have an actual or suspected effect on the labour market in the metropole.

Studies in the field of economic history generally regard human labour power as being of only peripheral significance in the course and level of economic development. Thus although the United States is a country that imported practically its entire workforce, this is barely reflected at all in literature in the field of economic history; whilst Landauer (1981), Poulson (1981), and Puth (1982) all refer in their economic histories of the USA to the procurement of labour power and its related processes and problems, the matter is most certainly not the subject of theoretical analysis or even considered to be a major factor affecting economic development.

Nor do more recent attempts at a general reassessment of the history of work solve the problem. Both the 1984 study by Jungbluth and the 1983 anthology edited by Schneider once again limit the 'history of the worker and work' to European (and male) history. Asian, African, and Latin American workers are not considered at all, and as a consequence slavery, coolieism, other forms of colonial forced labour and labour migration are also not discussed. The history of work since classical antiquity (Rome, Greece, Egypt) is limited to its evolution into European, capitalist wage labour, and the history of at least three quarters of the population of the world is ignored.

In the introduction I expressed the view that migration theory has little in common with development theory and also that it has not, at least in its West German variant, come up with any interconnections to speak of between migration and development, such as worldwide patterns of labour migration or an historical perspective which dates back further than the industrialization of Germany. It is for this reason that it is largely unsuitable as the basis for analysis of the world market for labour power.

That leaves only development theory. West German development theory has not suffered from the shortcomings already mentioned in particular in connection with migration theory. It does not limit itself in terms of national boundaries but has been greatly influenced, for example, by the Latin American dependency debate and also by French works on the subject. Nevertheless, this does not mean that it has adequately covered the processes of the world market for labour power.

A critique of recent theories of development

The majority of the more recent analyses in the field of development theory make no mention of workers in or from Asia, Africa and Latin America or their role in the development of capitalism, either in the past or in the present. This is also the case for those approaches that take the labour theory of value as their starting point and have evolved and come to regard themselves as counterpoles to the theories of growth, dualism and modernization.[1] On the occasions when the more recent theories of imperialism, most sections of the dependency debate, and the related theory of peripheral capitalism analyse structures inside those countries that have not been permitted to develop and the relationships between such countries and the metropole (that is to say, between the periphery and the centre), they rarely discuss living labour or its acquisition in any great detail. One needs only leaf through the bibliographies and guides to the subject to be convinced of that.

The following examination of the major works within the more recent debate on imperialism in Western Europe, on the concept of 'marginality' as a component part of many theories of dependency, on the debate on unequal exchange, and on theories of peripheral capitalism as expounded by Senghaas is not intended as a thorough analysis or overall assessment of these theories. Neither will I discuss the circumstances in which the studies came about, for what purpose they were written, or the effect, whether positive or negative, each one has had or will have on future political tactics. Instead the works will be examined exclusively from the following points of view:

1. Do they pose the question of the importance of labour forces in and from countries which have not been permitted to develop?
2. How is this question answered?
3. Which forms of exploitation do they consider?
4. Which historical perspective do they reflect?

The recent debate on imperialism

Studies published in the German language by Magdoff in 1970 and Jalée in 1971 confirm the extent to which the early stages of the recent West German debate on imperialism were influenced by Leninist thought. These works, entitled *Die Zeitalter des Imperialismus* (The age of imperialism) and *Das neueste Stadium des Imperialismus* (The latest phase of imperialism), consider the importance of raw materials and capital exports, development aid and foreign trade, the financial system and the concentration and centralization of capital. Neither looks in any detail at labour power. The authors even undertake an analysis of the production and realization of surplus value at international level without any consideration of those producing it or the process by which living and/or objectified labour is acquired. Such labour is mentioned only in relation to export and investment statistics.

Nor were Magdoff and Jalée the last to expound the virtues of this approach to analysing imperialism, even outside Soviet Marxist circles. Senghaas's much-discussed 1972 anthology *Imperialismus und strukturelle Gewalt* (Imperialism and structural violence) contains several instances of this same basic attitude. Thus O'Connor, clearly relying heavily on Lenin, lists five major characteristics of modern imperialism: the concentration of capital, the operation of a 'free' international market, the active participation of state capital, the consolidation of an international ruling class and the intensification of these trends as a result of the socialist threat (O'Connor, 1972, p. 153). The essay bears the title *'Die Bedeutung des ökonomischen Imperalismus'* ('The importance of economic imperialism'), and, as the above list suggests, labour power in or from colonial territories is not a subject which interests O'Connor.

In the same volume Wolff explains present-day 'imperialism from the point of view of the metropole'. He does not have a single word to say on the subject of labour power, despite a definition of imperialism upon which he expands in the essay and which reads, 'The term is generally used to describe the many means of control which one economy (business enterprises and government) exerts over another.' This control is then broken down further in a more detailed explanation according to which 'A business enterprise and/or its government strives for control in order to guarantee the following: 1. The import of essential raw materials and foodstuffs, 2. Markets for its industrial exports, and 3. Investment opportunities for its capital' (Wolff, 1972, pp. 187f).

The above examples speak volumes for the extent to which recent debate has been influenced by Lenin's analysis of imperialism. Lenin does not examine the importance of the labour force in territories colonized or penetrated by imperialist powers at all, for he does not believe it to be of relevance to his theory. This belief has been accepted without question for so long that decades later many studies still work on this assumption, whether implicitly or explicitly. Indeed, the theoreticians regard the goods produced by workers in those countries that have not been permitted to develop (raw materials, industrial and agricultural products) and their marketing as more important than the living labour itself.

Dependency theories

The concept of marginality is a typical example of the way in which different versions of dependency theory approach the question of labour power in countries that have not been permitted to develop. It is one of the most widely circulated but also one of the most obscure concepts within the dependency debate. The problem begins with the term itself:

> Marginality means standing on the fringe, and in relation to a sociological field one is inclined at first glance to see the term as referring to a side issue or a residual category outside the normal scheme of things – a foolish word to choose to describe the situation of the majority of the population. (Bennholdt-Thomsen, 1979, p. 45)

Bennholdt-Thomsen puts forward an exhaustive critique of the term which I do not intend to repeat here.[2]

It is important to remember that the exclusion or insufficient incorporation of the population from or into capitalist production is central to the concept of marginality. The following examples demonstrate how little uniformity exists in the various definitions of the term:

- One version of the concept is to be found in Amin (1976). For him the crucial point is the over-expansion of the tertiary sectors in the economies of countries which have not been permitted to develop.
- According to Quijano, the 'marginalized' make up 'a new and separate section of the working population' which contributes to the accumulation of capital through its role as a reserve army of labour and a body of 'exploited consumers' (Quijano, 1974, pp. 315, 338).
- Sunkel maintains, 'One can therefore say that marginality, the greatest and most explosive of Latin America's problems, is primarily caused by the fact that the majority of the population does not earn an adequate and steady income...' (Sunkel, 1972, p. 271). Marginality simply as a synonym for poverty and destitution?

According to Sunkel, 'integrated' (the opposite of 'marginal') is a term that applies to only a tiny fraction of the Latin American population: entrepreneurs, the middle classes and workers employed in the modern capitalist sector of the economy (ibid., p. 311).

Sunkel also incorporates both domestic and international mobility of labour into his analysis. For him mobility of labour means movement not only between integrated and marginalized sections of society, but also between the capitalist metropole and the countries that have not been permitted to develop. This mobility, he writes, 'has every prospect of also creating an international market for human labour power'. He adds that this market for human labour power would operate in both directions and seeks to prove his assertion by referring to the brain drain and development experts. What Sunkel does not realize is that the processes he regards as marginalization are the result of the emergence and development of the sections of the economy and society which he describes as integrated. The 'international market for human labour power' he anticipates has actually existed since capitalism first began its worldwide expansion and has for centuries been dominated quantitatively and qualitatively by the transfer of labour power from the countries that have not been permitted to develop to the capitalist metropole.

The above examples demonstrate the unsuitability of the term 'marginality' for describing structures in countries that have not been permitted to develop and in particular show that it is incapable of contributing to any great extent to a theoretical assessment of the workings of the world market for labour power.

Singer likewise examines employment, production, and the reproduction of labour power in the 'undeveloped nations', as he calls them, within the context of the dependency debate. Above all, he rejects the suggestion that unemployment and underemployment in such countries may be regarded as the result of supply and demand. He aims to demonstrate that the supply of as well as the demand for labour power is determined by the movement of capital (Singer, 1977, p. 53). He formulates his view more or less as a doctrine:

> Capital thus *produces* and *reproduces* its own labour power ... to the extent that it actually purchases labour power from the workers and distributes to the wage worker such resources as allow him to support himself on a daily basis and compensation at the end of his productive life. (Ibid., p. 55)

Though this is to some extent true of the metropole today, it can hardly be said to apply to countries that have not been permitted to develop. In view of the wage levels and the scale of unemployment and underemployment in such countries, it might be more accurately described as an absurdity than as an explanation.

Thereafter Singer falls back on arguments also used by Mandel and Sternberg: that labour power in the metropole is valued more highly as a result of the labour movement, that the 'undeveloped nations' produce relatively little surplus value, and that productivity is limited and reduced by poor wages. The last point is not proven empirically in Singer's study, and it is worth noting that productivity in factories producing for the world market and free production zones at least is equal to, and may soon be even higher than, that in the metropole. Singer regards young people and women as 'secondary labour'.

The debate on 'unequal exchange'

Certain parties to the debate on unequal exchange deal more discriminatingly with the question of labour power. In the late 1960s the West Germans entered the debate, which had begun in France (Emmanuel, 1969), with great enthusiasm. The central question was whether violations or modifications of the law of exchange were causing unequal quantities of labour power to be exchanged, and whether unequal exchanges of this kind resulted in a flow of value out of those countries that had not been permitted to develop and into the capitalist metropole. In West Germany the debate focused primarily on a study published in 1975 by Amin and entitled *Die ungleiche Entwicklung* (Unequal development, 1976). Far from taking the debate any further forward, however, the contributions provoked by this initial study actually lag behind it.

According to Amin, there is indeed unequal exchange on the world market, not only in cases where productivity in the countries that have not been permitted to develop is lower than that in the metropole ('periphery' and 'centre' in his terminology), but also where equal productivity must be assumed due to the fact that the organic composition of capital is the same in both regions. The latter case, claims Amin, is the more prominent on the world market. The basis of unequal exchange is, then, that wages are considerably lower in countries that have not been permitted to develop than in the metropole. Empirical evidence shows that no average wage has been established on the world market.

Amin offers only a few hints on the crucial question of how it is possible for wages, which as the price of the commodity 'labour power' must necessarily fluctuate around its value (i.e. reproduction costs), to be generally and consistently lower in such underdeveloped countries than in the metropole: '... it [the reward of labour] can be lower in so far as the peripheral society is subordinated by all available means, economic and extraeconomic, to this new function of supplying cheap labour for the exporting sector' (Amin, 1976, p. 192). More bluntly, 'It is thus not the "laws of the market" that explain the way wages have evolved in the periphery (which is the basis of unequal exchange) but quite simply the policies of primitive accumulation that are practised there' (ibid., p. 149). The question is fundamental and merits thorough analysis, but this is surely not a satisfactory response to it. Nevertheless, Amin's remarks go considerably further than, say, Mandel's contribution to the ongoing debate.

Mandel accepts that there is an unequal exchange of quantities of labour on the world market, but maintains that there is still an equivalent exchange of values: 'The unequal exchange therefore leads to a transfer of value (a transfer of quantities of labour, i.e. of economic resources) which does not run contrary to the law of value, but which is in harmony with the law of value' (Mandel, 1972, p. 332). Mandel claims that wage development depends on long-term trends in the nature of the industrial reserve army:

> Once the accumulation of capital was no longer being accomplished primarily as a result of the disintegration of the pre-capitalist classes on the domestic market, but through expansion of the external market, it began to create more jobs in the metropole than it destroyed there, since it was the jobs in the underdeveloped nations which were destroyed. It is for this reason that the secular trend was one of gradual dissolution of the industrial reserve army in the metropole and gradual growth of the industrial reserve army in the underdeveloped nations, and this then explains the divergence between real wages in the two parts of the world. (Ibid., p. 335)

Ultimately this must mean that wage development, in particular the great discrepancy between wage levels in the metropole and those in countries that have still not been permitted to develop today, is a function of supply and demand. Such an explanation is inadequate chiefly because it suggests that it is not the value of the commodity 'labour power' but its price which determines wage levels – at least in those countries that have not been permitted to develop.

Moreover, Mandel also inclines to the view that colonial labour power does have a lower value than that in the metropole (ibid., p. 318). This is, essentially, an unsatisfactory attempt to evade the analytical dilemma which arises from the fact that although wages in the metropole are actually many times higher than in countries which have not been permitted to develop, they are still only sufficient to reproduce labour and do not allow for any accumulation of capital (something which would, of course, shake the very foundations of the political economy).

On the one hand, Mandel has no wish to question the theory of value. On the other, it is for this very purpose that he abandons its premises, since low productivity should mean that the value of labour in those countries which have not been permitted to develop is not lower, but on the contrary higher than in the metropole, since a greater proportion of the production in question is necessary production.

Thus not only does Mandel's analysis fail to settle the question raised by Amin and various others, but it also contributes to the confusion which is now beginning to surround the debate. Those taking part each interpret the same series of basically similar features in different ways and fight each other tooth and nail, until eventually not even a lowest common denominator can be found.

The contributions by Schöller and Senghaas are perfect examples.

Schöller works on the assumption – clearly differentiated from Amin's view, but relying heavily on Mandel's – that unequal exchange, if indeed it does take place, consists of an unequal exchange of labour time or of 'national quantities of labour' (Schöller, 1975, p. 174). This unequal exchange can be put down to the unequal development of productive forces and is therefore a derivative phenomenon. In conclusion he even claims that, 'Low wages are, in fact, one of the prerequisites for capitalist development in the Third World wherever the value of the product is relatively low in relation to labour time' (ibid., p. 175). In this respect his view differs from that of Mandel. Yet Amin is adamant that the problem of unequal exchange exists where the organic composition of capital in the periphery is both lower and equal to that in the metropole, and that exports from those countries that have not been permitted to develop are, to a large extent, produced under comparable technological conditions as those in the metropole, so that there can be no question of the value of such production being lower in relation to the time worked than production elsewhere. Fröbel, Heinrichs and Kreye (1977) have been able to demonstrate this clearly for production in free production zones and factories producing for the world market.

Senghaas's 1977 contribution to the debate assumes the 'relative immobility of the labour force' (Senghaas, 1977, p. 182), a theory which Mandel attributes to Amin but has not proved (Mandel, 1974, p. 325). Senghaas rejects the notion of perfectly equal productivity levels and explains low wages with the assertion that 'a defective reproductive system constantly recreates a huge pool of cheap labour' (Senghaas, 1977, p. 182). Unlike Schöller, Senghaas is of the opinion that the incorporation into the economy of the labour forces in countries that have not been permitted to develop, in particular geographical shifts in production, will maintain the 'traditional ("unjust and unreasonable") world economic order' (ibid., p. 184).

There are two questionable points in Senghaas's reasoning. First, in view of the large-scale and extensive transfers of labour power throughout the history of the world market, there must be some doubt as to the alleged 'relative immobility of the labour force'. This said, the *present* situation on the world labour market is characterized primarily by mobility being limited and to a large extent also prevented by the metropole. Second, there is the question of whether the reproductive system is really defective, or whether it might not, in fact, be functioning in the best possible way from the point of view of the capitalist metropole.

Despite raising some interesting points early on, the debate on unequal exchange has thus made no appreciable contribution towards explaining the matter under discussion.

Peripheral capitalism and 'learning from Europe'

Briefly, a final point from Senghaas's *Von Europa lernen: Entwicklungs-geschichtliche Betrachtungen* (Learning from Europe: some developmental reflections), published in 1982. In this study the author is concerned with the conditions under which 'it would be possible for underdeveloped countries to catch up in a world economy characterized by ever-increasing differences in levels of development' (p. 15). The study can be seen as a further stage in his evaluation of peripheral capitalism.

With these conditions constantly in mind, Senghaas examines development in a number of countries, mainly in Europe, and classifies them according to various developmental models. The factors which he examines in his analysis and which he describes as the economic prerequisites for a viable economy are: the growth of agricultural yields (as food base or as raw materials), the industrial production of mass-consumption and capital goods, the manufacture of semi-finished products and the building of an infrastructure (p. 325).

The interlinking of these factors permits the development of economies 'capable of specific basic achievements'. Senghaas considers one such 'basic achievement' to be 'the productive incorporation of the mass of the people into the economy'. People, he writes, 'find work, receive an income and become consumers . . .' (Senghaas, 1982, p. 325). Human labour power has no part to play here, since such an approach regards every economic system, all power relations and historic development in the abstract. *People* are merely regarded as consumers of agricultural and industrial goods. Their incorporation into the productive process does not come about because they themselves stimulate the process of development, but as a result of the process itself. The fact that 'people find work' is, therefore, one of the achievements of a developed economy.

All of the above points, some of which are drawn from noted authors and studies of recent years, are sufficient, in my opinion, to illustrate that in many sections of the debate on development theory the standard of theorization on the issue of labour power in and from countries that have not been permitted to develop today is unsatisfactory. This is particularly true where assumptions are based on a labour theory of value. Evidently we still lack the empirical and historical evidence necessary to settle the matter.

The labour theory of value and the world market, colonialism and imperialism

If more recent theories do not necessarily possess the theoretical and historical tools for analysing the world market for labour power, then recourse to the classics is completely justified, both to investigate to what extent they possess such tools and because they contain some of the root causes of the distortions found in today's debate. Basing our discussion around the terms 'labour theory of value', 'world market', 'colonialism' and 'imperialism', we will now look at the contributions made to the debate by Marx and Engels, Lenin and Luxemburg.

Marx and Engels

The labour theory of value as developed by Marx under the influence of Smith and Ricardo should be one of the most common starting positions for Marxist theories of imperialism. This may sound self-evident, yet in many studies of imperialism the theory plays no part at all, let alone that of a keynote.

The basis of Marx's theory of society is that human power is the only means of producing new value. 'Labour,' writes Marx, 'is the substance, and the immanent measure of value...' (*Capital*, vol. 1, p. 503). The various epochs of human society are characterized by the various structures by means of which newly created value is acquired, i.e. the various means by which the workforce is exploited. Human labour power, its nature, its volume, its origin and its method of reproduction are therefore the very basis of both capitalism and every other mode of production.

Under capitalism, labour power becomes a commodity which, according to Marx's analysis, is acquired and exploited by capitalists primarily in the form of wage labour. Its value, like that of any other commodity, is measured in terms of the quantities of labour which it contains. In the case of human labour this means the cost of reproduction. Wages, as the price of the commodity called labour power, are orientated towards the cost of reproduction and must, if an equivalent exchange is to take place, if the law of value is to hold good, and if labour power is to be reproduced, correspond in the longer term and on average to its value, that is to say, they must cover the longer term cost of reproduction.

This sequence of ideas contains a number of problems, each of which has played an important part in the recent debates both on female labour and on development and underdevelopment. At this point we should perhaps mention a notion of some significance both for the link between capitalism and the exploitation of foreign labour power and for the question of racism and sexism, even though it is taken from another context. Marx writes, 'The secret of the expression of value, namely, that all kinds of labour are equal and equivalent, because, and in so far as they are human labour in general, cannot be deciphered, until the notion of human equality has already acquired the fixity of a popular prejudice' (*Capital*, vol. 1, p. 65).

How little such fixity the idea has acquired, in particular with regard to the work of women on the production and reproduction line, is demonstrated in Marx's analysis itself. In fact, the entire history of the world market for labour power is the history of the unequal evaluation of labour. More recent developmentalist analyses confirm that the claim that 'all kinds of labour are equal and equivalent' not only fails to meet public perceptions, but is still regarded as anything but a foregone conclusion, even by theoreticians who see themselves as Marxists.

The critique of the political economy developed by Marx and Engels certainly contains no theory of imperialism. In fact, they did not even use the term 'imperialism'. Nevertheless, they repeatedly turned their attention to contemporary colonialism, and its by then already historic methods. Their version of history and theory of capitalism cannot be imagined without it.

The works of Marx and Engels are littered with descriptions, interpretations and analyses of colonialism, both colonialism as a whole and individual aspects of colonialism, for colonialism is closely linked with the emergence of the world market – of which the world market for labour power will be regarded here as a part. One idea that recurs frequently in Marx's work is that the emergence of the world market is inseparably linked with the capitalist mode of production. In the *Grundrisse* (p. 408) Marx writes:

> The tendency to create the *world market* is directly given in the concept of capital itself. Every limit appears as a barrier to be overcome. Initially, to subjugate every moment of production itself to exchange and to suspend the production of direct use values not entering into exchange, i.e. precisely to posit production based on capital in place of earlier modes of production, which appear primitive from its standpoint. *Commerce* no longer appears here as a function taking place between independent productions for the exchange of their excess, but rather as an essentially all-embracing presupposition and moment of production itself.

Though the idea is expressed here primarily in abstract economic terms and not directly linked with supremacy and subjugation on a world scale, in *Capital* it is expressed in concrete historical terms:

> The discovery of gold and silver in America, the extirpation, enslavement and entombment in mines of the aboriginal population, the beginning of the conquest and looting of the East Indies, the turning of Africa into a warren for the commercial hunting of black skins, signalised the rosy dawn of the era of capitalist production. These idyllic proceedings are the chief momenta of primitive accumulation... (*Capital*, vol. 1, p. 703)

The above quotation refers essentially to the connection between the world market for labour power and the world market for commodities.

A little further on Marx again emphasizes the importance of the colonies to the process of primitive accumulation, a matter which is still the subject of debate today.

> The colonies secured a market for the budding manufactures, and, through the monopoly of the market, an increased accumulation. The treasures captured outside Europe by undisguised looting, enslavement, and murder, floated back to the mother-country and were there turned into capital. (*Capital*, vol. 1, p. 705)

As is evident from the relationship between England and India, the link between colonialism and compulsion is just as close as that between colonialism and the world market.

The treasures brought to England from India during the eighteenth century were acquired less through the comparatively trifling amount of trade conducted than through the direct exploitation of this country. They were part of the huge fortune wrung out of it and transported to England. (*MEW*, vol. 9, p. 154)

Using India as an example, Marx again clearly expresses the view that the scale and importance of colonial exploitation cannot be explained merely, indeed not even primarily, by economic indicators and foreign trade figures – for 'Profits can also be made by cheating' (*MEW*, vol. 26.3, p. 101).

What the English receive each year in the form of interest, dividends for railways which are of no use at all to the Hindus, military and civil service pensions, what they take from the country for the Afghan and other wars etc. etc., what they receive without giving anything in return, and quite apart from what they expropriate each year inside India – I am speaking then only of the value of the goods which India is forced to send to England each year free of charge – comes in all to more than India's 60 million agricultural and industrial workers' total income! It is a process of bleeding which must be avenged! (*MEW*, vol. 35, p. 157)

Still on the subject of the colonies' importance to capitalism, Marx's work contains passages pointing out both the colonies' function as a market and their role in the export of capital, as well as the fact that the concentration of capital had already begun.

At the very moment when a national branch of industry completely conquers the domestic market, at that very moment exporting becomes absolutely vital to that industry. Under the capitalist system industry must either expand or shrivel. It cannot remain stationary. To hinder expansion is to bring on ruination: the progress being made in the field of mechanical and chemical invention is continually putting human labour out of work, whilst at the same time speeding up the growth and concentration of capital. In this way it creates a surplus of workers and capital in every stagnant industry, a surplus which cannot find equilibrium anywhere, since the same process is simultaneously underway in every other branch of industry. As a result, the transition from domestic to foreign trade becomes a matter of life and death for all these branches of industry... (*MEW*, vol. 21, p. 368)

This time using England as an example Marx writes, 'The last new market the development of which might temporarily be able to revive England's trade is the Chinese market. It is for this reason that English capital is insisting on building the Chinese railways' (*MEW*, vol. 38, p. 470). Lenin was later to take this, along with the significance which he attributed to raw materials, as the focal point of his analysis of imperialism. Nevertheless, it is Luxemburg who, unlike Lenin but like Marx, takes as the starting point and crux of her analysis the assumption that external markets are indispensable.

The later debate on the subject of unequal exchange was also initiated in Marx's writings. According to Marx, foreign trade can lead to 'three working days in one country being exchanged for one in another' (for more details see *MEW*, vol. 26.3, p. 101). The question remains as to whether an equal exchange is taking place in such circumstances. At another point Marx refers not only to the extraordinary profitability of colonial trade, but also to variations in the value of labour power. He writes:

> This also applies, for example, to colonial trade, where, as a result of slavery and the fertility of mother nature (possibly also because of the practical or legal non-development of land ownership), the *value of labour* is lower than in the old country. Were the motherland's capital *transferable at will to this new trade* then, although it would reduce surplus profit in this particular *trade*, the *general level of profit* would increase. (*MEW*, vol. 26.2, p. 438)

Though by no means complete, these remarks may nevertheless be enough to prove the existence in Marx's writings of elements of a theory of colonialism which embraces the workings of the world market for labour power. They are a first attempt at dealing with the question of the transfer of labour. Engels, for example, examines the living conditions of Irish immigrants in England and also refers several times to coolie migration (*MEW*, vol. 38, p. 470 and vol. 39, pp. 298f).

More illuminating, however, are the passages on slavery and immigration into the USA:

> The slave market maintains its supply of the commodity labour-power by war, piracy, etc., and this rapine is not promoted by a process of circulation, but by the actual appropriation of the labour-power of others by direct physical compulsion. Even in the United States, after the conversion of the buffer territory between the wage-labour states of the North and the slavery states of the South into a slave-breeding region for the South, where the slave thrown on the market thus became himself an element of the annual reproduction, this did not suffice for a long time, so that the African slave trade was continued as long as possible to satisfy the market. (*Capital*, vol. 2, p. 483)

There are two important points to note here: first, the reference to the constant influx of black labour power as a result of the continuing inadequacy of reproduction in the USA, and second, the idea that under capitalist conditions labour power is not always acquired in the form of wage labour, but also through 'natural procurement', here by means of direct physical compulsion. This form of acquisition, at least, is clearly a capitalist form, since the labour power acquired becomes a commodity.

The notion that it is not wage labour, but labour power as a commodity, which is the form of labour power characteristic of the capitalist mode of production, was introduced into the current debate by Wallerstein.

There is another major theoretical point to consider in relation to slavery, namely that, 'In fact, the veiled slavery of wage-workers in Europe needed, for its pedestal, slavery pure and simple in the new world' (*Capital*, vol. 1, p. 711). This points to the fundamental significance for the development of capitalism of slavery as a means of exploiting labour power, a matter which is also given particular prominence elsewhere:

> Direct slavery is just as pivotal to our industry today as machinery, credit and so on. Without slavery, no cotton; without cotton, no modern industry. It was slavery which first gave the colonies a value, it was the colonies which first created international trade, and international trade is a vital pre-requisite for large-scale mechanized industry. (*MEW*, vol. 27, p. 458)

The second foundation upon which the American labour market rests, and which dominates in the northern USA, is immigration from Europe. 'It might be said that not only capital, but also labourers, in the shape of emigrants, are annually exported from England' (*Capital*, vol. 1, p. 573). In order to force such workers into wage labour, free access to the soil is limited.

> The trick is how to kill two birds with one stone. Let the Government put upon the virgin soil an artificial price, independent of the law of supply and demand, a price that compels the immigrant to work a long time for wages before he can earn enough money to buy land, and turn himself into an independent peasant. The fund resulting from the sale of land at a price relatively prohibitory for the wage-workers, this fund of money extorted from the wages of labour by violation of the sacred law of supply and demand, the Government is to employ, on the other hand, in proportion as it grows, to import have-nothings from Europe into the colonies, and thus keep the wage-labour market full for the capitalists. Under these circumstances, tout sera pour les mieux dans le meilleur des mondes possibles. This is the greatest triumph of 'systematic colonisation'. (*Capital*, vol. 1, pp. 772f)

Taken as a whole, the observations of Marx and Engels on the emergence and development of the world market and colonialism (including those developments regarded here as processes of the world market for labour power), and their analysis of the methods employed and the effects which these had on the notions underlying the labour theory of value form the beginnings of a Marxist theory of colonialism. The debate that might otherwise have sprung from all this was, however, restricted by Lenin's analysis of imperialism to consideration of just a few points.

Lenin

In the title of a pamphlet first published in 1917 Lenin expresses the idea central to his analysis of imperialism: *Imperialism, the Highest Stage of Capitalism*. Regardless of the controversy over whether Lenin's 'highest' stage also meant the highest stage of development so far, or whether he merely wished to focus on the notion of the imminent collapse of the prevailing economic and social order (for transitional or dying capitalism see *LW*, vol. 22, p. 307), there is no doubt that Lenin regarded imperialism, in so far as he analysed it, unequivocally and exclusively as a *stage* of capitalism. 'Thus, the twentieth century marks the turning-point from the old capitalism to the new, from the domination of capital in general to the domination of finance capital' (*Imperialism, the Highest Stage of Capitalism*, p. 45).

Lenin, then, draws a clear distinction between imperialism and the capitalist colonial policies of earlier stages (see ibid., pp. 84f). For him imperialism represents a particular limited period of capitalism in which industrial capital is no longer the determining force.

> Imperialism emerged as the development and direct continuation of the fundamental characteristics of capitalism in general. But capitalism only became capitalist imperialism at a definite and very high stage of its development, when certain of its fundamental characteristics began to change into their opposites, when the features of the epoch of transition from capitalism to a higher social and economic system had taken shape and revealed themselves in all spheres. (Ibid., p. 83)

Thus it is primarily those features of capitalism that change in the course of its development which characterize imperialism. According to Lenin's concept of imperialism, the transformation of competition into monopoly was far more important than, for example, the drive for expansion which had accompanied, was partly to blame for and had characterized the development of capitalism from its very inception.

According to Lenin, monopolies are the deepest economic foundation of imperialism (ibid., p. 93), and represent 'the transition from capitalism to a higher order' (ibid., p. 83). The age of imperialism is accordingly the age of finance capital and monopoly (cf. ibid., pp. 115ff); finance capital has snatched the supremacy which was previously the territory of industrial capital (cf. ibid., p. 84). Consequently, Lenin lists the five basic characteristics of imperialism as:

1. the concentration of production and of capital (monopoly)
2. the merging of bank capital with industrial capital into finance capital
3. the export of capital

4. the formation of monopolist capitalist associations which share the world among themselves
5. the completion of the territorial division of the world among the biggest capitalist powers (see ibid., pp. 84f).

More important here than the idea that imperialism represents a particular stage in the development of capitalism is the idea that the fundamental processes characterizing it are found exclusively in the metropole. As a consequence, Lenin's analysis is almost exclusively concerned with developments in the metropole. Events in the colonized territories penetrated by imperialism are, both empirically and theoretically, at best of secondary importance.[3]

This definition and this analysis laid the foundations for the more general political, but also the economic, understanding of imperialism and gave rise to the phrase 'the quest for markets and raw materials', a phrase which shaped and still shapes the body of methods employed in the analysis of imperialism.

One early example of the extent to which Leninist methodology has influenced countless theoretical and empirical works on the subject of imperialism and the exploitation of colonial labour is that the anthology *Forced Labour in Colonial Africa* (Nzula et al., 1979), first published in Moscow in 1933, begins with a chapter on Africa's role in the world economic system: Africa as a supplier of raw materials, Africa as a consumer of European goods, Africa as a zone for capital exports. Looking at Africa in this way, forced labour appears to be a derivative, secondary phenomenon: Leninist analysis of imperialism regards the logic of capital as the central issue. Thus even studies on forced labour and labour movement in a colonized continent focus on the economics of capital and not the economics of work. This in itself begs the question as to whether the labour theory of value still carries any weight.

When considering the world market for labour power Lenin deals mainly with labour migration under capitalism, the cause of which he believes to be above average wage levels in the rapidly developing industrial nations. On the one hand, Lenin regards labour migration within and between the capitalist nations and emigration to the USA as a sign of progress, since they mean higher wages for the workers, put an end to debt bondage and drudgery, and promote the acquisition of knowledge, the attainment of a higher standard of education and a higher level of awareness among the workers (see among others *LW*, vol. 3, pp. 247, 249, 594). On the other hand, he also sees its negative effects: the loss of some of Russia's best workers and poverty and misery for the migrants in the cities of Europe and America (see *LW*, vol. 19, p. 449 and vol. 21, p. 364). In his analysis of imperialism he looks at the growth of hierarchies within the working class:

> In the United States, immigrants from Eastern and Southern Europe are engaged in the most poorly paid jobs, while American workers provide

the highest percentage of overseers or of the better paid workers. Imperialism has the tendency to create privileged sections also among the workers, and to detach them from the broad masses of the proletariat. (*Imperialism, the Highest Stage of Capitalism*, p. 100)

Finally Lenin makes certain political demands that come across as decidedly modern, including freedom of movement for all workers and the abolition of discriminatory legal status. In *'Die Aufgaben der linken Zimmerwalder in der Sozialdemokratischen Partei der Schweiz'* ('The tasks of the Zimmerwald left in the Social Democratic Party of Switzerland') Lenin writes: 'Foreign workers' lack of political right and their position as foreigners intensifies the already growing political reaction and weakens international solidarity!' (*LW*, vol. 23, p. 141). Lenin points out that labour migration is a means by which to divide the working class, since foreign workers are regarded as having no rights. The working class should, he maintains, counter this by adopting a uniform internationalist approach.

However, Lenin's observations on the subject of labour migration also reveal that it is only on the question of migration between the capitalist nations that he took up a position. He concerns himself exclusively with labour migration within Europe and emigration to the USA and does not examine the processes of labour migration then being forced upon the African peoples by imperialism, or even the already historic process whereby the African peoples were forced to migrate to America. In this sense Lenin's treatment of the question of labour migration is markedly Eurocentric.

Nevertheless, his observations contain a number of ideas still important for the analysis of labour migration today:

- labour migration as the export of labour power
- the lack of rights of foreign workers and their function
- the division and stratification of the working class by means of discrimination against foreign workers
- the effect on promotion prospects for the indigenous workforce of importing labour power.

He is also of the opinion that:

This kind of exploitation of the labour of low-paid workers from underdeveloped countries is particularly characteristic of imperialism. To a certain extent it is the very basis of the parasitism of the rich imperialist nations, which actually bribe sections of their own workforce with higher wages whilst at the same time they exploit the labour of 'cheap' foreign workers in a terrible and shameful fashion.

Luxemburg
Rosa Luxemburg's theory of imperialism, developed in *Die Akkumulation des Kapitals – Ein Beitrag zur ökonomischen Erklärung des Imperialismus*

(The accumulation of capital), was first published in 1913,[4] several years before *Imperialism, the Highest Stage of Capitalism*, which Lenin wrote in 1916 and published in 1917. Yet even today the Marxist term 'imperialism' is closely linked to the name of Lenin, and an entry under this key word in the 1972 *Marxistisch-Leninistischen Wörterbuch der Philosophie* (Marxist-Leninist Dictionary of Philosophy) actually refers exclusively to Lenin. Luxemburg's contribution to the debate is ascribed at best secondary importance in the literature.[5]

Even when her work is debated more thoroughly the argument is almost always restricted to two aspects of her theory: first the schema of accumulation she develops as part of her thesis on underconsumption, and second her so-called catastrophe theory, by which is meant her view that capitalism requires the existence of non-capitalist societies, yet for the most part destroys them and will, for this very reason, be destroyed itself.

Of the classical theories of imperialism, Luxemburg's is the only one that deals in detail and in an informed manner with the question of the production and reproduction of labour power and whose concept of imperialism is directly linked to this question. The depth of her analysis but also its lukewarm reception make it imperative that her position be explained in greater detail here.

Luxemburg's concept of imperialism
For Luxemburg imperialism is basically:

> ... nothing other than a particular *method* of accumulation... Its essence is to be found in the spread of capitalist rule from the old capitalist nations into new territories and in economic and political competition between those nations for such territories. (*GW*, vol. 5, pp. 431f)

But Luxemburg also regards imperialism as a stage in the development of capitalism:

> In fact, that passionate drive which characterizes capitalist production has been visible since this first appeared on the historical scene, has run like a red thread through its entire development, has assumed ever increasing importance, until in the last quarter of a century, during capitalist production's imperialist stage, it has shown itself to be a factor capable of determining and dominating the life of society. (*GW*, vol. 5, p. 434)

Such a view of capitalist imperialism identifies the continuous nature of overseas exploitation as a dominating factor, yet does not regard territories which are either non-capitalist, conquered or still to be conquered as being of secondary importance.

Luxemburg develops, on the question of the relationship between capitalist and non-capitalist territories and classes, a new approach in which the labour force takes the leading role. She is not bent on a systematic examination of non-capitalist economies and societies, but enquires instead primarily after their part in capitalist accumulation. In accounts which are often detailed and using countries like Turkey, Egypt, South Africa, India, Algeria and China as examples, she identifies the mechanisms, objectives and in particular the consequences of the capitalist penetration of such societies.[6]

The reproduction of labour power and imperialism

Luxemburg succeeds in producing a sophisticated analysis of important aspects of the question of the reproduction of labour power under capitalism, and her concept of imperialism is inseparably linked with the answer to this question. Her starting point is the observation that Marx's writings on the subject do not deal with the process of proletarianization undergone by the peasantry in Europe.

> Marx ... held that the rural workers who continually migrate to the towns belong to the wage proletariat since they were formerly dominated by agricultural capital and now become subject to industrial capital. He ignores, however, the problem which is of paramount importance for conditions on the continent of Europe..., the very process, that is to say, of incessant transition from non-capitalist to capitalist conditions of a labour power that is cast off by pre-capitalist, not capitalist, modes of production in their progressive breakdown and disintegration. (*The Accumulation of Capital*, p. 362)

Above all, this means that in Europe the dying feudal system supplied the evolving capitalist system with 'ready made workers' (Marx). Luxemburg, however, maintains that this process was not merely a transition from feudalism to capitalism, but that 'Besides the decay of European peasants and artisans we must here also mention the disintegration of a variety of primitive forms of production and social organisation in non-European countries'.

For Luxemburg the capitalist world's drive for expansion, that is colonialism and imperialism, is directed as much at the acquisition of foreign labour power as at the procurement of raw materials and agricultural products.

> Since capitalist production can develop fully only with complete access to all territories and climes, it can no more confine itself to the natural resources and productive forces of the temperate zone than it can manage with white labour alone. (Ibid., p. 362)

The following sentence asserts the inevitability of the world market for labour power, and suggests that it is a precondition for and equivalent to the world market for goods and capital.

Capital needs other races to exploit territories where the white man cannot work. It must be able to mobilise world labour power without restriction in order to utilise all productive forces of the globe – up to the limits imposed by a system of producing surplus value.

At another point Luxemburg systematically lists the reasons behind capitalism's conquest of societies using the barter economy:

1. to gain immediate possession of important sources of productive forces such as land, game in primeval forests, minerals, precious stones and ores, products of exotic flora such as rubber etc.
2. to 'liberate' labour power and to coerce it into service
3. to introduce a commodity economy
4. to separate trade and agriculture. (Ibid., p. 369)

The above activites are essential to further primitive accumulation, a subject which Luxemburg was responsible for introducing into the debate.[7] Central to her concept of accumulation is that 'Since the accumulation of capital becomes impossible in all points without non-capitalist surroundings, we cannot gain a true picture of it by assuming the exclusive and absolute dominion of the capitalist mode of production' (ibid., p. 365).

Marx describes exploitation at home and abroad as the two pillars upon which primitive accumulation rests. Particularly abroad, he maintains, primitive accumulation is inseparable from force. Luxemburg stresses that that was not merely the case during the early stages of capitalism.

> Accumulation, with its spasmodic expansion, can no more wait for, and be content with, a natural internal disintegration of non-capitalist formations and their transition to commodity economy, that it can to wait for, and be content with, the natural increase of the working population. Force is the only solution open to capital; the accumulation of capital, seen as an historic process, employs force as a permanent weapon, not only at its genesis, but further on down to the present day. (Ibid., pp. 370f)

Capitalism also employs force more than anything else to take control of the labour power it requires. The various stages in the development of the world market for labour power, such as slavery and colonial forced labour, to which Luxemburg repeatedly refers, are ample proof of this.

Luxemburg also explains the transition from the employment of direct, unmediated compulsion, such as that characteristic of slavery, to the employment of 'gentle force', which includes economic pressure.

> For the first genuinely capitalist branch of production, the English cotton industry, not only the cotton of the Southern States of the American Union was essential, but also the millions of African Negroes who were shipped to America to provide the labour power for the plantations, and who later, as a free proletariat, were incorporated in the

class of wage labourers in a capitalist system. Obtaining the necessary labour power from non-capitalist societies, the so-called 'labour problem', is ever more important for capital in the colonies. All possible methods of 'gentle compulsion' are applied to solving this problem, to transfer labour from former social systems to the command of capital. (Ibid., pp. 362f)

She suggests that as part of the process of accumulation non-capitalist modes of production are mutilated and tampered with by capitalism for the principal purpose of procuring labour power. Citing various examples, including India, she gives her version of how capitalism affects societies based on a barter economy:

Their means of production and their labour power no less than their demand for surplus products is necessary to capitalism. Yet the latter is fully determined to undermine their independence as social units, in order to gain possession of their means of production and labour power and to convert them into commodity buyers. (Ibid., p. 371)

The fact that she deliberately speaks here of the disintegration of pre-colonial society as an 'independent social unit' rather than of its complete disintegration, indicates that she prefers to think of the process as one of metabolism between the two systems.

Historically, the accumulation of capital is a kind of metabolism between capitalist economy and those pre-capitalist methods of production without which it cannot go on and which, in this light, it corrodes and assimilates. Thus capital cannot accumulate without the aid of non-capitalist organisations, nor, on the other hand, can it tolerate their continued existence side by side with itself. Only the continuous and progressive disintegration of non-capitalist organisations makes accumulation of capital possible. Accumulation is more than an internal relationship between the branches of capitalist economy; it is primarily a relationship between capital and a non-capitalist environment ... (ibid., p. 417)

She develops the relationship between capitalist societies and those based on a barter economy as a dialectical relationship, and in doing so indicates that she is disinclined to embrace the 'catastrophe theory' attributed to her. In addition, she makes it clear that capitalism is incapable itself of producing and reproducing the labour power which it requires.

Labour for this army is recruited from social reservoirs outside the dominion of capital – it is drawn into the waged proletariat only if need arises. Only the existence of non-capitalist groups and countries can guarantee such a supply of additional labour power for capitalist production. (Ibid., p. 361)

This additional labour power is acquired with the help of imperialism, namely through its reform of non-capitalist structures and its modification of their modes of production. Though they are producing for capitalism, societies based on a barter economy supply labour power which is reproduced in non-capitalist fashion. Taking Egypt as an example, Luxemburg observes that, 'As forced labour, the fellah also provided the labour power and what is more, he was exploited without payment and even had to provide his own means of subsistence while he was at work' (ibid., p. 435).

Today Luxemburg's elaboration of the links both between the exploitation of labour power from non-capitalist classes or countries and imperialism, and between imperialism and the reproduction of labour power, is probably regarded as *The Accumulation of Capital*'s greatest achievement. Finally, we will examine the importance to the development of capitalism which Luxemburg attributes to imperialism.

The importance of imperialism

Luxemburg believes that the exploitation of non-capitalist societies, and in particular of their labour power, is of paramount importance to capitalist accumulation. Accordingly, she does not regard the capitalist system as a sealed system, that is to say, a system whose production is based exclusively on wage labour and which reproduces its wage workers itself. She writes:

In addition, there is no obvious reason why means of production and consumer goods should be produced by capitalist methods alone... In the first half of the nineteenth century, a great part of the surplus value in England was produced in the form of cotton fabrics. Yet the material elements for the capitalisation of this surplus value, although they certainly represented a surplus product, still were by no means all capitalist surplus value, to mention only raw cotton from the slave states of the American Union, or grain (a means of subsistence for the English workers) from the fields of serf-owning Russia. How much capitalist accumulation depends upon means of production which are not produced by capitalist methods is shown for example by the cotton crisis in England during the American War of Secession, when the cultivation of the plantations came to a standstill, or by the crisis of European linen-weaving during the war in the East, when flax could not be imported from serf-owning Russia. We need only recall that imports of corn raised by peasants – i.e. not produced by capitalist methods – played a vital part in the feeding of industrial labour, as an element, that is to say, of variable capital, for a further illustration of the close ties between non-capitalist strata and the material elements necessary to the accumulation of capital. (Ibid., p. 357)

Elsewhere Luxemburg points out that the exploitation of foreign labour power is linked with particularly high levels of profitability:

Yet if the countries of those branches of production are predominantly non-capitalist, capital will endeavour to establish domination over these countries and societies. And in fact, primitive conditions allow a greater drive and of far more ruthless measures than could be tolerated under purely capitalist social conditions. (Ibid., p. 365)

Luxemburg postulates that non-capitalist societies are essential to capitalist accumulation and does not regard capitalism as a sealed system. One of the many reasons for this view is that capitalism requires influxes of labour power, another the fact that a certain amount of overlap exists at an economic level between non-capitalist, structurally deformed societies and capitalism. For Luxemburg imperialism is basically a means of procuring foreign labour power which is not produced or reproduced under capitalist conditions and the exploitation of which is therefore particularly profitable.

Unlike Lenin, she recognizes the immediate importance to capitalism or imperialism of labour in the colonies, exposes the basic mechanisms by means of which it is incorporated into capitalist production and circulation, and analyses this process as an integral part of capitalist imperialism.

Yet in no way does she see this personpower as having revolutionary potential. In the Junius pamphlet (*Die Krise der Sozialdemokratie* – The crisis of social democracy), for example, she writes:

The signal for the social revolution that will free mankind can, when the hour is ripe, only come from Europe, from the oldest capitalist countries. Only the English, French, Belgian, German, Russian, Italian workers together can lead the armies of the exploited and oppressed of the five continents. Only they can, when the time comes, call capitalism to account and retaliate for its centuries of crimes against all primitive peoples and for its destructive deeds throughout the world. (*GW* 'Collected Works', vol. 4, p. 162)

Luxemburg's belief that only the European proletariat could rise up and pass into history is a view disproved by history itself. In this regard Rosa Luxemburg remains rooted in the Eurocentric thinking prevalent among European theorists at the time and in the political theory and practice linked with that thinking.

Nevertheless, living labour in colonized territories is an important, today surely the most important, facet of Luxemburg's analysis of imperialism.

In contrast, the authors of every other classical analysis of imperialism, from Bucharin to Lenin to Hilferding, focus on derived categories such as markets and raw materials, questions of superstructure or financial aspects. Analyses of the logic of capital are adapted accordingly.

Today the study of imperialism still lacks basic research into living and working conditions in the colonized continents. Whereas Engel's study *The*

Condition of the Working Classes in England laid the foundations for the formulation of a critique of the political economy of capitalism, no one has so far laid the foundations for an analysis of colonialism and imperialism, except perhaps in fragmentary form.

However, at least three of the more recent contributions to the debates on the theory of imperialism and development may well prove influential when it comes to tackling the question of the world market for labour power in the future.

Some elements of the developmental analysis of the world market for labour power

In my introduction I refer to the study of Fröbel, Heinrichs and Kreye which introduced into the debate the concept of a 'world market for labour power' and which produced evidence in support of the existence of such a market. The many contributions to the debate (including Simonis, 1977; Jacobson et al., 1980; Olle, 1980; Junne, 1980; and Fröbel, Heinrichs and Kreye, 1980) which the study provoked do not, however, focus on the importance of labour power or its reproduction.

Nor does the original study concentrate unequivocally on theoretical examination of the above, but rather on empirical aspects. Despite producing impressive evidence which shows that the 'new international division of labour' is aimed first and foremost at more intense exploitation of female wage workers, the authors fail to develop a theory on the sexual division of labour. Moreover, the term 'world market for labour power' is used solely in relation to geographical shifts in production. It is given no historical dimension and basically refers – since it is only the goods produced which are exported – to the transfer of objectified labour. Whereas technical advance has resulted in a large-scale mobilization of capital, labour power has been mobilized only in a restricted form.

Whereas this form of international division of labour appears to be new, it does not, in fact, violate the principle according to which countries which have not been permitted to develop supply raw materials and agricultural produce whilst the metropole monopolizes manufacturing industry. To all intents and purposes human labour power is merely being utilized as a raw material *in situ*. Transfers of labour power to other continents or to the metropole have, to some extent at least, become superfluous.

Accordingly, it is not necessary for us to further consider the debate on the new international division of labour. Instead, we will look at Meillassoux's 1976 study *Die wilden Früchte der Frau: über häusliche Production und kapitalistische Wirtschaft* (The wild fruits of woman: domestic production and the capitalist economy). We will examine this study first, since the author, taking Luxemburg's concept and analysis of imperialism as his starting point, gives a detailed and actualized account of the reproduction of labour power under capitalism and in doing so focuses on imperialism.

The section on Meillassoux will be followed by an examination of the subsistence debate in its feminist variant and by a review of various particularly relevant theses relating to the 'world system' approach to development and migration.

Imperialism as a means of reproducing cheap labour (Meillassoux)
The very title which the author gives the second part of his analysis, *'Die Ausbeutung der häuslichen Gemeinschaft: der Imperialismus als Mittel zur Reproduktion billiger Arbeitskräfte' (The exploitation of the household community: imperialism as a means of reproducing cheap labour)*, indicates clearly that he has taken Luxemburg's position as his starting point. Like Luxemburg, Meillassoux is of the opinion that the capitalist system is not a sealed system, especially when it comes to the supply of labour power.

Meillassoux is rightly critical of the fact that in the development debate underdevelopment is normally considered from the point of view of exchange. He maintains that if underdevelopment could be proved to be a result of the over-exploitation of labour then this would have important political consequences.

The central question which Meillassoux endeavours to answer is that of the circumstances under which labour in the colonized countries is over-exploited (Meillassoux, 1976, p 111).

He works on the assumption that the artificial preservation of non-capitalist modes of production in countries that have not been permitted to develop is part of an imperialist strategy to exploit such modes of production as a community and to siphon off value from them on a permanent basis. It is for this reason, claims Meillassoux, that large sections of agriculture in such countries remain uncapitalized, and that the mode of production found in such countries, a form of household economy, continues to exist, albeit in a mutilated form. This is the case particularly in territories where capitalist forms of agriculture would not be profitable due to soil conditions, the transport system etc.

The exploitation of the household economy is based on the fact that although it is not incorporated into capitalist production, it is incorporated into capitalist circulation, since it supplies cheap export goods (above all agricultural produce) and, more importantly, cheap or even free labour for the capitalist system. The worker, who is thus at the disposal of the capitalist system, has grown up outside the capitalist mode of production. According to the requirements of capitalism, he or she is either incorporated – in various ways – into the capitalist productive process or thrown back into the household. This household feeds the worker during unproductive periods, and thus reproduces the worker's labour power. This is as true for workers producing for the capitalist system at home, i.e. inside countries that have not been permitted to develop, as for those forced to do so, for example, in Europe as migrant workers.

Meillassoux writes:

Until now this process has accompanied the development of capitalism constantly, in fact at an ever-increasing pace and to an ever-increasing extent, with the result that, like the other mechanisms of capitalist reproduction, it *must be regarded as immanent in it.* (Meillassoux, 1976, p. 114)

Thus primitive accumulation takes place continuously. One of the consequences of this is that although capitalism is superior to all previous modes of production in terms of production levels, it is nevertheless still dependent in world terms on the household economy and non-capitalist modes of production for the reproduction of labour power.

The process described above leads to organic overlap between non-capitalist modes of production in those countries that have not been permitted to develop and capitalism, with both being simultaneously preserved and destroyed through over-exploitation. Thus capitalism exploits not only 'free workers', but also entire productive communities. Meillassoux also describes the actual historical course of this process and maintains that ever since primitive accumulation first began the capitalist system has experienced a constant influx of labour power produced outside of that system – first from disintegrating feudal modes of production, then from other non-capitalist modes of production.

The development in the metropole (and only there) of structures which reproduce labour power primarily in a capitalist manner by paying an indirect as well as a direct wage which is then distributed through a 'community organism' has been a lengthy process, and even then structures still exist which are remnants of a household economy and which in the main exploit female workers outside the sphere of waged employment.

Workers in and from colonized territories do not receive an indirect wage, or if they do then in an extremely reduced form, and the reproduction of their labour power continues to take place almost exclusively in the non-capitalist sector, a sector which is maintained specifically for this purpose. As a result, the exploitation of such labour power is particularly profitable, since the capitalist not only acquires the surplus value produced by the workers, but also a capital income from labour.

Using African forced and migrant labour as an example, Meillassoux outlines the development of the various methods of incorporating labour power from colonized territories into the capitalist system and divides such labour into three phases. In the first phase the worker is employed in the capitalist sector only during the dead season. Non-capitalist production is not interrupted, but instead guarantees the reproduction of the worker's labour power. This therefore costs the capitalist nothing whatsoever. In the second phase the worker is likewise employed only during the dead season, but this time away from home, with the result that the capitalist must keep the worker for as long as the latter is in his employ. Characteristic of the next phase is that the worker is employed in the capitalist sector both during and outside the dead season and must therefore be compensated for losses of production in the non-capitalist sector by means of a wage.

This third phase also serves as the model for present-day labour migration; here too responsibility for keeping the worker in periods of non-employment within the capitalist sector (old age, illness, or unemployment) and to a large extent also the training of new workers remains with the non-capitalist sector.

Meillassoux gives numerous examples in support of his thesis on the importance of influxes of labour power, including South Africa's homeland system, the Nazi concentration camps, and present-day labour migration to Western Europe.

On the one hand, he succeeds on the whole in producing a convincing, politico-economically and historically sound analysis of imperialism as a means of reproducing cheap labour power, but on the other hand the fact that he bases this on the concept of the 'household community', as developed by him in the first part of his study, is not altogether unproblematic. Although his attempt at evolving an anthropo-economic theory is not at the centre of this discussion, it should nevertheless not be ignored, if for no other reason than because of the way in which the concept of the household community itself is evolved.

Meillassoux defines the household community as the basal cell 'of a mode of production which results from the totality of such communities, these being organized amongst themselves for the purposes of producing and reproducing in the economy and in society the productive preconditions for that mode of production' (ibid., p. 47). It is associated with a certain level of development of productive resources that involves neither animal tractive force nor collective means of production. In its definitive form the household community is organized on a patriarchal basis and 'custody of the wives' progeny is awarded to the husbands' community' (ibid., p. 46).

The concept has been debated thoroughly, especially in France (see, for example, Adler, 1976; Bonte, 1976; Suret-Canale, 1977; and Panoff 1977), and I do not intend to go into the ethnological or anthropological debate surrounding the subject in detail here. It is, however, worth highlighting two points of particular importance to the matter with which we are concerned.

First, although Meillassoux clearly points out the paramount importance to the household community of female labour, and in particular how crucial the female's reproductive capabilities are, he nevertheless regards the subjugation of womankind, a characteristic feature of the household community, exclusively as a prerequisite (see also Mackintosh, 1977). It is a fact, not a problem. Meillassoux ultimately regards women as objects, and his analysis and therefore his view of history are distinctly mechanistic as a result. This, of course, also has an effect on the second part of his study. By way of a deduction from his analysis, many aspects of which are totally original, he advances an old thesis so detrimental to many women in countries that have not been permitted to develop that it can no longer be ignored. He writes:

The struggle for emancipation conducted by young people and women (progressive though it may be in so far as it subordinates itself to the class struggle in order to strengthen this) is actually orientated towards the development of capitalism in society. (Meillassoux, 1976, p. 162)

Second, Meillassoux maintains that societies like those in his model of the household community no longer exist, whereas in fact today's household community still contains millions of productive cells which are being incorporated to varying degrees into capitalist society (ibid., p. 106). Under these circumstances the question must naturally be posed as to whether this controversial and problematic concept could not be replaced with one which does not reduce women to the status of objects under male control, but which regards them as the individuals who not only guarantee the primary production and the reproduction of life, but also do so as more than mere tools.

The subsistence debate and the first feminist approaches
The concept of subsistence may be regarded as an alternative to the concept of the 'household community' and its anthropological origins. It has been topical ever since the latter half of the 1970s, above all as a result of the subsistence debate[8] which has been in progress since then and from which have evolved the first feminist approaches to development theory in West Germany.

The participants, both male and female, in the subsistence debate have not yet reached agreement on a standard interpretation of the concept of subsistence, but are instead developing different versions of it. Aside from its meaning within development theory, the term is basically used to mean 'having a livelihood'. The term 'subsistence production' is accordingly taken to refer to production orientated towards goods which supply utility value for personal use. The working group of the Bielefeld development sociologists defined its starting point thus:

> It is our central working hypothesis that only the inclusion in the debate on development theory of agrarian and urban subsistence production, as well as that done in the home, will lead to a wider understanding of underdevelopment, as well as of development. (Otto-Walter, 1979)

Although the importance of this new perspective is undeniable, the way in which the concepts and theorems have developed is contradictory: Elwert and Wong (1979, p. 257), for example, view subsistence production as complementing commodity production, although they are keen not to restrict the latter to its capitalist form, but also to include simple commodity production. For them, subsistence production is just as likely as commodity production to be found in the agricultural, handicraft, domestic and other sectors. Fett and Heller (1982, p. 70), however, talk in terms of subsistence production and reproduction and regard 'housework, that is, preparing meals, fetching water and wood, cleaning, and raising the children', i.e. the work done by women, as reproduction. Production, on the other hand, covers the cultivation of the land, gathering (in which women participate), hunting and handicrafts. Particularly in countries that have not been permitted to develop this distinction is decidedly artificial, and the first feminist utterings on development theory rightly reject such a breakdown on the grounds that it takes no account of the work women do.

Bennholdt-Thomsen, Werlhof and Mies are the leading exponents of a feminist variant on the concept of subsistence. For them, the most essential part of any analysis is quite rightly its inclusion of the work done by women in the metropole and in those countries which have not been permitted to develop, since they, unlike Meillassoux for example, see the oppression of and discrimination against women as a problem. Accordingly, they are coming to regard subsistence production as the opposite to waged labour. Mies (1983, p. 117), for example, writes:

> Within the wider debate, the term 'subsistence production' also covered the work done by those who have been marginalized (slum-dwellers, retailers, small craftsmen etc.), that is by those who have to produce the means of their own survival without actual wage labour.

Subsistence production, then, evidently also includes certain forms of commodity production and is therefore seen as an analytical category within which to examine non-waged labour, not least the work of housewives in capitalist countries. The same sequence of ideas may also be found in the writings of Bennholdt-Thomsen and Werlhof. The latter, for example, writes:

> Our criticism of the modes of production debate is that it defines all non-waged labour as being outside capitalism and therefore also fails to accuse capitalism of the related forms of exploitation. Imperialist theory, on the other hand, only takes account of waged employment. Accordingly, 'work' is equated with 'paid work', and the whole vast question of unpaid work does not arise at all. (Werlhof, 1978a, p. 182)

The introduction of the two terms 'paid work' (i.e. waged labour) and 'unpaid work' (i.e. the work done by housewives, peasants etc.), both of which are used frequently by all three authors, into a conceptual framework which is orientated towards a critique of the political economy[9] is problematic to say the least. For on the surface a wage is (at best – as Meillassoux points out), after all, only payment for work done, merely the value of the work required. Under capitalism all additional work is unpaid labour.

Moreover, the criticism is altogether too strident: Although it certainly applies to the dominant strains of the *debates* on imperialism and modes of production, it does not apply to Luxemburg's contribution to the *theory* of imperialism, and from a feminist perspective this contribution cannot, of course, be ignored. A similar problem arises with regard to the modes of production debate, one of the contributions to which is that by Meillassoux, which we have already discussed. Meillassoux's stated view is that imperialism causes organic overlap between the 'household community' and capitalism, and that capitalism preserves this undeniably non-capitalist mode of production in order to exploit it as a community and to permanently siphon off value from it.

The reception accorded Luxemburg's work is of particular significance here. In various essays her work is positively held up as a counterpole to more prevalent theories of imperialism and development. Werlhof, for example, writes:

> And did not Rosa Luxemburg – whom I mention so often... for this very reason – evolve a similar stance on the question of imperialism and colonialism which was so broad and so fundamental that it could, even then, have produced almost all of the analysis with which we are wrestling today? (Werlhof, 1983, pp. 52f)

The personal assessment of *Die Akkumulation des Kapitals* published by Bennholdt-Thomsen in 1981 is somewhat different. She considers Luxemburg's work, as usual, in terms of 'accumulation schema' and 'collapse theory', but goes on to accuse Luxemburg of expounding a concept of value in which subsistence work is not regarded as socially useful labour (Bennholdt-Thomsen, 1981, p. 38).

On the one hand, then, the feminist strand of the subsistence debate rightly criticizes the fact that the work done by women in the political economy continues to be ignored (Werlhof talks of a 'blind spot', see in particular Werlhof, 1978b). Indeed, it is thanks to this strand that the work done by women in countries that have not been permitted to develop is now being examined in detail in the West German debate on development and imperialism. On the other hand, in addition to flaws in its reception of Luxemburg's work, its handling of terms – both those already in existence and those newly developed – is somewhat superficial and decidedly problematic. A particularly good example of this is the crucial concept of *Hausfrauisierung*, literally 'housewife-ization'.

Bennholdt-Thomsen, Mies and Werlhof (1983, p. 10) write:

> We cannot yet claim to have found other, more valid concepts. This would require a great deal of theoretical and practical work. Nevertheless one crucial concept has crystallized as a result of our theoretical and empirical work: the concept of 'housewife-ization'.
> ... The housewife is the classic non-wage worker whose labour is nevertheless acquired by the capitalist system. Using this model,

capitalism divides all work into wage labour and non-wage labour, and throughout the world non-waged labour, or housewife-type labour, is the most common basis of capital accumulation. The characteristic feature of such labour is that it is *acquired, not purchased.*

Here we find the same terminological lack of definition as we found in relation to 'paid' and 'unpaid' labour, for purchase is, in fact, *one* form of acquisition.

If, as Bennholdt-Thomsen, Mies and Werlhof write, it is usual for the process of 'housewife-ization' to occur at the same time as the process of proletarianization in the metropole, then one needs only to study the history of the world market for labour power to see that in the history of capitalism the 'classic non-wage worker' is not the housewife, but Indian forced labour (male and female) and the African slave (male and female). Whereas the work done by the metropolitan housewife is a function of waged labour – it presupposes that the man or the woman or both are earning a wage or have an income – slaves and forced labour, and to a large extent also coolies, have no access to waged employment.

The very term 'housewife-ization' limits the debate by failing to take account of the diversity of the methods of exploitation employed under capitalism or during the capitalist era. The old, orthodox Marxist thesis on the proletarianization of all countries, which history itself has shown to be inaccurate and which we must regard as having been superseded, has now acquired a feminist variant whose Eurocentrism exceeds even that of the original and is totally unfounded.

The export of the housewife ideology, which can actually be observed, should not be confused with the process by means of which the material and social situation of the majority of the population, and especially women, in those countries that have not been permitted to develop is adapting to the standard model of the 'housewife' in the metropole.

Though the feminist version of development theory has not yet been able to produce any serviceable new concepts and consequently no compelling theoretical overall analysis, it has nevertheless succeeded in posing some important questions, in particular on the situation and role of women in countries that have not been permitted to develop and on the subject of conflict. It has also conducted a certain amount of scientific analysis. The result is an overdue, but for that all the more necessary, body of empirical research, at least some of which is of such high quality that it will form an important foundation for the future formulation of theory. Examples of such research may be found in Mies's 1982 study of female Indian lacemakers, in Reddock's 1983 study of female slaves in the Caribbean, and in the studies of Werlhof (1980) and Bennholdt-Thomsen (1980) of the women's struggle in Latin America.

The term 'subsistence production' has come to apply in particular to a theorization of the work done by women. As a descriptive category at least it is preferable to the term 'household community'.

A synthesis of development and migration theories: the world-system approach (Wallerstein and others)

The starting point for and central proposition of the world-system approach to development and migration is the view that between 1450 and 1550 a 'modern world system' developed with a world economy centred on Europe, and that as a result interdependent societies and nation states took over from autonomous societies and nation states as the basis for the analysis of society.

According to Hopkins and Wallerstein, (1979, p. 187; see also Wallerstein, 1983):

> If there is one thing which differentiates a world-system concept from every other concept then it is the conviction that the analytical standard for comparison is a world system which is defined according to *economic* processes and relations and not according to any legal, political, cultural geographical, or any other standard!

For Wallerstein, then, it is not waged labour which defines capitalism, but labour power as a commodity (see Wallerstein, 1979, p. 45) – an idea also expressed by Marx when he speaks of the 'labour-power commodity' in relation to the slave trade (*MEW*, vol. 24, p. 475). For Wallerstein, slavery, debt bondage and other forms of unfree labour are capitalist 'modes of labour control'. Capitalist expansion is closely linked with the question of labour power. As Wallerstein says, 'The search for markets is not an adequate explanation. A much more plausible explanation is the search for cheap labour power' (Wallerstein, 1984, p. 33).

The following quotation indicates that Wallerstein's line of argument is based, at least in part, on a variant interpretation of the concept of subsistence:

> Historically speaking, every single territory newly incorporated into the world economy set real income at a level which lay at the lower end of the international wage table. Such territories had almost no fully proletarianized households and were in no way encouraged to develop any. (Ibid.)

A further link with both Meillassoux's stance and the subsistence debate becomes visible when Wallerstein points out that it is not the individual as the smallest unit which forms the basis of the capitalist mode of production, but the household.

The content of Wallerstein's theories is also based to some extent on Luxemburg's analysis of imperialism, which likewise views primitive accumulation as a crucial phase. The essential distinction between the two theories is, however, that Wallerstein has a completely different concept of imperialism. The world-system approach as formulated by him is clearly not a theoretical concept of imperialism. For Wallerstein, imperialism is a secondary category, a phenomenon not specifically capitalist, which occurs on the political plane. This political plane, however, has little bearing on the economic processes and relations which characterize the world system. Thus for Hopkins and Wallerstein the difference between competing hegemonic powers and an imperialist power (which seeks to subjugate 'peripheral' states) is that 'the former operate primarily through the market' (Hopkins and Wallerstein, 1979, p. 164). This concept of imperialism is closer to Kautsky's than to Lenin's or Luxemburg's.

Next Wallerstein puts forward another decidedly orthodox Marxist proposition: he is of the opinion that the prognosis of absolute pauperization has proven correct for the overwhelming majority of the world labour force, (although not for industrial workers, who still constitute only a small part of the world's population), and that the rate of exploitation has increased very sharply for them. This, then, is his concept of the ethnicization of the world labour force. Wallerstein (1984, pp. 67f, 72) views institutionalized racism as a means of controlling direct producers on a world scale.

Whereas this idea is well defined, a similar analysis of institutionalized sexism remains conceptual in nature and considerably more superficial in content. For example, Wallerstein states that, 'non-productive (subsistence) labour became the prime responsibility of the adult woman/mother', that 'non-productive work was done in the household', and that 'the correlation between the division of labour and the value of labour was a function of historic capitalism and meant a permanent devaluation of the work done by women ...', but does not explain in any more detail what he means by 'productive' or 'value'.

Despite the weaknesses I have pointed out, it should be noted that the world system approach regards the question of labour power as crucial, and that – unlike in the subsistence debate – a systematic historical perspective is developed to which dating makes a contribution (the fifteenth/sixteenth century as the beginning of the capitalist world system). By looking at 'labour power as a commodity' within the framework of a world system it is possible and has been possible to observe the diversity of capitalist-dominated forms of exploitation in all continents.

As the last of six research objectives in their attempts to further develop the concept of a world system, Hopkins and Wallerstein quote the 'incorporation into the world economic order of the formation of the labour force', meaning both the study of the various institutionalized forms of labour in history and in the present and also its quantifications. Transfers of labour power and labour migration are expressly covered by their research (Hopkins and Wallerstein, 1979, p. 197).

Under the title 'The global labor market in the modern world economy', McLean Petras gives a breakdown of labour specifically for this field of research: forced transfers, transplanted labour groups, the import/export of reserve labour forces and the brain drain. Her essay too is regarded as a programme for future research.

To date the findings of those who adopt the world system approach have been published primarily in the form of anthologies. Such anthologies include *Labor in the World Social Structure* (Wallerstein, 1983) and *Labor in the Capitalist World-Economy* (Bergquist, 1984). Although the essays contributed to both works by the individual authors deal specifically with problems of a purely historical and/or geographical nature, the analyses do not cover the whole field of research and do not contain a systematic overview, partly because of the dissimilarity of the positions the authors adopt. Moreover, the first of the two anthologies in particular concentrates on the question of labour movements and pays less attention to general methods of incorporating the labour force into capitalist production. Consequently, further development of the research approach is still to come.

Finally, I should also mention a study, entitled *Labor, Class and the International System* (Portes and Walton, 1981), which although it is part of the debate on the concept of a world system, is also in critical dispute with it. On the one hand the authors differentiate clearly between 'colonizing migrations' and labour migrations (pp. 22f), but on the other they point out that the usual distinctions drawn between labour migration and the brain drain, between legal and illegal, internal and international migration hinder analysis rather than assist it. One of their major findings is recorded in the proposition that labour – both qualified and unqualified – moves in a mobile, flexible and elastic fashion within a broad international framework, from which, in combination with various forms of capital mobility, numerous possible variations result.

Summary

Many theories of imperialism and development leave the structures and workings of the world market for labour power largely or completely unconsidered. The last three theories discussed – that of Meillassoux with his concept of the 'household community' and imperialism as a means of reproducing cheap labour power, the subsistence debate in its feminist variant, and the world-system approach, which takes as its starting point the notion that 'capitalism is characterized by labour power as a commodity' – are, despite the criticisms I have levelled, those of the more recent versions of development theory most suited, structurally, to discern the importance of labour power, in particular in the colonies and countries still not permitted to develop. They are also most suited to recognize the importance to the development of capitalism of the various methods of acquiring labour, and to take steps towards an analysis.

When all is said and done, there has as yet been no satisfactory appraisal in development theory in general of the world market for labour power, or of the acquisition of labour power from non-capitalist societies for capitalist production and the capitalist market from the beginning of its expansion until the present day. This is particularly the case for the historical aspects: Meillassoux's study, for example, does not begin until the relatively late colonial penetration of Africa, and the subsistence debate does not yet have a systematic historical perspective.

When one considers the difficulties more recent theories have experienced with the subject, the value of Rosa Luxemburg's analysis becomes particularly evident: for a long time the fact that her work contained important ideas on the connection between capitalist production and the labour forces from non-capitalist classes and societies was overlooked. To this extent her theories are still fundamental.

Using the historical and empirical evidence presented in chapters 1 to 5 my next and final chapter will draw together those ideas which serve to complement and extend the analytical framework.

Notes

1. We can dispense with an explanation of theories of growth, dualism and modernization. These regard human labour as only one of several factors of production and, unlike theories based on the labour theory of value, they are therefore not inconsistent with their basic assumptions if they do not regard the processes covered here by the term 'world market for labour power' as crucial elements of their analyses.

2. See Meinardus (1982) on the subject of this criticism.

3. This intensive and thorough critique of the Leninist concept of imperialism may also be found in Grohs (1976), Tibi (1975), Geiger and Mansilla (1983) and elsewhere.

4. All quotations from this work are taken from the 1951 edition published in London and translated by Agnes Schwarzschild.

5. This is demonstrated not only by the fact that Lenin's work is regarded in the socialist countries as virtually canonical (the model is *Lenins Imperialismustheorie und die Gegenwart*, Berlin 1980), but also by the fact that the West German debate ascribes paramount importance to his work, possibly because it is regarded as the most adequate theory of its time (Wöhlcke, Wogau and Martens, 1977, p. 11), possibly because it is regarded as *the* further development of Marx's theory (Grimm, 1979, p. 128), possibly because great importance is attributed to it 'within the science of Marxism' (Datta, 1982, p. 26), or possibly because each of the more recent theories of imperialism either criticizes or adheres to it (Grohs, 1976, p. 38).

6. See, for example, *The Accumulation of Capital*, pp. 371–7 on India, pp. 377–85 on Algeria, pp. 429–39 on Egypt, pp. 439–45 on Turkey.

7. For the more recent debate on the subject see among others Amin (1974) and Frank (1977).

8. For documentation on the numerous contributions to this debate see Krogbäumker (1980) and Schiel and Stauth (1981, pp. 142f).

9. Bennholdt-Thomsen summarizes her position on the Marxist theory thus:

> Nevertheless, we in no way claim that the theory of value as a tool for analysing unwaged forms of work is of no use. On the contrary, it must be emphasized that only the consistent application of the labour theory of value guarantees a serviceable result. This means extending the theory of value and applying it in an orthodox yet productive fashion. (Bennholdt-Thomsen, 1981, p. 139)

Elsewhere Werlhof writes, 'The only thing which I, as a woman, can do and must attempt to do is to extend – you may say 'overstretch' – this theory in such a way as to also cover women' (Werlhof, 1983, p. 49).

7. Elements of a Theory of the World Market for Labour Power

The principal stages in its development and its characteristics

The methods by which foreign labour power is and has been incorporated into the world market for labour power – beginning with the enslavement of the Indians and Indian forced labour, through African slavery and coolieism, to colonial forced and migrant labour, and finally labour migration and the brain drain – may be regarded and described as stages in that market's development.

It was not supply and demand which determined that development. Labour power was indeed bought and sold on this market from very early on and traded as a commodity, but since the owners did not offer their labour power on a labour market formed in the usual way, physical compulsion was employed to press-gang them into working. For centuries the world market for labour power functioned in this violent fashion and by doing so helped to bring about an inversion of the usual relationship between supply and demand. The diversion of numerous producers from traditional autochthonous economies accelerated the decline of those economies and liberated large numbers of workers, with the result that in many parts of the world today the demand for jobs in the capitalist sector vastly exceeds the supply. Seen within the context of the world market for labour power, this is a relatively recent development and did not assume worldwide significance until the second half of this century.

Not until fairly recently did the 'doubly free wage worker' first appear on the world market for labour power. In fact, the history of that market relativizes the claim that waged labour is *the* capitalist method of exploitation and demonstrates clearly that the development of methods of exploitation does not lead directly from the dependent, enslaved peasant to the wage worker, nor from the slave to the wage worker, but that various forms of unfree or half-free labour lie along the way. For a long time these forms of labour were the dominant forms, especially in the colonized continents.

Diagram 2 on page 211 shows how the individual stages in the development of the world market for labour power follow on from each other through the course of history. Each main stage is dated, and it is clear that each stage develops during the final phase of the previous stage. Furthermore, the time scale indicates a growing dynamism, a rapid succession and the increasingly shorter duration of each individual stage and therefore of each system of recruitment.

Map 8 demonstrates clearly that the world market for labour power was indivisibly linked with colonialism well into the twentieth century. Indeed, it was within this framework that its various forms developed: for a long time the major function of the world market for labour power was to provide a solution to the so-called labour question in the colonies, that is to say, its function was to satisfy demand for workers for colonial production on behalf of the colonial rulers, and this it did by means of both intra- and inter-continental transfers of labour in and to the colonized continents.

Map 8 also outlines the form which these migrations, largely induced by force or economic pressure, have taken. It was through such migrations that from the sixteenth century onwards America, Africa, and Asia gradually became reservoirs of labour power and/or operational areas. At least since the beginning of the eighteenth century transfers of labour power have formed an important part of the developing capitalist world market, but although in the nineteenth century Europe was still the major controller of such transfers and the major user of colonial labour power in its own interests, it was not itself a component part in territorial terms of the world market, either as a host region or, to any great extent, as a supplier of labour power.

The large-scale export of labour power from Europe that began in the 19th century has not been taken into account on the map, since the process cannot really be equated, for example, with the transatlantic slave trade or the coolie migrations.

One of the fundamental differences is that European emigration was generated by developments within European society (capitalization of the agricultural sector, industrialization) and also by the fact that the target areas (primarily the USA, then Canada and Australia) were little more than the extension of European societies to other continents. Moreover, for a considerable length of time, West European emigrants had a real chance of gaining possession of the means of production in their 'new homes'. Workers from the colonies and countries that have not been permitted to develop were not imported into the metropole (Europe and the USA) to any great extent until the twentieth century.

Consequently, the world market for labour power may be roughly divided into two main historical phases. The first encompassed the emergence and development of the world market for labour power under colonialism; the second began with industrialization and resulted in the direct incorporation into the world market of the capitalist metropole. From then on labour power acquired abroad was not only integrated into

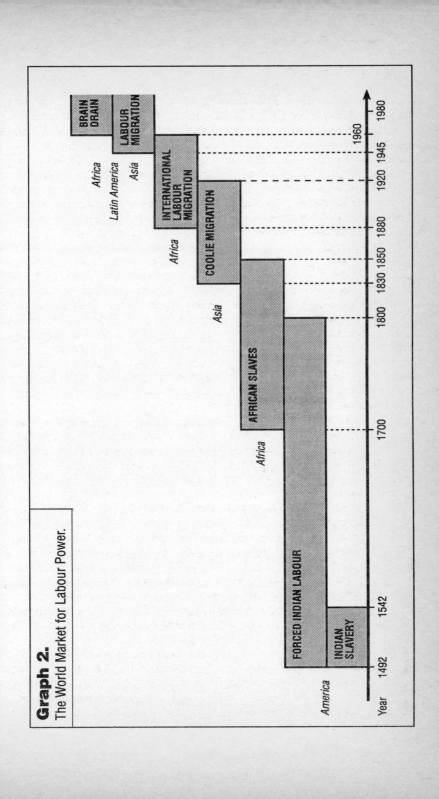

Graph 2.
The World Market for Labour Power.

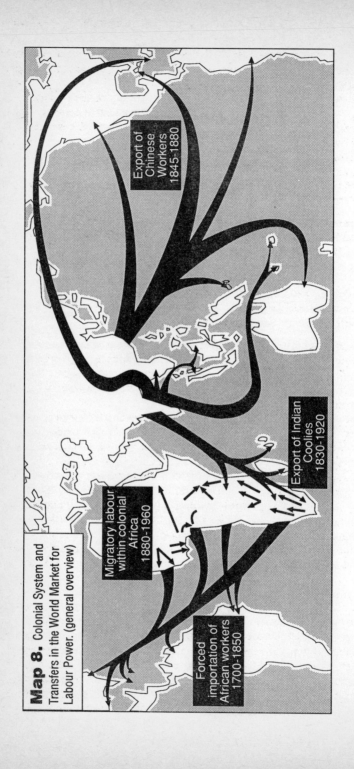

Map 8. Colonial System and Transfers in the World Market for Labour Power. (general overview)

Export of Chinese Workers 1845-1880

Export of Indian Coolies 1830-1920

Migratory labour within colonial Africa 1880-1960

Forced importation of African workers 1700-1850

the productive process outside the capitalist societies, but also inside them, and it was thus not until labour migration began that foreign labour power first appeared in the metropole.

The world market for labour power in its colonial variant did not disappear when the second phase began. Instead it reached new peaks in the nineteenth and twentieth centuries, and the two phases became closely interwoven.

Since the end of World War Two labour migration has been the leading phenomenon on the world market for labour power; it has been possible to discern three basic varieties of labour migration, though this may not be the complete picture. They are:

a) migration within Europe between countries at different levels of economic development (for example, Italy and West Germany, Ireland and Great Britain, Spain and France)
b) migration between countries that have not been permitted to develop (including Jordan and Saudi Arabia, Ghana and Nigeria)
c) migration from countries that have not been permitted to develop to the metropole (for example, Turkey and West Germany, the Maghreb and France, Mexico and the USA).

The way in which delimited reservoirs of labour power are divided among the individual nations that constitute the metropole has resulted in labour migration being regarded primarily as a binational process or a series of binational processes, not as a worldwide structure or a manifestation of the world market for labour power.

Just as the development of the world market for labour power may be divided into two main phases, so it is possible to divide the internal development of capitalism into two main phases. The turning point came in the nineteenth century when industrial capitalism gained supremacy over trading capitalism. Until the abolition of the transatlantic slave trade – and for as long afterwards as the American and Caribbean domestic slave trades continued to operate – trading capital was basically concerned with making profits on the world market for labour power. Abolition weakened trading capitalism and the coolie recruitments shook it still further, until eventually it completely lost its influence over and significance to the world market for labour power. A study published in 1935 outlines the process thus:

At first employers obtained coolies through middlemen, either Europeans or natives of the area in which they were recruiting. But since these middlemen demanded unreasonably high prices in times of increased demand, the employers endeavoured to become independent of them and joined forces to this end. The labour question was, in fact, the sole reason behind the establishment of planters' consortia. Through joining together the planters hoped to force down recruitment costs and improve the quality of the incoming labour force. Accordingly, they avoided, wherever possible, using the services of middlemen and went over to the 'kangani, sardar, and laukeh systems of recruitment'. In Dutch as well as in English colonies the recruitment of labour power through middlemen, whether for the benefit of employers or workers, is still forbidden today. Only in southern China is it still practised. (Pelzer, 1935, p. 112)

The costs incurred by the users of transferred labour power were no longer entered in the books as invested capital, as the cost of slaves had been. Under coolieism, as in the employment of wage workers everywhere, labour power became variable capital. The supersession of trading capitalism thus marked the impending conclusion of the colonial phase of the world market for labour power and highlighted one of the fundamental differences between the two main phases. After the onset of industrialization trading capitalism no longer played any appreciable part in importing labour power into the capitalist metropole and played only a minor part in twentieth-century transfers of labour power within the colonial system.

Those labour systems characteristic of the first phase of the world market for labour power – Indian slavery and forced labour, African slavery and forced migration, the export of the Chinese and Indians as coolies, and numerous forms of intra-continental forced and migrant labour, i.e. all the systems already discussed by means of which workers from and in the colonies were exploited, in particular by the Europeans – are closely connected. For one thing they were all structural elements of European colonialism, for another those who deployed the labour power recruited under such systems, namely the European colonial rulers, regarded two or more of these systems during any one phase as being in competition with each other. As early as the sixteenth century the profitability of the forcible deployment of Indian labour was being compared to that of the deployment of African slaves (see Chapter 1). Later the Caribbean planters debated the relative profitability of the various forms of slave ownership, and in the nineteenth century the costs of the coolie system were compared with those of slavery (see Chapter 3).

However, it was not merely a case of contrasting two particular labour systems. By the time the late nineteenth-century era of imperialist expansion began, users were investigating what else they could learn from various labour systems. One such investigation from 1883, entitled *'Die Kolonisation Senegambiens'*, looked like this:

The country, then, is not lacking in fertility. What it lacks is *workers*. Only the black man is capable of working in Senegambia's climate. Europeans can at best supervise the work ... We know from past experience that one cannot rely on the negro as a free worker. It is thus necessary to turn to foreigners, for example the Chinese, for temporary assistance ... Only in this way can we achieve the quickest and easiest possible intensive increase in profits from the land. Of course, we will have to advance with the energy of the early Spanish and English conquerors and use armed force not merely to guard the country adequately, but also to force the natives to totally vacate the terrain.

Here African forced labour and the coolie system, as well as experience of the early colonization of America (including genocide), are viewed in terms of how they can best help the exploiter.

One further example is labour migration within Europe, which had already begun by the end of the nineteenth century. Sartorius von Waltershausen regards the Polish workers employed in Germany as a 'second-grade working class' which in Germany had much the same function as 'the negro in the eastern states of North America, the Chinese in California, the East Indian coolie in the British West Indies, the Japanese in Hawaii and the Polynesian in Australia' (cited in Bade, 1983, p. 46).

It was not unusual for comparative argumentation to be based on calculations in which were included average and empirical values for the cost of labour power (purchase price and expenditure on maintenance or wages), life span and productivity. The results were then reduced to simple arithmetical formulas: an African slave does the same amount of work as four Indians (see Mannix, 1971, p. 5), or the cost of a coolie is less than half that of a slave.

What gave Indian labour and Asiatic contract, forced and migrant labour the edge over African slaves, so far as those who exploited the labour power of others was concerned, was that it did not require them to invest in replacements. If an Indian worker became unavailable for work then the worker's village community had to replace the worker. Coolies even bore the cost of their crossing themselves, but black slaves who died, who were unfit for work or who had run away could only be replaced by purchasing new slaves or by those bred on the plantation. During the initial phase of the world market for labour power this meant that for as long as Indian workers were available they were by far the 'cheapest' form of labour. Not until the American population had been decimated to such an extent that the supply of labour power to the colonial society became threatened did it become profitable to import large numbers of African slaves. Not until the coolie system was introduced in the nineteenth century was a solution finally found to the problem encountered by the user of this labour power, namely the problem of having to invest heavily in order to replace the labour power which he had acquired through the transatlantic slave trade. This indicates that the period between the beginning of the slave trade and the emergence of the coolie system not only witnessed the creation of the basis for industrialization in the capitalist metropole, but also the development of the methods used in colonization.

Not until Britain's colonization of India and China were large numbers of workers finally liberated and mobilized, that is, excluded from all access to the means of production and therefore every opportunity to support themselves. Earlier colonizations had lacked the vital preconditions for such a liberation and mobilization, partly because of the free access to the soil enjoyed by the populations of many regions of Africa and partly because of the still markedly feudal structure of Portugal and Spain, the colonial powers which initiated the slave trade.

Between the colonial phase of the world market for labour power and the second phase, which extends into the present day and encompasses the import into the metropole of living labour, there have been a number of developments of a continuous nature. Present-day labour migration and the brain drain, like the slavery and the coolie systems and the fascist system of forced labour, are all methods of importing living labour. The fact that the calculations of profitability used by slave-traders as early as the sixteenth century have been further developed since then and are still common is a clear indication of this. The calculation of profitability for the hire of forced labour from Nazi concentration camps reproduced earlier is just one extreme illustration of the fact that the inhumanity which underlies the slave-traders' calculations is still intensifying (see Chapter 5).

Ultimately these calculations were forerunners of the markedly economics-orientated, often hugely mathematical cost-benefit analyses that were for a long time commonly used in the study of labour migration.[1]

Competition between labour systems not only exists during the first phase of the world market for labour power, but also in the second. The debate surrounding various forms of labour migration conducted in West Germany primarily in the 1960s, which was characterized by catchwords such as 'rotation' and 'integration', was part of this trend. Since the 1970s geographical shifts of production to countries that have not been permitted to develop have been regarded and debated as a competitive alternative to labour migration. This view is expressed clearly in the 1977 and 1979 studies by Hiemenz and Schatz. The conclusion reached by the 1977 essay is that by 1985 almost 10 per cent of all those working in the manufacturing industry in West Germany should be expected to have experienced 'liberation as a result of foreign trade', with foreign workers becoming unemployed in larger numbers than German workers (Hiemenz and Schatz, 1977, p. 56).

They continue:

> To sum up, one should say that the empirical findings of this study lead us to the conclusion that one may regard international trade and the international migration of capital to distant lands as an alternative to the international migration of workers. Nevertheless, it is hardly to be expected that the employment of workers abroad will become totally unimportant in the future. One reason for this is that there is still, and will continue to be, inadequate integration into the international division of labour both in West Germany and in other countries which import labour power, as well as a tendency to replace the import of labour-intensive goods with the import of labour power. (Ibid., p. 58)

Among other things, geographical shifts in production facilitate the tapping of sources of labour that cannot take part in labour migration for cultural, social and economic reasons. Young women between the ages of seventeen and twenty-five, who make up the bulk of those employed in relocated factories, have as a result of the socialization of women acquired qualifications that are vital to the productive process, but that cannot be translated into demands for higher wages because they do not count as formal qualifications. Since the women remain in their countries of origin, geographical shifts in production neither interfere to any great extent with the reproduction of labour power, nor cause social problems in the metropole. The wages paid to such workers are far lower than those paid to migrant workers.

The very fact that labour migration and geographical shifts in production are seen as alternatives indicates that for the time being at least it is not only the various methods by which living labour power is directly transferred that are regarded as being in competition on the world market for labour power, but also those that create a world market for labour power through the import of objectified labour.

Capitalism and its policy of maintaining supremacy and control on the world market for labour power

A glance at the history of the world market for labour power reveals that this market is controlled by the users of labour power, and that the level of economic and social development in the colonizing countries and the hegemony within Europe are ultimately the factors that have most influence over which system is used to exploit foreign labour power.

In the fifteenth and early sixteenth centuries Spain and Portugal, countries which had initially divided up the New World between themselves and which controlled the slave trade, were the dominant powers in Europe and therefore determined the form which the employment of foreign workers should take and the level of that employment. During the sixteenth century England began to establish its supremacy on the oceans, and this supremacy also manifested itself in Britain's control of the slave trade and establishment of colonies in every corner of the world. Through Great Britain slavery developed into the dominant system on the world market for labour power. Though there was a certain degree of continuity in the system, there were also some internal modifications.

At the beginning of the nineteenth century, a still dominant Great Britain finally put a stop to the transatlantic slave trade. The abolition of slavery itself, on the other hand, was spread across almost the entire century: slavery was outlawed in the British colonies in 1834, in the French colonies in 1848 and in the USA in 1865. It was 1870 and 1888 respectively before Brazil and Cuba followed suit. The order in which slavery was abolished corresponded with the order in which industrialization took place in Europe and the USA – Great Britain as the outrider, with France and the USA in pursuit and Spain and Portugal failing to catch up.

The abolition of slavery was also important to Great Britain because in the nineteenth century the British began intensive colonization of Africa and needed African workers there in order to produce goods to meet demand in Europe. In view of this, the abolition of the transatlantic slave trade, which deprived Africa of workers, was more important than the abolition of slavery itself.

Thereafter the coolie system was the basic means by which workers were moved around the British Empire. As long as there were surpluses Britain was also prepared to supply workers to colonial territories belonging to other powers.

In the nineteenth century, but above all in the second half of the twentieth century, the scale, structure and course of labour migration has been controlled unequivocally and exclusively by the countries that play host to migrant workers. It is they who determine the composition of the waves of migration in terms of qualifications, age, marital status and gender. The scale and timing of arrivals and departures and the pattern of immigration and remigration are directly dependent on the economic climate and the state of the labour market in host countries and on those countries' prognoses of how such factors might change in the future.

Labour migration to West Germany and Switzerland are particularly clear examples of how perfectly the metropole is able to direct such processes. In times of crisis the metropolitan labour markets and 'social networks' are relieved of strain by sending migrant workers home, and the host countries are careful to select those whom they expel in their own interests. Thus, to give but one example, the return home of Turkish migrant workers yielded the West German social insurance fund DM1,760 million in 1984 alone; the financial inducements offered to migrants in order to encourage them to return home (the capitalization of claims for unemployment benefit and pension contributions) not only successfully relieved the strain on the labour market without affecting costs, but also proved decidedly lucrative for West Germany (see *Frankfurter Rundschau*, 23 January 1985).[2]

The geographical shifts in production that took place primarily in the 1970s were proof of the fact that the structures of the world market for labour power are also adapted directly to short-term economic and in particular technological developments in the metropole and are extremely flexible.

Supremacy in and control of the world market for labour power often create antagonisms, however, between the short-term interests of private capital and the longer term interests of the state. During the first stage in the development of the world market for labour power the colonial nations attempted to use government measures to regulate the nature and scale of the recruitment of labour power in colonized territories. Examples of such measures include the Indian Protection Laws, the debate on the *encomienda*, the Black Code in British colonies and the USA, and the *code noir* in the French colonies. The sixteenth century saw the creation of the first public office whose holder was responsible for the exploitable labour force: in Spanish America the holder of this office was known as the *protectores y defensores de indios* (Konetzke, 1965, p. 180); during the slavery age the holder was known as the 'protector of slaves', and under coolieism as the 'protector of emigrants' in India and the 'protector of immigrants' in the host countries (Tinker, 1974, p. 14).

Measures and offices of this kind reflected government endeavours to secure the long-term supply of labour power. These endeavours necessitated countering the most extreme forms of the over-exploitation to which Indian forced labour in particular, but also slaves and coolies were exposed, since this led to the annihilation of the workforce.

During the early stages in the development of the world market for labour power this meant direct confrontation and conflict of interest between governments and colonizers; protective regulations had no effect. State intervention became more effective as the world market for labour power developed and after trading capital was superseded. This was especially so since it was in principle limited to an absolute minimum in the interests of the colonizers and private capital and did not jeopardize the particular high profit levels associated with the exploitation of foreign labour power.

Contrary to popular belief, then, it was the states constituting the metrople that from the very beginning accepted responsibility for protecting the world market for labour power. Böhning (1984, p. 32) writes:

> There was no international labour migration until the nation state, first in Europe, assumed a concrete form and the colonies became independent. Of course, during the phase in which nation states were still forming the private sector operated an infamous pre-form of international labour migration (black slaves and white bondsmen), which was transformed between the abolition of the slave trade and World War One under state supervision, above all from Great Britain, into a pure form of labour migration (the engagement of Indians and others in East and South Africa and in the Caribbean).

Nevertheless, it must be said that even today certain stages in the process of labour migration, in particular recruitment, are still handled by the private sector, for example directly by firms. From the very beginning governments made at least some attempt to supervise the exploitation of foreign labour power, as the examples given indicate. They even had some success with the slave trade. State supervision did not begin in the nineteenth or twentieth centuries, but has been one of the continuities of the world market for labour power, although state influencing control has increased and its forms have been modified and perfected.

The organization of supremacy and control on the world market for labour power did not, however, remain at state level: the capitalist countries had a collective interest in ensuring the continual over-exploitation of foreign labour power, and at the beginning of the twentieth century this community articulated its interests in the nascent international organizations and elsewhere. The Internal Labour Association of the League of Nations, as today's International Labour Organization was officially known in its early days, played a particularly important part in this process.

At its first general meeting in November 1919 the organization voted in favour of an eight-hour day and a forty-eight hour week for Europe and the USA. China, Persia and Siam were explicitly excepted under this ruling, and British India fixed its own standard working week at sixty hours (Senghaas-Knobloch, 1979, p. 43). It has to be said that the choice of the countries named here was not random: the organization was intent on protecting crude oil interests and therefore on maintaining the unique levels of profitability associated with the exploitation of both Chinese and in particular Indian workers by extending the working day to something approaching its absolute limits.

Additional proof of the International Labour Office's role as the guarantor of the collective interests of the capitalist countries is the fact that by 1929 it had still not been able to agree on a declaration in favour of the abolition of forced labour. A memorandum on the current level of forced labour in the world (the Grey Report) drawn up in Geneva for the International Labour Conference in the same year restricted itself 'basically to reproducing the legal provisions in force in the individual colonies'. 'The extensive use in the French colonies of military service as a form of forced labour first came to light in a "supplementary report" which was handed out to delegates at the close of the conference' (Furtwängler, 1929, p. 795).

The conference resulted in a questionnaire being sent out to governments. Although only two representatives of the workers in colonized territories attended the conference and these, as Furtwängler, who acted as a technical adviser to the German delegation, reports, were kept under surveillance by plainclothes policemen, the conference organizers attempted to suppress the customary general debates. 'Obviously they feared that such a highly political debate might result in delegates dividing themselves into beneficiaries and victims of the Versailles world order – a little bit of "class conflict between the nations"' (ibid., p. 795).

Even today the international organizations are still acting out this role. UNIDO, for example, encourages the establishment of free production zones and factories, which produce for the world market as part of a political and development programme whose first task is to create jobs and thereby eradicate unemployment. Its second purpose, however, is to guarantee the formation of a skilled industrial labour force and access to modern technology (see Fröbel, Heinrichs and Kreye, 1977, pp. 552f). In view of wage levels, working conditions, the amount of work carried out previously on the infrastructure and technological standards in factories producing for the world market and free production zones, UNIDO's support for such geographical shifts in production is obviously part of a strategy to safeguard this particular method of exploiting labour power in the collective interest of the countries which make up the metropole.

Though the development of the world market for labour power is and has been basically determined by the economic interests of the metropole and its technical potential, this does not mean that those exploited have always reacted passively. On the contrary, they have developed countless forms of resistance and non-acceptance, many of them well known, and some of which have always been regarded as such. Still more in all probability went unnoticed by the colonial rulers and other users of colonial labour power and have not been covered in the literature on the subject.

One of the forms of overt and covert resistance and non-acceptance used by the exploited in order to damage the interests of the exploiters and which they could, under the force of circumstances, only direct against their own person, was suicide. This method was used by Indians, slaves and coolies as a last resort. Other methods included the refusing of food until death intervened, and collective or individual drowning. The folding back of the tongue for the purposes of suffocation and mass hangings were also methods used. In fact, the latter form of resistance was linked for certain African tribes with notions of the transmigration of the soul and was believed to result in the soul returning to Africa after death and in reunion with one's loved ones. Some regarded slaves from tribes with such beliefs as unsaleable. In the same vein, the fact that slaves from Santo Domingo frequently committed suicide earned them the reputation of having nothing but contempt for death and of being absolutely fearless to the extent that even torture could have no effect on them.

Between April 1839 and November 1846 1,337 suicides were officially recorded in Cuba, of which 86.7 per cent were accounted for by slaves, 8.7 per cent by whites, and 3.9 per cent by free coloureds. It is fair to assume that a high percentage of suicides, especially among the slaves, went undetected, since for a slave owner the reporting of a suicide meant having to pay the costs of various investigations. Yet even according to official statistics, the suicide rate among slaves during that period was almost eight times higher than among whites.

Speculation that the number of suicides would fall after the abolition of the transatlantic slave trade proved to be false. Chinese contract workers, who found themselves in the same desperate position as the slaves, turned to the same last resort. In 1862 346 suicides were recorded in Cuba, of which 173 were committed by Chinese workers, 130 by black slaves, and the remaining 43 by free coloureds and whites (cf. Hall, 1971, pp. 20ff and Mannix, 1971, pp. 19, 118ff).

German colonial rulers also encountered suicide among their plantation workers. They treated the matter with unsurpassable cynicism. One book published in Germany in 1905 states:

> Unfortunately our Chinese were of almost hysterical sensitivity. The smallest trifle, just five public strokes, offended them. And without even considering that they were wasting foreign currency and were badly damaging the company, they would kill themselves at the slightest provocation. If they didn't like the food they would hang themselves. If they were deprived of their opium they would hang themselves. If it was raining they would hang themselves. A Chinaman does not place much value on life. But I had never dreamed just how little he does actually value it. At the slightest offence they would say that it would serve the company right if they hanged themselves – and did so straight away. (Cited in Mamozai, 1982, p. 49)

Several of the other forms of resistance employed by Indians, slaves, and coolies have already been mentioned in the appropriate chapters. Resistance included running away and open rebellion, industrial action in the form of refusing to bear children, the destruction of foodstuffs, the refusal to cultivate the land, the development of certain individual and collective modes of behaviour, the way in which they brought up their children, types of music, stories and the religion of the oppressed.

Between 1791 and 1804, at the time of the French Revolution, the black slaves in Haiti in the Antilles conducted a war of independence against France. More than 30,000 French soldiers lost their lives without Napoleon being able to countermand by force the emancipation of the slaves (cf. Buch, 1976). There were still so many escaped slaves on the loose that there was actually a word for them. Derived from the Spanish term *cimarron*, which was used for runaway domestic animals which had become wild again, the term applied to such slaves in the English-speaking world was 'maroons'. The Spanish-speaking world continued to use *cimarron* without any modification (Tinker, 1984, p. 77).

Just as the workers forcibly recruited and transported abroad during both world wars resisted, so too did slave labourers in Africa. Even migrant workers developed specific forms of resistance and non-acceptance, as the part they have played in strikes in the metropole demonstrates; the high incidence of psychosomatic illness among female migrant workers in particular can be regarded as a refusal to accept metropolitan ways of life.

No systematic, coherent account of the various forms of resistance and non-acceptance has ever been written, and the ways and means which women in particular have invented have been paid no attention at all. This last point is demonstrated most forcibly in the foreword to *Der Cimarron: die Lebensgeschichte eines entflohenen Negersklaven aus Cuba* (The maroon: the biography of a runaway negro slave from Cuba). Miguel Barnet writes:

The woman was 100 years old, the man 104. The woman had been a slave. In addition, she practised the Yoruba veneration of slaves and was a spiritualist. In the man's words ... one could discern a leaning towards superstition and esoteric notions of religion. His life was interesting ... We forgot the old lady.

On the basis of their work with the man the authors wrote a study which has been translated into several languages.

The various forms of resistance and non-acceptance employed by the exploited, particularly women, are largely unresearched – and not only in relation to the history of the world market for labour power. As a result, this account must remain incomplete and unsatisfactory.

Racism, sexism and the reproduction of labour power

Not only did Europe create the external, material conditions necessary to the exploitation of the colonized peoples, it also created the corresponding racist ideologies.

Since Las Casas it is the Africans who have been considered particularly suited to working on the plantations and in the mines. The Indians, on the other hand, have been associated with a disastrously high incidence of death. During the Age of Imperialism racist ideologies, which since the Enlightenment have rested upon scientific foundations, were expounded and assimilated in a particularly aggressive manner. The economic motives behind various countries' colonial endeavours were veiled with talk of educational, religious or some such missions in which the teaching of Africans in particular to work was a central issue. As one German colonialist put it, 'First we must create the preconditions under which trade can exert an influence on culture and, in fact, on the cultural development of our natives. This can be done by educating them to work systematically' (cited in Bald et al., 1978, p. 112).

Whereas Africans were regarded as lazy but strong, Chinese coolies were described, not only by the German colonial rulers, as 'this diligent, modest, if disagreeable people' (cited in Mamozai, 1982, p. 49).

From the very beginning the world market for labour power operated according to racist principles, which permitted the highest degree of exploitation of those at the base of racial hierarchy. Of the American Indians, for example, the Europeans singled out the Caribs as a special group and declared that the members of this group could be enslaved without hesitation. Further examples of hierachization include the placing of American half-castes into a hierarchical sequence, the ban on the enslavement of Indians and simultaneous intensification of the enslavement of Africans, and the allocation of slave status exclusively by reference to the status of the mother, a practice which resulted in the repeal of the patriarchal norm in favour of a racist one.

Examination of racist structures is made more difficult by the fact that some of these structures were to some extent modelled on those which existed in the colonized societies themselves. Such structures manifested themselves, for example, in avowed or unavowed awareness of the superiority of the whites, but also in each colonized people's perception of its own superiority or inferiority in relation to other colonized peoples. Even today such assumptions of superiority or inferiority may still be found, even in critical works written by the descendants of those affected. The following quotation from one of the best studies written of the history of Africa's underdevelopment is just one example:

> The native Indians had no resistance to new European illnesses such as smallpox, nor were they able to survive the organized drudgery of the slave plantations and the slave mines, since they had only just outgrown the hunting-tribe stage in their development. Thus it happened that in Cuba and Hispaniola, for instance, the Indian population was practically annihilated by the white interlopers. At the same time Europe itself had only a small population and could not dispense with any of its workers. In Africa the population had long been well versed in agriculture and in many regions was accustomed to disciplined work. These objective conditions existed before the beginning of the European slave trade, and are some of the reasons that the European capitalist class used its control of international trade to force Africa to specialize in the export of prisoners. (Rodney, 1976, pp. 65f).

It is not important that the above statement fails to take account of major elements of the initial phase of the world market for labour power. What is important is that the arguments which it contains are untenable in more than one respect. Rodney endeavours to explain away the genocide inflicted upon the Indians with biological factors whose pertinence he neither defines in detail nor proves. His reference to differences in the stage of civilization which the Indians and Africans had reached is misleading: it cannot be said, for example, of the Incas, Mayas and Aztecs that they 'had only just outgrown the hunting-tribe stage in their development'. By restricting discussion to a population well versed in agriculture and accustomed to disciplined work in Africa, Rodney is simply applying the arguments used by the European colonizers to justify their penetration of Africa, and belief in the inferiority of the Africans, to the relationship between Africa and America.

Like racism, the phenomena of sexism, categorization and discrimination on the grounds of membership of the female sex are also a generally accepted principle on the world market for labour power. At first glance women play a seemingly rather insignificant part in many of the stages in the development of this market. It was primarily the men in colonized societies who were obliged, directly or indirectly, to carry out forced labour; every cargo of slaves from Africa is said to have contained two thirds men and only one third women and children; under the coolie system women formed only a minority of the workers exported, and labour migration is always portrayed as a male-dominated process.

Nevertheless, the reality of colonialism is that large numbers of women were recruited as forced labour: as bearers, mine workers, gatherers, and servants. The slave-owning societies of the Caribbean and the USA made hardly any distinction between male and female slaves when assigning work. In the USA there was an equal number of enslaved men and women, unlike in the Caribbean where female slaves were in the minority.

It is difficult to discover the history of women on the world market for labour power from the literature on this subject, for colonized women were of even less interest to the historians of Europe than their men. Such women also had less opportunity to pass on or rediscover their own history.

This is still the case today. The literature on the subject of labour migration, for example, paints a picture dominated by the male or apparently sexless migrant, and women are included at best as dependent relatives. Even in the field of women's studies female migrant workers are not discussed, especially in relation to the formulation of theory.

Yet every form of colonial or capitalist exploitation affected women more intensely than it did men. Exploitation was not restricted to the recruitment of women for colonial production and as servants, but also extended to their sexual and reproductive capacity. This is particularly evident in the case of Indian women when one considers the emergence of the race of half-castes which replaced the original population of America, but it also holds true for African female slaves and the women in Africa, Asia and Australia who lived through the colonization of their continents (for Africa see Mamozai, 1982).

Moreover, as a result of forced and migrant labour, men became unavailable to help produce the means of subsistence so this burden had to be borne by women, possibly assisted by children and the elderly. Every form of forced and migrant labour, even those that directly affected only men, increased the workload of the women in colonized societies.

Women were thus more important to the world market for labour power as producers and reproducers of labour power than through their incorporation into capitalist commodity production. This in no way means that they were treated more considerately, for example by being exempted from hard physical labour, but meant above all that their specifically female capabilities were used in the interests of the users of labour power.

Through every stage in the development of the world market for labour power women have resisted being used in this way. The problems encountered when the USA and the Caribbean attempted to breed slaves is proof enough. Industrial action of the sort where women refuse to bear children has probably been used in all colonized territories and is only possible if women apply knowledge handed down to them through the ages. Indian women, female African slaves in America and colonized women in Africa, Australia and the South Seas, as well as female coolies, all resorted to this form of non-acceptance.

The Europeans' desire to gain control over the reproductive capacities of colonized women – until well into the first few decades of the 20th century this meant prevailing upon women to bear more children – manifested itself in the inducements, such as bonuses and privileges, offered to mothers, midwives, overseers etc. By making use of the usually relatively small number of women involved in the transfer of labour power (particularly under the coolie system) the colonizers attempted to ensure that the societies to which these women belonged would continue to function as reservoirs and suppliers of labour power.

The reproductive capacity and labour power of the female was purposefully deployed to preserve this most important prerequisite for the continued existence of the world market for labour power. If the structures created for the purposes of reproducing labour power during the market's colonial phase point to its operation according to sexist principles, from the slave age through to the present day, then this is confirmed by the way in which women were incorporated into capitalist production. The work done by women on the world market for labour power, including those affected by geographical shifts in production and labour migration, is the lowest paid work of all. One American study (Chiswick, 1980) found that on the basis of the 1970 USA census it generally takes a male immigrant in the USA 11 to 15 years to reach the height of his earning power, as determined by his ethnic origin, whereas women reach that level after only five years. The sting in the tail is that female immigrants' incomes are generally far more affected by their ethnic origin – an indication of the complex interrelation between racism and sexism. In 1976 American firms paid average hourly rates of between $0.17 (Indonesia) and $0.62 (Singapore) in countries which have not been permitted to develop. The majority of the employees in their factories are women (Hancock, 1983, p. 136).

Chiswick's findings point to discrimination against female migrant workers on three counts: as women, as migrant workers or foreigners, and as members of another racial or ethnic group. Morokvasic (1983, p. 26) presents the case for the oppression of this group of women on four counts: as women, as members of the working class, as members of a migrant minority group, and finally because they regard discrimination as their destiny, as natural and normal, since they carry the oppression within themselves.

Thus in all there would appear to be five counts on which female migrant workers suffer discrimination:

1. as women
2. as members of the working class
3. as migrant workers/foreigners
4. as members of another race/ethnic group
5. since they carry the oppression within themselves.

In terms of methodology and content this list is undoubtedly not unproblematic, yet it illustrates that female migrant workers constitute a source of labour power which is exploitable to an extreme degree. As both reproducers of labour power and as female wage workers they are regarded both by Western European and USA capitalism, as well as by the capitalism of the Arab oil states, as a 'highly attractive form of labour power' (Phizacklea, 1983, p. 5).

The idea that race and gender have similar functions as criteria for oppression and discrimination has often been debated in recent years (see among others Davis, 1982, Benard, 1981). In fact, it is a point of view introduced very early on into the debate on the exploitation of labour power: Olivier (1906, pp. 27f), for example, refers to it at the beginning of this century. What the analogy between race and gender clearly means is that women from races that suffer discrimination are even lower down the social hierarchy than men of the same race. They are, therefore, the most exploitable.

On the world market for labour power demographic evolution and population policy are closely connected with the forced reproduction of labour power by women. Indeed it was not until the Spaniards arrived in America that they first became a problem. Although various forces among the colonizers soon emerged which regarded the people, i.e. the labour force, as the actual wealth of America, such voices did not dominate the process of colonization. This was dominated instead by those who sought gold, silver and precious stones to satisfy demand in the late-feudal motherland and who strove – at least during the crucial first years and decades of colonization – to obtain these not so much through the deployment of workers as through compulsory gifts, plunder and collections. Tropical produce, at first mainly sugar cane, only became important to the Spaniards and Portuguese in America where there were no more treasures to carry off as booty.

America was the first continent to be colonized and its conquest took place before capitalism had become established. As a result Portugal and Spain were not interested at first in raw materials or agricultural produce, but in precious metals and precious stones.

The annihilation of the Indian labour force, whether during the conquest, during the establishment of foreign rule, or through overwork, was therefore largely acceptable, since it did not strike at the heart of Spain's or Portugal's still largely feudal colonial interests. Moreover, the reservoir of labour power must surely have appeared at first to be inexhaustible, with the result that measures designed to reproduce labour power for the colonial rulers were not really one of the major subjects on which agreement had to be reached.

In Latin America the tendency to reduce entire Indian populations to a source of labour power for the European colonizers led to the destruction of both the material and the immaterial basis for the reproduction of pre-colonial society. Accordingly, the need to reproduce labour power in the colonies and the world market for labour power emerged simultaneously. Whilst the Indians were being exterminated, it was considered 'unnecessary' to conquer Africa, although parts of the continent were already known: there was fast becoming plenty of scope for deploying labour power in America.

With the shift in emphasis from colonial exploitation in the form of Indian slavery and forced labour to the deployment of enslaved African labour power in America, Europe entered a new phase in its acquisition of labour power from abroad. The forced migration of the African peoples was the first method developed by the colonialists for siphoning off labour power from other societies on the one hand, whilst preserving the pre-colonial basis of reproduction, though in a badly distorted form, on the other.

As a result of the subsequent colonizations of Africa and Asia and through the coolie system this method, which was initially rather uncomplicated, evolved and became more sophisticated. In the course of this evolution various new solutions were found to the problem of how to reproduce labour power. Under slavery the middle-term and long-term reproduction of labour power in particular was relatively costly for the user, since regular investment was needed in replacing the labour force, either through importation or breeding. Even direct daily reproduction was often quite costly for the slave owner, since it had to be guaranteed in a minimal form even in unproductive times. This all puts into some perspective the slave owner's calculation already quoted, according to which an African worker achieves as much as four Indians: high replacement costs limit this advantage considerably.

Under the coolie system and the various other systems of forced and migrant labour in the colonies, the cost of replacing the labour force largely disappeared: wages were paid only for productive time, and the profits made by traders either vanished or were borne by the workers themselves. The workers even bore the cost of their transportation. Not least because they reproduced themselves, a coolie cost only half as much as a slave.

Now let us glance at another important aspect of the reproduction of labour power: during the age of the African slave the world market for labour power operated at an intercontinental level, with Africa supplying America with labour for the benefit of Europe. During subsequent stages in the development of the market the units which served as reservoirs of labour power and which undertook the long-term reproduction of the labour force became increasingly smaller: for the coolie system it was the British Empire, then, later, individual states or specific territories within these states. From the point of view of the deployment and reproduction of the labour force the system became increasingly complex and therefore also more difficult to oversee – something demonstrated, for example, by the multitude of waves of migration which took place within colonial Africa.

The problems involved in reproducing labour power are closely linked with the question of demographic evolution and population policy. As we have seen, the colonialists experienced difficulty for almost the entire duration of the colonial phase of the world market for labour power in maintaining their stocks of labour power and avoiding decreases in population. During this time the population in what is now the capitalist metropole grew considerably, whilst high mortality and low birth rates were recorded in the colonized territories. In 1906 a prize of DM6,000 was offered for the study which contained the best suggestions for raising the birth rate in Cameroon (Mamozai, 1982, p. 53).

The following statement relates to the demographic evolution both of the metropole on the one hand and of the colonies or countries that have not been permitted to develop on the other:

> Looking at it in this way, it is possible to distinguish two phases since 1750 in which the population movement in both regions changed direction. The first extends from 1750 to 1900, the second from 1900 to the present day. It is a feature of both phases that whenever the population of one region is showing an upward trend, the population in the other shows a downward trend. (Khalatbari, 1977, p. 108)

What this means is that the users of the labour power of countries that have not been permitted to develop (the former colonies) are faced with the opposite problem in the second half of the 20th century than that which they faced in the colonial age: with an increase in the population or 'population explosion' and the resulting surplus of labour power.

Nowadays schemes designed to control the reproductive capacity of women in Asia, Africa and Latin America are no longer aimed, as they were in the colonial phase, at increasing the birth rate, but at cutting it. To this end numerous measures are debated, and most are adopted. Control over and regulation of population growth are to be achieved through ideological influence (by promoting contraception, small families and so on), pecuniary benefits and disincentives (bonuses for sterilization, fiscal policy etc.), and even overt and covert force (sterilization at birth for those giving birth in hospital or for women having other operations, also without their knowledge). By 1965, for example, 34 per cent of Puerto Rican women between the ages of 20 and 49 had been sterilized. The agencies involved include both the state institutions of most of the countries that have not been permitted to develop and international development aid organizations and institutions ('Bevölkerungspolitik', 1977, *Materialien*, 1984).

The object of the measures adopted during both phases of the world market for labour power and of demographic evolution was to control the ability of women to bear children and thereby to find a level of reproduction high enough on the one hand to guarantee the supply to the capitalist sector, nationally and internationally, of a sufficient number of suitable workers, but also so low and socially selective that social and political development would remain controllable.

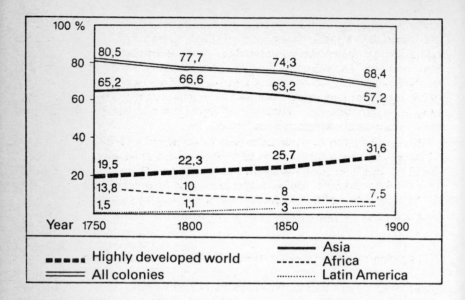

Diagram 3 (Khalatbari, 1977: 115)
The populations of developed and less developed regions as a percentage of world population, 1700–1900

At present the metropole is attempting to supplement its attempts at restricting population growth in those countries that have not been permitted to develop with measures designed to achieve an increase in the birth rate for indigenous white women. Its aim is to halt the decline in population within its own borders and among such groups. In order to achieve this, use is also being made of the section of the population which has entered the metropole as migrant labour. The West German government's scheme to reunite the families of migrant workers in West Germany, which along with the embargo on recruitment shaped West German migration policy in the 1970s, served basically to ward off for the middle term the effects on the labour market of the decline in the birth rate.

Only a quarter of the foreign women in West Germany entered the country on their own work permits. The majority of the remaining 75 per cent entered under the scheme to reunite families, and accordingly, their right of residence is dependent on that of their husbands. (cf. *'Deutsch muß die Familie sein'*, 1984, p. 51.) At first migrant families in West Germany tended to have more children than German families (in 1974 17.3 per cent of all the children born in West Germany were foreign nationals), but very soon a trend emerged which showed that migrant couples were beginning to conform to the generative behaviour of the West German couple

(Münscher, 1979, pp. 6ff). The reuniting of families had thus served its purpose in terms of population policy, and in 1980 the West German Federal Ministry of Education and Science predicted that 'in 1989 approximately 85,000 foreigners (absolute peak) will leave general education, i.e. when the large numbers of Germans now leaving school have done so'. The subsequent phase of this policy (from the beginning of the 1980s on) consisted on the one hand of selectivity as regards this source of labour power (the repatriation of young people and adults who are not integrated into the labour market), and on the other of a purposeful family policy towards the German population.

This combination of population policy, the import and reproduction of labour power and not least the gainful employment of women may also be found in other countries. It was attempted in France after the end of World War Two (Lannes, 1953, p. xiv), and looking at Switzerland Haug (1978, p. 238) finds that, 'The dynamic element in the demographic history of Switzerland is... international labour migration.'

The economic importance of the world market for labour power

Some of the more recent works on the subject of development theory attempt, by using computer models, statistical evidence and so on, to prove that colonial and/or imperialist exploitation did not appreciably influence the industrialization and economic development of the metropole and was not the cause of underdevelopment in the colonized territories. Such stances have been adopted, among others, by Senghaas and Elsenhans. Elsenhans, for example, writes:

> The only contribution made by the Third World to 'primitive accumulation', i.e. the liberation of labour power for the purposes of producing capital goods, before the industrial revolution must therefore be the fact that the supply of luxury goods from the south to the European upper classes enabled European factors of production to be employed to a lesser extent on such luxury consumption and therefore to remain available to produce capital goods and mass-consumption goods.

According to Elsenhans, the situation did not change fundamentally during the colonial age, when the export of raw materials began, and he therefore comes to the conclusion that 'The economic growth of today's Western industrialized nations cannot be put down to the exploitation of the Third World' (Elsenhans, 1984, p. 19).

The concepts which underlie this argument are problematic: primitive accumulation is reduced to the liberation of labour power, value to international purchasing power, and exploitation to the seizure of value (ibid., p. 11). It thus becomes logical to ask, 'How can the value of a fitter's labour power be compared with the value of a Third World smallholder's labour power?' (ibid., p. 131).

Wirz poses the question for slavery which Elsenhans endeavours to answer for the world economy as a whole and in general reaches the same conclusion:

> And although international trade may have facilitated and accelerated the industrial revolution by opening up new markets, making new materials available, and allowing the domestic market to expand, it was nevertheless, so far as we know, neither the reason nor the cause of this secular event.

He goes on to separate development and underdevelopment from each other: 'However, theories which regard development and underdevelopment as two necessarily mutually dependent phenomena of the capitalist world market are, at least as far as the 18th century is concerned, empirically unfounded' (Wirz, 1984, pp. 213f). Wirz favours the view that the significance of slavery to the development of the world system has long been overestimated and puts forward the following arguments (pp. 204ff) in support of this proposition:

1. The amount of revenue earned from the slave trade between 1761 and 1807 was never more than 7.9 per cent of England's entire investment in industry, and even then this figure is unrealistically high since the slave traders invested their profits elsewhere. (Wirz is of the opinion that realistically the figure could not have been more than 0.11 per cent.)
2. Income from the slave trade ran at a maximum of 1 per cent of England's national income, so that for England one must assume 'the economic marginality of the slave trade and profits from the slave trade'.
3. Even England's profits from her Caribbean colonies, which relied on slave labour, did not alter the picture, since the rate of return on capital there was less than 2 per cent. 'Even the acquisition of government debentures would have yielded more...'

Wirz and Elsenhans both fail to question the relevance of their calculations or at best do so gradually. They take into account only the transfer of goods and capital. The fact that the motherland or the metropole controls the basis of their calcuations is not important to them. In models of the capitalist economy the transfer and acquisition of labour power is not measurable, i.e. expressible in money terms, and cannot be so.

Using this method, the entire world market for labour power might well also be classified as being at best of secondary importance, perhaps because the labour power which it was responsible for supplying was not deployed at all in Europe until the 19th century; even after the 19th century there have only been a few countries and brief periods in which migrant workers constituted 10 per cent or more of the workforce. Moreover, the suggestion that migrant workers might have had any fundamental effect on the economic development of Europe and the USA could be denied on the grounds that they were often unqualified.

There are, however, both qualitative and quantitative arguments which point to the importance of the world market for labour power to the development of capitalism since the slave age: one thing which can be proved unequivocally is the fact that the labour power supplied through the world market for labour power was primarily deployed in those spheres which were of *fundamental* importance to the economic development of the individual nations which constitute the metropole. The Southern states of the USA produced cotton and other agricultural produce with labour power supplied by slaves, the industrialization of the North was sustained by an industrial proletariat made up of new immigrants and also by 'free' black workers.

In Europe industrialization began with the English textile industry. Not only was its basic raw material, cotton, produced by black slaves and later Egyptian *fellah*s, but the processing of that raw material was essentially carried out by Irish migrant workers. The mines in the Ruhr, which played a crucial part in Germany's industrialization, relied on Polish labour power.

Even today the world market for labour power is still important to the metropole, especially in periods of peak prosperity. In 1974, for example, 10.9 per cent of all those employed in West Germany were migrant workers. In France the figure was 11.1 per cent, in Switzerland 21.2 per cent, and in Belgium 8.8 per cent. At that particular time at least, those employed in free production zones and factories producing export goods for the world market should also have been added. So too should a substantial number of the migrant workers in the oil states, since many of these were working for European, American or Japanese firms.

One of the major areas in which the structures of the world market for labour power have played a crucial role is in the building of the world's infrastructure: the Panama and Suez canals, just to name the biggest canal construction projects, the railways of the USA and Canada, but also of Asia and Africa (which were made possible and completed as a result of colonial and imperialist exploitation there), were all built by slaves, coolies, forced labour and migrant workers. The same is true of the roads, motorways and underground systems of Western Europe, which were constructed primarily by migrant workers and forced labour.

In the final analysis it is debatable whether the world market for labour power has contributed more to the development of the metropole or to the underdevelopment of the colonized territories. This is particularly questionable as regards the initial stages in the development of the market, for one cannot be blind to the tremendous waste and destruction of labour power which occurred, labour power which was lost to the countries of origin, yet was never or only briefly deployed in the host countries and which was additionally deprived of every opportunity to pursue any kind of creative activity. Slavery was just one extreme example of this waste. The economic losses alone incurred by the colonies and countries still today not permitted to develop as a result of slavery, coolieism, colonial forced and migrant labour, the brain drain and labour migration – if it were possible to quantify them objectively – must surely be many times greater than the huge profits which the metropole drew from these forms of exploitation.

From what we have learned about the processes of the world market for labour power in this study it is more than evident that the over-exploitation of these untold millions of workers, above all from the colonized continents, was and is a permanent and integral part of the Western European and North American economies, and that this has been the basis of their development to present-day levels.

Notes

1. Examples include Bahadir's 1978 study of labour migration from Turkey, Lakhoua's detailed calculations for Tunisian labour migration (1976), works by Leuschner (1973), Blitz (1977), Nagel (1979), and others on the employment of foreigners in West Germany, and by Lebon (1978) on France.

2. Another calculation works on the assumption that German social insurance funds saved DM4,000 million on payments made to 120,000 workers and that in addition, bonuses of DM161 million paid to those returning home were offset by a saving of DM330 million that no longer had to be paid out in the form of unemployment benefit, shortened working week allowances and family allowance (*Frankfurter Rundschau*, 27 September 1985).

Bibliography

Adamson, Alan H., 1984, The Impact of Indentured Immigration on the Political Economy of British Guiana. In, Kay Saunders (ed.), *Indentured Labour in the British Empire 1834–1920*, London, Canberra, pp. 42–56.

Aderinto, Adeyemo, 1978, Toward a Better Understanding of Brain Drain. In, *Human Resources and African Development*, New York, p. 320–32.

Adler, Alfred, 1976, L'ethnologie marxiste: vers un nouvel obscurantisme? In, *L'homme*, Oct.–Dec. 1976, XVI (4), pp. 118–28.

Albertini, Rudolf von, 1976, *Europäische Kolonialherrschaft: die Expansion in übersee 1880–1940*, Zurich.

Alouane, Youssef, 1979, *L'émigration maghrébine en France*, Tunis.

Amin, Samir, 1974, Zur Theorie von Akkumulation und Entwicklung in der gegenwärtigen Weltgesellschaft. In, Senghaas, Dieter (ed.), *Peripherer Kapitalismus*, Frankfurt am Main, pp. 71–97.

———— 1976, *Unequal Development: An Essay on the Social Formations of Peripheral Capitalism*, Sussex.

ANBA (Amtliche Nachrichten der Bundesanstalt für Arbeit).

Anti-Slavery Society for the Protection of Human Rights (various material), London.

Arbeitsgruppe Bielefelder Entwicklungssoziologen, 1979, *Subsistenzproduction und Akkumulation*, Saarbrücken, Fort Lauderdale.

Auernheimer, Georg, 1984, Ausländerforschung (Migrationsforschung). In, *Handwörterbuch Ausländerarbeit*, Weinheim, Basle, pp. 58–62.

Aufhauser, Keith R., 1974, Profitability of Slavery in the British Caribbean. In, *Journal of Interdisciplinary History*, Cambridge, Mass., 5 (1974) 1, pp. 45–69.

Ausländerbeschäftigung und Imperialismus, 1971. In, *Das Argument*, 68, Berlin.

Ausländer raus aus Nigeria! Massenausweisung als Heil allen wirtschaftlichen Übels?, 1983. In, *Blätter des iz3w*, 108, Freiburg, pp. 35–40.

Ausländische Arbeitnehmer in Westeuropa, 1980, *Aktuelle JRO Landkarte*, vol. 27 8/80, Munich.

Avineri, Shlomo, 1968, *Karl Marx on Colonialism and Modernization*, New York.

Bade, Klaus J., 1983, *Vom Auswanderungsland zum Einwanderungsland? Deutschland 1880–1980*, Berlin.

Bahadir, Sefik Alp, 1978, Volkswirtschaftliche Kosten und Nutzen des Exports von Arbeitskräften. In, *Außenwirtschaft*, 33, 1978/4, pp. 350–4.

Bald, Detlef, Heller, P., Hundsdörfer, V. and Paschen, J., 1978, *Die Liebe zum Imperium: Deutschlands dunkle Vergangenheit in Afrika*, Bremen.

Barnet, Miguel (ed.), 1976, *Der Cimarron: die Lebensgeschichte eines entflohenen Negersklaven aus Cuba, von ihm selbst erzählt*, Frankfurt am Main.

Barth, Gunter, 1964, *Bitter Strength: A History of the Chinese in the United States 1850–1870*, Cambridge.

Bauer, Otto, 1906–7, Proletarische Wanderungen. In, *Die Neue Zeit*, no. 41, vol. 25/2, pp. 476–94.

Becker, Carl, 1933, *The Declaration of Independence*, New York.

Becker, Ruth, Dörr, G. and Tjaden, K. H., 1971, Fremdarbeiterbeschäftigung im deutschen Kapitalismus. In, *Das Argument*, 68, 9/10, pp. 741–56.

Beer, Ursula, 1983, Marx auf Füße gestellt? Zum theoretischen Entwurf von Claudia von Werlhof. In, *Probleme des Klassenkampfes*, 50, pp. 22–37.

Benard, Cheryl, 1981, *Die geschlossene Gesellschaft und ihre Rebellen: die internationale Frauenbewegung und die Schwarze Bewegung in den USA*, Frankfurt am Main.

Bennholdt-Thomsen, Veronika, 1979, Marginalität in Lateinamerika. In, *Lateinamerika, Analysen und Berichte*, 3, Berlin, pp. 45–85.

———— 1980, Die stumme Auflehnung der Bauersfrauen: Bericht aus einem Dorf im Süden Mexikos. In, *Beiträge 3 zur feministischen Theorie und Praxis, Frauen und 'dritte' Welt*, Munich, pp. 49–56.

———— 1981, Subsistenzproduction und erweiterte Reproduction. In, *Gesellschaft – Beiträge zur Marxschen Theorie*, Frankfurt am Main, pp. 30–51.

———— Mies, Maria and Werlhof, Claudia von, 1983, Frauen, die letzte Kolonie. In, *Technologie und Politik*, 20, Reinbek.

Bergquist, Charles (ed.), 1984, *Labor in the Capitalist World-Economy*, Beverly Hills.

Bevölkerungspolitik und Sterilisationsmißrauch, 1977. In, *Clio* 4.

Birks, J. S. and Sinclair, C. A., 1980, *International Migration and Development in the Arab Region*, Geneva.

Blaschke, Jochen and Greussing, Kurt (eds), 1980, *'Dritte Welt' in Europa: Probleme der Arbeitsimmigration*, Frankfurt am Main.

Blitz, Rudolf C., 1977, A Benefit-Cost Analysis of Foreign Workers in West Germany, 1957–1973. In, *Kyklos*, vol. 30, no. 3, pp. 479–502.

Bodley, John H., 1983, *Der Weg der Zerstörung: Stammesvölker und industrielle Zivilisation*, Munich.

Bogues, Tony, 1982, Eine 400 Jahre alte Plantage – zur politischen Ökonomie Jamaikas. In, *Dub Version*, Berlin, pp. 44–64.

Böhning, Wolf Rüdiger, 1984, Arbeitsmigration. In, Auernheimer, Georg (ed.), *Handwörterbuch Ausländerarbeit*, Basle, pp. 32–5.

Bonte, Pierre, 1976, Marxisme et anthropologie: les malheurs d'un empiriste. In, *L'homme*, Oct.–Dec. 1976, XVI (4), pp. 129–36.

Bowser, Frederick P., 1974, *The African Slave in Colonial Peru: 1524–1650*, Stanford, California.

Braig, Marianne and Lentz, Carola, 1983, Wider der Enthistorisierung der Marxschen Werttheorie: Kritische Anmerkungen zur Kategorie Subsistenzproduktion. In, *Probleme des Klassenkampfes*, 50, pp. 5–21.

Brand, J. van den, 1902, *De millioenen uit Deli*, Amsterdam.

Brandes, Volkhard and Tibi, Bassam (eds), 1975, *Handbuch 2 – Unterentwicklung*, Frankfurt am Main, Cologne.

Brückner, Reinhard and Hättig, Walter, 1985, Der Apartheidstaat 1985: Wirtschaftskrise, 'Reformen', Bürgerkrieg. In, *Blätter des iz3w*, 126, June 1985, pp. 20–27.

Buch, Hans Christoph, 1976, *Die Scheidung von San Domingo: wie die Negersklaven von Haiti Robespierre beim Wort nahmen*, Berlin.

Bucharin, N., 1926, *Der Imperialismus und die Akkumulation des Kapitals*, Berlin, Vienna.

―――― 1929, *Imperialismus und Weltwirtschaft*, Berlin, Vienna.

Bundesanstalt für Arbeit, 1970, *Ausländische Arbeitnehmer*, Nuremburg.

Bundesministerium für Bildung und Wissenschaft, 1980, Daten zur Situation der Ausländerfamilien. In, *Der Arbeitgeber*, 3/32, 1980.

Burakumin/Japan, 1983, Die Diskrimierung einer Minderheit in Japan. In, *Pogrom 98*, pp. 22–5.

Callinicos, Luli, 1982, *Die Geschichte des südafrikanischen Volkes, Vol. 1: Gold in Südafrika: Schwarze Arbeit – Weißer Reichtum*, Bonn.

Campbell, Persia Crawford, 1923, *Chinese Coolie Emigration within the British Empire*, London.

Castles, Stephen, 1987, *Migration und Rassismus in Westeuropa*, Berlin.

Cespedes, Augusto, 1982, *Teufelsmetall*, Bornheim.

Chapa, Jorge, 1981, Wage Labor in the Periphery: Silver Mining in Colonial Mexico. In *Review*, 4 (1981) 3, Fernand Braudel Center for the Study of Economics, Historical Systems and Civilization, Binghamton, New York, pp. 509–34.

Chattopadhyay, Amal Kumar, 1959, *Slavery in India*, Calcutta.

Chen, Jack, 1981, *The Chinese of America*, San Francisco.

Chiroux, René, 1979, Les travailleurs étrangers et le développement des relations internationales. In, *Les travailleurs étrangers et le droit international*, Societé Française pour le Droit International, Colloque de Clermont Ferrand, Paris, pp. 3–174.

Chiswick, Barry R., 1980, Immigrant Earning Patterns by Sex, Race, and Ethnic Groups. In, *Monthly Labour Review*, vol. 103/10, pp. 22–5.

Christian Science Monitor (weekly international edition), Boston, 7 February 1983.

Columbus, Christopher, 1981, *Schiffstagebuch*, Frankfurt am Main.

Conan Doyle, Arthur, 1985, *Das Congoverbrechen*, Frankfurt am Main.

Cordova, Armando, 1974, Rosa Luxemburg und die Dritte Welt. In, Pozzoli, Claudio (ed.), *Rosa Luxemburg oder die Bestimmung des Sozialismus*, Frankfurt am Main, pp. 65–93.

Curtin, Philip De Armond, 1970, *Atlantic Slave Trade: A Census*, Madison.

Datta, Asit, 1982, *Ursachen der Unterentwicklung – Erklärungsmodelle und Entwicklungspläne*, Munich.

Davidson, Basil, 1966, *Vom Sklavenhandel zur Kolonisierung: Afrikanisch-europäische Beziehungen zwischen 1500 und 1900*, Hamburg.

Davis, Angela, 1982, *Rassismus und Sexismus: schwarze Frauen und Klassenkampf in den USA*, Berlin.

Davis, Kingsley, 1951, *The Population of India and Pakistan*, Princeton, New Jersey.

Demps, Laurenz, 1974, Einige Bemerkungen zur Veränderung der innenpolitischen Situation im faschistischen Deutschland durch den Einsatz ausländischer Zwangsarbeiter. In the series *Fremdarbeiterpolitik des Imperialismus*, issue 1: *Wesen und Kontinuität der Fremdarbeiterpolitik des deutschen Imperialismus*, Rostock (unnumbered), pp. 97–118.

Dettloff, Ariane and Kirchmann, Hans, 1981, *Arbeitsstaat Japan: Exportdrohung gegen die Gewerkschaften*, Reinbek.

Deutsch muß die Familie sein: zur Vertreibungspolitik gegen Ausländer, 1984. In, *Materialien gegen Bevölkerungspolitik*, Hamburg, pp. 50–1.

Dieterich, Heinz, 1981, *Produktionsverhältnisse in Lateinamerika: Inkareich, hispano-amerikanische Kolonisation und kapitalistische Entwicklung; zur Kritik der Dependenz-Theorie*, Giessen.

Dohse, K., 1981, *Ausländische Arbeiter und bürgerlicher Staat: Genese und Funktion von staatlicher Ausländerpolitik und Ausländerrecht*, Königstein.

Drescher, Seymour, 1977, *Econocide: British Slavery in the Era of Abolition*, Pittsburgh, Pennsylvania.

Duchac, R., 1973, Chronique de l'émigration. In, CRESM (ed.), *Annuaire de l'Afrique du Nord*, Paris.

Eckstein, Gustav, 1903–4, Chinesische Kuli. In, *Die Neue Zeit*, nos. 2 and 3, vol. 22/1, pp. 52–8 and 85–90.

———— 1906–7, Zur Kulifrage. In, *Die Neue Zeit*, no. 13, vol. 25/2, pp. 548–55.

———— 1910, Der Parteitag von Chicago und die Kulifrage. In, *Die Neue Zeit*, no. 48, vol. 28/2, pp. 786–96.

Economist, The, London.

Ehrke, Michael, 1981, *Mexikanische Einwanderung in die USA: Analysen aus der Abteilung Entwicklungsländerforschung*, no. 88, Jan. 1981, Friedrich-Ebert-Stiftung, Bonn.

Ehrlich, A., Ehrlich, P. R. and Bilderback, L., 1979, *The Golden Door – International Migration between Mexico and the United States*, New York.

Eichholtz, Dietrich, 1974, Das Zwangsarbeitersystem des faschistischen deutschen Imperialismus in der Kontinuität imperialistischer Fremdarbeiterpolitik. In the series *Fremdarbeiterpolitik des Imperialismus*, no. 1: *Wesen und Kontinuität der Fremdarbeiterpolitik des deutschen Imperialismus*, Rostock (unnumbered), pp. 77–96.

Elsenhans, Hartmut, 1978, Mobilität der Arbeitskraft und Akkumulation: Aspekte einer sozioökonomischen Theorie des internationalen Systems. In, *Migration und Wirtschaftsentwicklung*, Frankfurt am Main, New York, pp. 9–30.

———— 1979, Grundlagen der Entwicklung der kapitalistischen Weltwirtschaft. In, Senghaas, Dieter (ed.), *Kapitalistische Weltökonomie: Kontroverse über ihren Ursprung und ihre Entwicklungsdynamik*, Frankfurt am Main, pp. 103–50.

———— 1984, *Nord-Süd Beziehungen: Geschichte – Politik – Wirtschaft*, Stuttgart.

Elsner, Lothar, 1974, Zum Wesen und zur Kontinuität der Fremdarbeiterpolitik des deutschen Imperialismus. In the series *Fremdarbeiterpolitik des Imperialismus*, no. 1: *Wesen und Kontinuität der Fremdarbeiterpolitik des deutschen Imperialismus*. Rostock (unnumbered), pp. 2–76.

Eltis, D., 1972, The Traffic in Slaves Between the British West Indian Colonies, 1807–1833. In, *Economic History Review*, Cambridge, Ser. 2.25 (1972) 1, pp. 55–64.

Elwert, Georg and Wong, Diana, 1979, Thesen zum Verhältnis von Subsistenzproduktion und Warenproduktion in der Dritten Welt. In, Arbeitsgruppe Beilfelder Soziologen, *Subsistenzproduktion und Akkumulation*, Saarbrücken, Fort Lauderdale, pp. 255–78.

Emmanuel, Arghiri, 1969, *L'échange inégal*, Paris.

Emmer, Pieter, 1984, The Importation of British Indians into Surinam (Dutch Guiana), 1873–1916. In, Marks, Shula and Richardson, Peter, *International Labour Migration: Historical Perspectives*, London, pp. 90–111.

Endt, Peter, 1918, Die Wanderarbeiterverhältnis in Indien. In, *Die Neue Zeit*, nos. 24 and 25, vol. 36/2, pp. 560–4 and 585–9.

Engl, Luise and Theodor, 1975, *Die Eroberung Perus in Augenzeugenberichten*, Munich.

Ennew, Judith, 1981, *Debt Bondage: A Survey*, Anti-Slavery Society, London.

Ernst, Angelika, 1980, *Japans unvollkommene Vollbeschäftigung*, Institut für Asienkunde, Hamburg.

Ernst, Klaus and Schilling, Hartmut (eds), 1981, *Entwicklungsländer: sozialökonomische Prozesse und Klassen*, Berlin (GDR).

Ersu, P.-H. and Wagner, Michael, no date, *L'insertion professionelle des travailleurs migrants qui retournent dans leur pays d'origine*. Report presented to CAHRS (Comité des Conseillers du Représentant spécial pour le réfugiés de Population) of the Council of Europe.

Esser, Hartmut, 1980, *Aspekte der Wanderungssoziologie: Assimilation und Integration von Wanderen, ethnischen Gruppen und Minderheiten*, Darmstadt, Neuwied.

———— 1983, Ist das Ausländerproblem in der Bundesrepublik Deutschland ein 'Türkenproblem'? In, Italiaander, Rolf (ed.), *'Fremde raus?' Fremdenangst und Ausländerfeindlichkeit*, Frankfurt am Main, pp. 169–79.

Evans, Raymond, 1984, 'Kings' in Brass Crescents: Defining Aboriginal Labour Patterns in Colonial Queensland. In, Saunders, Kay (ed.), *Indentured Labour in the British Empire 1834–1920*, London, Canberra, pp. 183–212.

Faulwetter, Helmut, 1977, The Reverse Transfer of Technology (Brain Drain) – Instrument of Neo-colonialist Exploitation and an Impediment to the Development of Science and Technology in Developing Countries. In, *Wissenschaftliche Beiträge*, Berlin (GDR), 12 (1977) 3, pp. 5–13.

Ferencz, Benjamin B., 1981, *Lohn des Grauens: die verweigerte Entschädigung für jüdische Zwangsarbeiter*, Frankfurt am Main, New York.

Ferenczi, Emerich, 1913, *Die Arbeitslosigkeit und die internationalen Arbeiterbewegungen*, Jena.

Fett, Roland and Heller, Elenor, 1982, Von der Subsistenzökonomie zur Marktproduktion – die Transformation der bäuerlichen Ökonomie der Boko in Nord-Bénin. In, Elwert, Georg and Fett, Roland (eds), *Afrika zwischen Subsistenzökonomie und Imperialismus*, Frankfurt am Main, New York, pp. 70–92.

Fieldhouse, David Kenneth, 1965, *Die Kolonialreiche seit dem 18. Jahrhundert*, (*Fischer Weltgeschichte*, Vol. 29), Frankfurt am Main.

Fischer, Cornelia and Heier, Dieter, 1983, *Entwicklungen der Arbeitsmarkttheorie*, Frankfurt am Main, New York.

Fischer, Emil, 1906–7, Die Verwendung von Kuli als Lohnarbeiter in der deutschen Seeschiffahrt. In, *Die Neue Zeit*, no. 19, vol. 25/2, pp. 790–6.

Fonck, T., 1917, *Farbige Hilfsvölker – die militärische Bedeutung für unsere koloniale Zukunft*, Berlin.

Frank, Andre Gunder, 1968, *Kapitalismus und Unterentwicklung in Lateinamerika*, Frankfurt am Main.

———— 1977, On So-called Primitive Accumulation. In, *Dialectical Anthropology*, no. 2, pp. 87–106.

Franklin, John Hope, 1983, *Negro: die Geschichte der Schwarzen in den USA*, Frankfurt am Main, Berlin, Vienna.

Friederici, Georg, 1925, 1936, 1936a, *Der Charakter der Entdeckung und Eroberung durch die Europäer*, vols. I–III, Stuttgart.

Fröbel, Folker, Heinrichs, Jürgen and Kreye, Otto, 1977, *Die neue internationale Arbeitsteilung*, Reinbek.

———— 1980, Weltweite Reorganisation der Produktion - eine Replik. In, *Kritik*, no. 25, pp. 73–85.

———— 1982, Die Ware Arbeitskraft. In, *Der Überblick*, 1/82, pp. 1–5.

_____ 1986, *Umbruch in der Weltwirtschaft*, Reinbek.

Furtwängler, F. J., 1929, Koloniale Zwangsarbeit. In, *Arbeit*, 6, pp. 789–96.

Galeano, Eduardo, 1980, *Die offenen Adern Lateinamerikas*, Wuppertal.

Galenson, David, 1979, The Slave Trade to the English West Indies, 1673–1724. In, *Economic History Review*, 32 (1979) 2, Hertfordshire, pp. 241–9.

Gandhi, Mahatma, 1983, *Mein Leben*, Frankfurt am Main.

Geiger, Wolfgang and Mansilla, H. C. F., 1983, *Unterentwicklung; Theorien und Strategien zu ihrer Überwindung*, Frankfurt am Main.

Geiselberger, Siegmar (ed.), 1972, *Schwarzbuch: ausländische Arbeiter*, Frankfurt am Main.

Genovese, Eugene D., 1972, *In Red and Black: Marxian Explorations in Southern and Afro-American History*, New York.

Gernet, Jacques, 1979, *Die chinesische Welt*, Frankfurt am Main.

Gervasi, Sean, 1972, *Industrialisierung, Fremdkapital und Zwangsarbeit in Südafrika*, Offenbach.

Goslinga, Cornelius C., 1979, *A Short History of the Netherlands, Antilles and Surinam*, The Hague, Boston, London.

Graves, Adrian, 1984, The Nature and Origins of Pacific Islands Labour Migration to Queensland, 1863–1906. In, Marks, Shula and Richardson, Peter, *International Labour Migration: Historical Perspectives*, London, pp. 112–39.

Grebeler, Leo, Moore, Joan and Guzman, Ralph, 1970, *The Mexican American People: the Nation's Second Greatest Minority*, New York.

Green, Willian A., 1984, The West Indies and Indentured Labour Migration – the Jamaican Experience. In, Saunders, Kay (ed.), *Indentured Labour in the British Empire 1834–1920*, London, Canberra, pp. 1–41.

Griese, Hartmut M. (ed.), 1984, *Der gläserne Fremde: Bilanz und Kritik der Gastarbeiterforschung und der Ausländerpädagogik*, Opladen.

Grieshaber, Erwin P., 1979, Hacienda: Indian Community Relations and Indian Acculturation: an Historiographical Essay. In, *Latin American Research Review*, 14 (1979) 3, pp. 107–29, Chapel Hill, NC.

Grimm, Klaus, 1979, *Theorien der Unterentwicklung und Entwicklungsstrategien*, Opladen.

Grohs, G., 1976, Probleme der Imperialismustheorie. In, TU Berlin, *Probleme der Entwicklungsländer und der Entwicklungspolitik, TUB – Dokumentation aktuell 2*, pp. 24–37.

Gross, Bernd, Stevens, Willi and Werth, Manfred, 1982, *Akademiker aus Entwicklungsländern in der Bundesrepublik Deutschland: zwischen Brain-Drain und Rückkehr*, Saarbrücken, Fort Lauderdale.

Häbler, Konrad, 1895, Die Anfänge der Sklaverei in Amerika. In, *Zeitschrift für Sozial- und Wirtschaftsgeschichte*, vol. IV, 1895, pp. 176–223.

Hall, Gwendolyn Midlo, 1971, *Social Control in Slave Plantation Societies: a Comparison of St Domingo and Cuba*, Baltimore and elsewhere.

Halliday, Fred, Labor Migration in the Middle East. In, *MERIP Reports*, no. 59, pp. 3–17.

Hancock, Mary, 1983, Transnational Production and Women Workers. In, Phizacklea, Annie (ed.), *One Way Ticket: Migration and Female Labour*, London, pp. 131–46.

Harbach, Heinz, 1976, *Internationale Schichtung und Arbeitsmigration*, Hamburg.

Hättig, Walter, 1985, Zwangsumsiedlung – die häßlichste Seite der Apartheid. In, *Blätter des iz3w*, no. 126, June 1985, pp. 32–6.

Haug, Werner, 1978, *Einwanderung, Frauenarbeit, Mutterschaft: Probleme der schweizerischen Bevölkerungsentwicklung und Bevölkerungspolitik 1945–1976*, Bern.

Heckmann, Friedrich, 1981, *Die Bundesrepublik – ein Einwanderungsland*, Stuttgart.

Hein, Wolfgang, 1981, Fachübersicht: zur Theorie der Unterentwicklung und ihrer Überwindung. In, *Peripherie*, 5/6, pp. 64–91.

Hell, Jürgen, 1981, Das Schiffstagebuch des Columbus im Kontext der großen Entdeckungen. In, Columbus, Christoph, *Schiffstagebuch*, Frankfurt am Main, pp. 169–90.

Hertzmann, Lewis, 1980, Canada: L'Immigration au Canada avant et après la Confédération. In, *Les migrations internationales de la fin du 18e siècle à nos jours*, Paris, pp. 79–107.

Hiemenz, Ulrich and Schatz, Klaus-Werner, 1977, Internationale Arbeitsteilung als Alternative zur Ausländerbeschäftigung – der Fall der Bundesrepublik Deutschland. In, *Die Weltwirtschaft*, 1, pp. 35–58.

–––––– 1979, *Trade in Place of Migration*, Geneva.

Hilferding, Rudolf, 1974, *Das Finanzkapital*, 2 vols., Frankfurt am Main.

Hoffman-Nowotny, Hans-Joachim, 1970, *Migration: ein Beitrag zu einer soziologischen Erklärung*, Stuttgart.

–––––– 1973, *Soziologie des Fremdarbeiterproblems*, Stuttgart.

–––––– 1981, A Sociological Approach Toward a General Theory of Migration. In, *Global Trends in Migration*, New York, pp. 64–83.

Hopkins, Terence K. and Wallerstein, Immanuel, 1979, Grundzüge der Entwicklung des modernen Weltsystems: Entwurf für ein Forschungsvorhaben. In, Senghaas, Dieter (ed.), *Kapitalistische Weltökonomie: Kontroversen über ihren Ursprung und ihre Entwicklungsdynamik*, pp. 151–200.

Houdaille, J. and Sauvy, A., 1974, L'Immigration clandestine dans le monde. In, *Population*, no. 4–5.

Hübner-Dick, Giesela and Seidelmann, Raimund, 1978, Der Faktor Arbeit in der Südafrikanischen Republik. In, Elsenhans, Hartmut (ed.), *Migration und Wirtschaftsentwicklung*, Frankfurt am Main, New York.

L'Immigration en France en 1977, 1978. Statistiques du Travail Supplement au Bulletin Mensuel, Paris.

Jacobi, Carola and Niess, Thomas, 1980, *Hausfrauen, Bauern, Marginalisierte: Überlebensproduktion in 'Dritter' und 'Erster' Welt*, Saarbrücken, Fort Lauderdale.

Jacobson, David, Wickham, Ann and Wickham, James, 1980, Babbage und Dependenztheorie: eine untaugliche Synthese zur Erklärung der neuen internationalen Arbeitsteilung. In, *Kritik*, no. 24, pp. 121–8.

Jain, Ravindra K., 1984, South Indian Labour in Malaya, 1840–1920: Asylum, Stability and Involution. In, Saunders, Kay (ed.), *Indentured Labour in the British Empire 1834–1920*, London, Canberra, pp. 158–82.

Jalée, Pierre, 1971, *Das neueste Stadium des Imperialismus*, Munich.

James, Ibrahim, 1983, Nigeria, Alien Influx and the ECOWAS Treaty: National Sovereignty Versus Supranational Allegiance. In, *Genève-Afrique*, 21 (1983) 1, Geneva, pp. 7–24.

Jungbluth, Adolf, 1984, *Die arbeitenden Menschen: ihre Geschichte und Schicksal*, Cologne.

Junne, Gerd, 1980, Entwicklungstendenzen und Folgen der internationale Arbeitsteilung. In, *Kritik*, no. 26, pp. 84–99.

Kamara, Sylviane, 1980, Personne n'en veut. In, *Jeune Afrique*, no. 1032, 15 October 1980.

Kammerer, Peter, 1980, Arbeitsimmigration, Zusammensetzung der Arbeiterklasse und sozio-ökonomische Stabilität. In, Blaschke, Jochen (ed.), 'Dritte Welt' in Europa: Probleme der Arbeitsimmigration, Frankfurt am Main.

Kaneko, Martin, 1979, Soziale Schichtung und Arbeitsstruktur in diskriminierten Buraku. In, Beiträge zur Japanologie, Institut für Japanologie, Vienna, pp. 295–319.

Kapitalismus in Entwicklungsländern, 1983, research findings, Berlin.

Karstedt, Oskar and Werder, Peter von, 1941, Die Afrikanische Arbeiterfrage, Berlin.

Katayama, S., 1910, Japanisch-amerikanische Probleme. In, Die Neue Zeit, no. 67, vol. 28 (2), pp. 732–43.

Katsoulis, Haris, 1978, Bürger zweiter Klasse – Ausländer in der Bundesrepublik, Frankfurt am Main, New York.

Kautsky, Karl, 1883, Auswanderung und Kolonisation, eine Entgegnung II. In, Die Neue Zeit, no. 9, vol. 1, pp. 393–404.

———— 1910, Der Kongreß von Kopenhagen. In, Die Neue Zeit, no. 48, vol. 28 (2), pp. 772–9.

Keely, Charles B., 1978, Vereinigte Staaten von Amerika. In, Gehmacher, Ernst, Kubat, Daniel and Mehrländer, Ursula (eds), Ausländerpolitik im Konflikt, Bonn, pp. 21–34.

———— and Elwell, Patricia J., 1981, International Migration: Canada and the United States. In, Global Trends in Migration, New York, pp. 181–207.

Khalatbari, Parviz, 1977, Bevölkerungsdynamik und Gesellschaft, Berlin.

Kidd, Charles V., 1967, Migration of Health Personnel, Scientists, and Engineers from Latin America, Washington D.C. Pan American Health Organization Scientific Publication no. 142.

Killingray, Davis and Matthews, James, 1979, Beasts of Burden: British West African Carriers in the First World War. In, Canadian Journal of African Studies, 13 (1979) 1–2, Ottawa, pp. 5–23.

Ki-Zerbo, Joseph, 1979, Die Geschichte Schwarz-Afrikas, Wuppertal.

Klein, Herbert S. and Engermann, Stanley L., 1979, A Note on Mortality in the French Slave Trade in the Eighteenth Century. In, Gemery, Henry A. and Hogendorn, Jan S., The Uncommon Market: Essays in the Economic History of the Atlantic Slave Trade, New York and elsewhere, pp. 261–72.

Kloosterboer, Willemina, 1976, Involuntary Labour since the Abolition of Slavery: a Survey of Compulsory Labour Throughout the World, Westport (Connecticut). Reprint of the Leiden Edition, 1960.

Knight, Franklin W., 1978, The Caribbean: The Genesis of a Fragmented Nationalism, New York.

Kogon, Eugen, 1948, Der SS-Staat, Munich.

Köhne, 1901, Arbeiterverhältnisse. In, Festschrift zum VIII. Allgemeinen Deutschen Bergmannstag in Dortmund am 11.–14. September 1901.

Die Kolonisation Senegambiens: ein Beitrag zur Kolonisationsfrage, 1883. In, Das Ausland: Wochenschrift für Länder- u. Völkerkunde, no. 21, vol. 56 (21 May 1883), pp. 413–14.

Kondapi, C., 1951, Indians Overseas 1838–1949, Bombay, Calcutta, Madras, London.

Konetzke, Richard, 1960, Die Mestizen in der kolonialen Gesetzgebung: zum Rassenproblem im spanischen Amerika. In, Archiv für Kulturgeschichte, vol. 42, no. 2, pp. 131–77.

———— 1965, Süd- und Mittelamerika I (Fischer Weltgeschichte vol. 22),

Frankfurt am Main.

Die Konkurrenz der indischen Kulis, 1883. In, *Die Neue Zeit*, vol. 1, no. 4, pp. 198f.

Kornberger, Reiner, 1980, *Noviembre Negro – Massaker und Widerstand in Bolivien*, Frankfurt am Main.

Kossok, Manfred and Markov, Walter, 1955–56, Konspekt über das spanische Kolonialsystem. In, *Wissenschaftliche Zeitschrift der Karl-Marx-Universität*, no. 111, Leipzig, pp. 230–65.

Krogbäumker, Beate, 1980, *Dokumentation neuerer Arbeiten zum 'Verhältnis von Subsistenz- und Warenproduktion'*, Universität Bielefeld, Universitätsschwerpunkt Lateinamerikaforschung, working paper no. 22, October 1980.

Kung, Shien-woo, 1962, *Chinese in American life: Some Aspects of their History, Status, Problems and Contributions*, Seattle.

Kwok, Viem and Leland, Hayne, 1982, An Economic Model of the Brain Drain. In, *American Economic Review*, vol. 72, no. 1, pp. 91–100.

Lakhoua, Mohamed F., 1976, *Cost-benefit Analysis of Exporting Workers: the Tunisian Case*, Michigan State University, thesis.

Lal, Brij V., 1984, Labouring Men and Nothing More: Some Problems of Indian Indenture in Fiji. In, Saunders, Kay (ed.), *Indentured Labour in the British Empire 1834–1920*, London, Canberra, pp. 126–57.

Landauer, Carl, 1981, *Sozial- und Wirtschaftsgeschichte der Vereinigten Staaten von Amerika*, Stuttgart.

Lang, James, 1979, *Portuguese Brazil: the King's Plantation*, New York.

Lannes, Xavier, 1953, *L'Immigration en France depuis 1945*, La Haye.

Las Casas, Bartolomé, 1981, *Kurzgefaßter Bericht von der Verwüstung der Westindischen Länder*, Frankfurt am Main.

Lebon, 1978, Les Migrations externes (Approches diverses de quelques aspects significatifs du fait migratoire en France). In, *Revue Française des Affaires Sociales*, vol. 32, April–June.

Lemoine, Maurice, 1983, *Bitterer Zucker: Sklaven heute in der Karibik*, Zurich.

Lenin, V. I., 1959, *Werke*, vols. 3, 19, 21, 22, 23, Berlin.

———— 1978, *Imperialism, the Highest Stage of Capitalism*, 17th Edition, Moscow.

Lenins Imperialismustheorie und die Gegenwart, 1980, Berlin.

Leuschner, Dieter, 1973, Volkswirtschaftliche Kosten und Erträge der Beschäftigung ausländischer Arbeitnehmer. In, *Zeitschrift für die gesamte Staatswissenschaft*, vol. 129, no. 4, pp. 702–13.

Lewis, G. J., 1982, *Human Migration: a Geographical Perspective*, London.

Linhart, Robert, 1980, *Der Zucker und der Hunger*, Berlin.

Loewen, James W., 1971, *The Mississippi Chinese: Between Black and White*, Cambridge (Harvard East Asian Series, 63).

Loth, Heinrich, 1981, *Sklaverei: die Geschichte des Sklavenhandels zwischen Afrika und Amerika*, Wuppertal.

Luxemburg, Rosa, 1951, *The Accumulation of Capital*, London.

———— 1975, Die Akkumulation des Kapitals — eine Antikritik. In, Luxemburg, Rosa, *Gesammelte Werke*, vol. 5, Berlin, pp. 415–23.

———— 1974, Die Krise der Sozialdemokratie. In, Luxemburg, Rosa, *Gesammelte Werke*, vol. 4, Berlin, pp. 51–164.

Mackintosh, Maureen, 1977, Reproduction and Patriarchy: A Critique of Claude Meillassoux, 'Femmes, Greniers et Capitaux'. In, *Capital and Class* 1977 (summer), pp. 119–27.

Magdoff, Harry, 1970, *Das Zeitalter des Imperialismus: die ökonomischen*

Hintergründe der US-Außenpolitik, Frankfurt am Main.

Mamozai, Martha, 1982, *Herrenmenschen: Frauen im deutschen Kolonialismus*, Hamburg.

Mandel, Ernest, 1968, *Marxistische Wirtschaftstheorie*, 2 vols., Frankfurt am Main.

———— 1972, *Der Spätkapitalismus*, Frankfurt am Main.

Mandeng, Patrice, 1973, *Auswirkungen der deutschen Kolonialherrschaft in Kamerun: die Arbeitskräftebeschaffung in den Südbezirken Kameruns während der deutschen Kolonialherrschaft 1884–1914*, Hamburg.

Mannix, Daniel P., 1971, *Black cargoes: a History of an Atlantic Slave Trade, 1518–1865*, New York.

Marks, Shula and Richardson, Peter (eds), 1984, *International Labour Migration: Historical Perspectives*, London.

Martin, Jean I., 1978, *The Migrant Presence*, Canberra.

Marx, Karl, 1954, *Capital*, vol. I, London.

———— 1974, *Capital*, vol. II, reprint of the 1957 edition, London.

———— 1977, *Gundrisse (GR)*, English reprint of the 1973 edition, London.

———— and Engels, Friedrich, 1976, *Werke (MEW)*, various volumes, Berlin.

Massey, Douglas S. and Schnabel, Kathleen M., 1983, Recent Trends in Hispanic Immigration to the United States. In, *International Migration Review*, vol. 17, no. 2.

Materialien gegen Bevölkerungspolitik, 1984, Hamburg.

McGregor Ross, W., 1927, *Kenya from Within: a Short Political History*, London.

McLean Petras, Elizabeth, 1981, The Global Labor Market in the Modern World-Economy. In, *Global Trends in Migration*, New York, pp. 44–63.

Meillassoux, Claude, 1976, *Die wilden Früchte der Frau: über häusliche Produktion und Kapitalistische Wirtschaft*, Frankfurt am Main.

Meinardus, Marc, 1982, *Marginalität – Theoretische Aspekte und entwicklungspolitische Konsequenzen*, Saarbrücken.

Meinicke-Kleint, 1961, Der deutsche Imperialismus und die Verschärfung der Widersprüche zwischen den imperialistischen Ländern in Nordafrika (Marokko, Algerien, Tunesien). In, *Konferenz Probleme des Neokolonialismus, 5–8.4.1961 in Leipzig*, interim report.

Meuschel, Sigrid, 1981, *Kapitalismus oder Sklaverei: die langwierige Durchsetzung der bürgerlichen Gesellschaft in den USA*, Frankfurt am Main.

Michels, Peter M., 1976, *Wetbacks, Koyoten und Gorillas: Arbeitskämpfe der Farmarbeiter in den USA*, Frankfurt am Main.

Mies, Maria, 1982, *The Lace Makers of Narsapur*, London.

———— 1983, Subsistenzproduktion, Hausfrauisierung, Kolonisierung. In, *Beiträge zur feministischen Theorie und Praxis, no. 9/10: Zukunft der Frauenarbeit*, Cologne, pp. 115–24.

Minces, Juliette, 1973, *Les travailleurs étrangers en France*, Paris.

Minchinton, Walter E., 1979, The Triangular Trade Revisited. In, Gemery, Henry A. and Hogendorn, Jan S., *The Uncommon Market: Essays in the Economic History of the Atlantic Slave Trade*, New York, pp. 331–52.

Morel, Edmund D., 1904, *King Leopold's Rule in Africa*, London.

Morokvasic, Mirjana, 1983, Women in Migration: Beyond the Reductionist on Hook. In, Phizacklea, Annie (ed.), *One Way Ticket: Migration and Female Labour*, London and elsewhere, pp. 13–32.

Mühlenberg, Friedrich, 1967, *Wanderarbeit in Südafrika: Ursachen eines Arbeitsmarktphänomens dualistischer Wirtschaftsgesellschaften*, Stuttgart.

Mukherjee, Santos, 1981, 'Pseudo-Entwicklung' und Arbeitslosigkeit – Perspektiven der Beschäftigung in Industrie- und Entwicklungsländern. In, Bruchstellen, *Industrialisierung und Planung in der Dritten Welt*, Frankfurt am Main.

Müller, Fritz Ferdinand, 1962, *Kolonien unter der Peitsche*, Berlin.

Münscher, Alice, 1979, *Ausländische Familien in der BRD: Familiennachzug und generatives Verhalten*, Munich.

Nagel, Gerhard, 1979, *Volkswirtschaftliche Kosten von Wanderungen*, Hanover.

Negt, Oskar and Kluge, Alexander, 1981, *Geschichte und Eigensinn*, Frankfurt am Main.

Newland, Kathleen, 1979, *International Migration: The Search for Work*, Worldwatch Paper 33.

Newton, John R. and Osborn, T. Noel, 1980, A Profile of Legal Mexican Migration to the United States. In, Poulson, Barry W. and Osborn, T. Noel, *US–Mexico Economic Relations*, Boulder (Colorado).

Nichtweiss, Johannes, 1959, *Die ausländischen Saisonarbeiter in der Landwirtschaft der östlichen und mittleren Gebiete des deutschen Reiches: ein Beitrag zur Geschichte der preußisch-deutschen Politik von 1890–1914*, Berlin.

Nikolinakos, Marios, 1973, *Politische Ökonomie der Gastarbeiterfrage*, Hamburg.

———— 1980, Anmerkungen zu einer allgemeinen Theorie der Migration im Spätkapitalismus. In, Blaschke, Jochen and Greussing, Kurt (eds), 'Dritte Welt' in Europa: Probleme der Arbeitsimmigration, Frankfurt am Main, pp. 60–71.

Nohlen, Dieter and Nuscheler, Franz (eds), 1982, *Handbuch der Dritten Welt*, vol. 1: *Unterentwicklung und Entwicklung: Theorien – Strategien – Indikatoren*, Hamburg.

———— 1982, *Handbuch der Dritten Welt*, vol. 4: *Westafrika und Zentralafrika: Unterentwicklung und Entwicklung*, Hamburg.

North-Coombes, M. D., 1984, From Slavery to Indenture: Forced Labour in the Political Economy of Mauritius 1834–1867. In, Saunders, Kay (ed.), *Indentured Labour in the British Empire 1834–1920*, London, Canberra, pp. 78–125.

Nzula, A. T., Potekhin, I. I. and Zusmanovich, A. Z., 1979, *Forced Labour in Colonial Africa* (reprint of the 1933 Moscow edition), London.

Oberem, Udo, 1980, Über den indianischen Adel im kolonialzeitlichen Ecuador. In, *Lateinamerikastudien*, Munich, pp. 31–41.

O'Connor, James, 1972, Die Bedeutung des ökonomischen Imperialismus. In, Senghaas, Dieter (ed.), *Imperialismus und strukturelle Gewalt: Analysen über abhängige Reproduktion*, Frankfurt am Main, pp. 123–86.

Oguzkan, Turhan, 1975, The Turkish Brain-Drain: Migration Tendencies among Doctoral Level Manpower. In, R. E. Krane, *Manpower Mobility Across Cultural Boundaries*, Leiden, pp. 205–21.

Olivier, Sydney, 1906, *White Capital and Coloured Labour*, London.

Olle, Werner, 1980, Neue Weltarbeitsteilung und Ausländerbeschäftigung der westdeutschen Industrie. In, *Kritik*, no. 24, pp. 107–20.

Onoh, J. K., 1983, *The Nigerian Oil Economy: From Prosperity to Glut*, London.

Otto-Walter, Renate, 1979, *Unterentwicklung und Subsistenzreproduktion – Forschungsansatz der Arbeitsgruppe Bielefelder Entwicklungssoziologen (ed.): Subsistenzproduktion und Akkumulation*, pp. 7–12.

Paczensky, Gert von, 1979, *Weiße Herrschaft: eine Geschichte des Kolonialismus*, Frankfurt am Main.

Padmore, G., 1931, Forced Labour in Africa. In, *Labour Monthly*, vol. 13.

Panoff, Michel, 1977, Claude Meillassoux et le mode de production domestique. In,

Revue Française de Sociologie, vol. 18, no. 1, Jan.–Mar. 1977, pp. 133–43.

Patterson, Orlando, 1982, *Slavery and Social Death*, Cambridge, Mass.

Pelzer, Karl Josef, 1935, *Die Arbeiterwanderungen in Südostasien*, Hamburg.

Phizacklea, Annie (ed.), 1983, *One Way Ticket: Migration and Female Labour*, London and elsewhere.

Piel, Jean, 1980, Pérou – immigration et démarrage de l'agriculture spéculative au Pérou au 19e siècle. In, *Les Migrations internationales de la fin du 18e siècle à nos jours*, Paris, pp. 147–60.

Pierenkemper, T. and Tilly, R. (eds), 1982, *Historische Arbeitsmarktforschung: Entstehung, Entwicklung und Probleme der Vermarktung von Arbeitskraft*, Göttingen.

Piore, Michael, 1980, *Birds of Passage: Migrant Labour and Industrial Societies*, Cambridge and elsewhere.

Pogarell, Hans-Herrmann, 1984, Von der Sklaverei zur Zwangsarbeit: Entwicklungen in Südnigeria. In, *Der Überblick*, 20 (1984) 4, pp. 68–70.

Portes, Alejandro, 1976, Determinants of the Brain Drain. In, *International Migration Review*, vol. X, no. 4, pp. 489–508.

———— and Walton, John, 1981, *Labor, Class and the International System*, New York.

Postma, Johannes, 1979, Mortality in the Dutch Slave Trade, 1675–1795. In, Gemery, Henry A. and Hogendorn, Jan S., *The Uncommon Market: Essays in the Economic History of the Atlantic Slave Trade*, New York, pp. 239–60.

Poulson, Barry W., 1980, The Brain Drain from Mexico to the United States. In, Poulson, Barry W. and Osborn, T. Noel (eds), *US–Mexico Economic Relations*, Boulder (Colorado), pp. 245–60.

———— 1981, *Economic History of the United States*, New York.

Power, Jonathan, 1979, *Migrant Workers in Western Europe and the United States*, Oxford.

Prien, Hans-Jürgen, 1978, *Die Geschichte des Christentums in Lateinamerika*, Göttingen.

Puth, Robert C., 1982, *American Economic History*, New York.

Qualey, Carlton C., 1980, Etats-Unis – Immigration to the United States Since 1815. In, *Les Migrations internationales de la fin du 18e siècle à nos jours*, Paris, pp. 35–78.

Quijano, Anibal, 1974, Marginaler Pol der Wirtschaft und marginalisierte Arbeitskraft. In, Senghaas, Dieter (ed.), *Peripherer Kapitalismus*, Frankfurt am Main, pp. 298–341.

Ramesar, Marianne D., 1984, Indentured Labour in Trinidad 1880–1917. In, Saunders, Kay (ed.), *Indentured Labour in the British Empire 1834–1920*, London, Canberra, pp. 57–77.

Randall, Peter (ed.), 1973, *Südafrika: Macht, Armut und Privilegien*, report of the Economics Commission of the Study Project on Christianity in Apartheid Society, Stuttgart, Bonn.

Rathgen, 1920, Kuli. In, Schnee, Heinrich (ed.), *Deutsches Koloniallexikon*, Leipzig, pp. 386–8.

Reddock, Rhoda, 1983, Frauen und Sklaverei in der Karibik. In, *Beiträge zur feministischen Theorie und Praxis*, 9/10, Cologne, pp. 125–34.

Richardson, Peter, 1984a, Chinese Indentured Labour in the Transvaal Gold Mining Industry, 1904–1910. In, Saunders, Kay (ed.), *Indentured Labour in the British Empire 1834–1920*, London, Canberra, pp. 260–90.

———— 1984b, Coolies, Peasants and Proletarians: the Origins of Chinese

Indentured Labour in South Africa, 1904–1907. In, Marks, Shula and Richardson, Peter (eds), *International Labour Migration: Historical Perspectives*, London, pp. 167–86.

Ripken, Peter, 1978, *Südliches Afrika: Geschichte, Wirtschaft, politische Zukunft*, Berlin.

———— and Wellmer, Gottfried, 1978, Bantustans und ihre Funktion für das südafrikanische Herrschaftssystem. In, Ripken, Peter, 1978, pp. 194–203.

Röben, Bärbel, 1985, Die Inselstaaten in der Pazifik. In, *Der Überblick*, 3/85, pp. 10–17.

Roberts, G. W. and Byrne, G., 1966, Summary Statistics on Indenture and Associated Migration Affecting the West Indies, 1834–1918. In, *Population Studies*, 20, pp. 124–34.

Roberts, Janine, 1978, *From Massacres to Mining: the Colonization of Aboriginal Australia*, London.

Rockett, Ian R. H., 1976, Immigration Legislation and the Flow of Specialized Human Capital from South America to the United States. In, *International Migration Review*, vol. X, no. 1, pp. 47–61.

Rodney, Walter, 1976, *Afrika – die Geschichte einer Unterentwicklung*, Berlin.

———— 1981, Guyana: the Making of the Labour Force. In, *Race and Class*, vol. 22, no. 4, pp. 331–52.

Röhrbein, Karin and Schultz, Reinhard, 1978, *Puerto Rico: Geschichte, Kultur, Gegenwart*, Berlin.

Röhrich, Wilfried, 1983, *Politik und Ökonomie der Weltgesellschaft*, Opladen.

Roth, K.-H., 1977, *Die 'andere' Arbeiterbewegung*, Munich.

Russel-Wood, A. J. R., 1982, *The Black Man in Slavery and Freedom in Colonial Brazil*, London.

Samuel, Michel, 1978, *Le prolétariat africain noir en France*, Paris.

Sartorius von Waltershausen, A., 1925, Kuli. In, *Handwörterbuch der Staatswissenschaften*, vol. 6, Jena, pp. 100–3.

Saunders, Kay, 1984, The Workers Paradox: Indentured Labour in the Queensland Sugar Industry to 1920. In, Saunders, Kay (ed.), *Indentured Labour in the British Empire 1834–1920*, London, Canberra, pp. 213–59.

———— (ed.), 1984, *Indentured Labour in the British Empire 1834–1920*, London, Canberra.

Schiel, Tilman and Stauth, Georg, 1981, Unterentwicklung und Subsistenzproduktion. In, *Peripherie*, no. 5/6.

Schipulle, Hans Peter, 1973, *Der Ausverkauf der Intelligenz aus Entwicklungsländern*, Munich.

Schmidt, Fred, 1938, *Sklavenfahrer und Kuli-Klippper*, Berlin.

Schmidt, Heinz G., 1985, *Der neue Sklavenmarkt: Geschäfte mit Frauen aus Übersee*, Basle.

Schmitt, Eberhard (ed.), 1984, *Dokumente zur Geschichte der europäischen Expansion, Vol. 2: Die großen Entdeckungen*, Munich.

Schnee, Heinrich (ed.), 1920, *Deutsches Koloniallexikon*, Leipzig. Entries: Arbeiter, Arbeiterverhältnisse, Arbeitsweise der Naturvölker, Arbeitszwang, Körperliche Züchtigung.

Schneider, Helmuth (ed.), 1983, *Geschichte der Arbeit: vom Alten Ägypten bis zur Gegenwart*, Frankfurt am Main, Berlin.

Schöller, Wolfgang, 1975, Unterentwicklung und ungleicher Tausch auf dem Weltmarkt. In, Tibi, Bassam and Brandes, Volkhard (eds), *Handbuch 2 – Unterentwicklung*, Frankfurt am Main, Cologne, pp. 140–75.

Schubert, Alex, 1978, *Panama: Geschichte eines Landes und eines Kanals*, Berlin.

Seeber, Eva, 1964, *Zwangsarbeiter in der faschistischen Kriegswirtschaft*, Berlin.

Senghaas, Dieter (ed.), 1972, *Imperialismus und strukturelle Gewalt: Analysen über abhängige Reproduktion*, Frankfurt am Main.

———— 1977, *Weltwirtschaftsordnung und Entwicklungspolitik: Plädoyer für Dissoziation*, Frankfurt am Main.

———— 1982, *Von Europa lernen: Entwicklungsgeschichtliche Betrachtungen*, Frankfurt am Main.

Senghaas-Knobloch, Eva, 1979, *Reproduktion von Arbeitskraft in der Weltgesellschaft*, Frankfurt am Main, New York.

Serageldin, Ismail et al., 1983, *Manpower and International Labor Migration in the Middle East and North Africa*, World Bank, New York and elsewhere.

Sherman, William L., 1971, Indian Slavery and the Cerrato Reforms. In, *Hispanic American Historical Review*, 51 (1971) 1, Durham, N.C., pp. 25–50.

Simon, Gildas, 1977, *Etat et perspectives de l'émigration tunisienne*, Republique Tunisienne, Ministère du Plan.

———— and Noin, Daniel, 1972, La migration maghrébine vers l'Europe. In, *Cahiers d'outre-Mer*, no. 99, 25 (1972), Bordeaux, pp. 241–76.

Simonis, Georg, 1977, Die Bundesrepublik und die neue internationale Arbeitsteilung. In, *Leviathan*, 1/1977, pp. 36–56.

Simpson, Lesley Byrd, 1966, *The Ecomienda in New Spain: the Beginning of Spanish Mexico*, Los Angeles.

Sinclair, Michael, 1979, Canadian involvement in the Brain Drain from Africa: Opportunities for Action. In, *Issue*, 9 (1979), 4, Waltham, Mass., pp. 19–25.

Singer, Paul, 1977, Beschäftigung, Produktion und Reproduktion der Arbeitskraft. In, Bennholdt-Thomsen, Veronika (et al.) (eds), *Lateinamerika, Analysen und Berichte* 1, Berlin, pp. 53–69.

Slicher van Bath, Bernard, 1979, Economic Diversification in Spanish America Around 1600: Centres, Intermediate Zones and Peripheries. In, *Jahrbuch für Geschichte von Staat, Wirtschaft und Gesellschaft Lateinamerikas*, 16 (1979), Cologne, pp. 53–95.

Smith, Clifford Thorpe, 1970, Depopulation of the Central Andes in the 16th Century. In, *Current Anthropology*, 11 (1970) 4/5, Chicago, Ill., pp. 453–64.

Spear, Percival, 1979, *Oxford History of Modern India: 1740 to 1975*, Oxford.

Specker, Johann, 1951, Kirchliche und staatliche Siedlungspolitik in Spanisch-Amerika im 16. Jahrhundert. In, *Missionswissenschaftliche Studien*, 1951, Aachen, pp. 426–38.

Spiegel, Der, no. 6, 1983, Hamburg.

Stahl, C. W., 1981, Migrant Labour Supplies Past, Present and Future; with Special Reference to the Gold-mining Industry. In, Böhning, W. R., *Black Migration to South Africa: a Selection of Policy Oriented Research*, Geneva, pp. 7–44.

Statistisches Jahrbuch der Bundesrepublik Deutschland, 1983, 1984, 1985, 1986, Wiesbaden.

Sternberg, Fritz, 1971, *Der Imperialismus*, Frankfurt am Main (Berlin 1926).

Strahm, Rudolf H., 1975, *Überentwicklung – Unterentwicklung*, Nuremburg.

Sunkel, Osvaldo, 1972, Transnationale kapitalistische Integration und nationale Desintegration: der Fall Lateinamerika. In, Senghaas, Dieter (ed.), *Imperialismus und strukturelle Gewalt: Analysen über abhängige Reproduktion*, pp. 258–315.

Suret-Canale, Jean, 1977, Economies et sociétés d'Afrique tropicale. In, *La Pensée*, vol. 194, pp. 121–32.

Talha, Larbi, 1974, L'evolution du mouvement migratoire entre le Maghreb et la

France. In, *Maghreb-Machrek*, no. 61/1974, Paris.

———— 1976, Genèse et essor de l'offre de travail migrant: le cas du Maghreb. In, Ruf, W. K. et al. (eds), *Rapports de Dépendance au Maghreb*, Paris.

Tannenbaum, Frank, 1972, Contrast: North American and South American Slavery. In, Simmons, Charles W. and Morris, Harry W. (eds), *Afro-American History*, Columbus (Ohio), pp. 27–35.

Thiam, Awa, 1981, *Die Stimme der schwarzen Frau: vom Leid der Afrikanerinnen*, Reinbek.

Tibi, Bassam, 1975, Zur Kritik der sowjetmarxistischen Entwicklungstheorie. In, *Handbuch 2 – Unterentwicklung*, Frankfurt am Main, Cologne, pp. 64–86.

Timmermann, Vincenz, 1982, *Entwicklungstheorie und Entwicklungspolitik*, Göttingen.

Tinker, Hugh, 1974, *A New System of Slavery: the Export of Indian Labour Overseas, 1830–1920*, London.

———— 1984, Into Servitude: Indian Labour in the Sugar Industry, 1833–1970. In, Marks, Shula and Richardson, Peter, *International Labour Migration: Historical Perspectives*, London, pp. 76–89.

Tomasi, Lydio F., 1982, Zur Situation der Migrationsforschung in den USA. In, Bischoff, Detlef and Heintzl, Maria (eds), *Arbeitsmigration und ihre sozialen Folgen: der Beitrag der Wissenschaft zu ihrer Bewältigung*, Berlin, pp. 29–42.

Totsuka, Hideo, 1980, Japan – Korean Immigration in Pre-war Japan. In, *Les migrations internationales de la fin du 18e siècle à nos jours*, Paris, pp. 263–79.

Trautmann, Wolfgang, 1981, Die sozio-ökonomische Struktur der kolonial-zeitlichen Latifundien in Tlaxcala, Mexico. In, *Vierteljahrschrift für Sozial-und Wirtschaftsgeschichte*, 68 (1981) 3, Wiesbaden, pp. 349–71.

Tung, William L., 1974, *The Chinese in America, 1820–1973: a Chronology and Fact Book*, Dobbs Ferry, NY, (Ethnic Chronology Series no. 14).

Twain, Mark, 1976, *Following the Equator: a Journey Around the World*, vols. I and II, New York, London, (*Writings of Mark Twain*, vols. VII and VIII).

Überleben sichern, Das, 1980, report of the North–South Commission (the Brandt Report).

Varl, Leroy and White, Landeg, 1978, 'Tawani, Machambero!': Forced Cotton and Rice Growing on the Zambezi. In, *Journal of African History*, 19 (1978) 2, pp. 239–63.

Vinke, Hermann, 1984, *Wir sind wie die Fische im Meer. Mikronesien: Verseucht, verplant, verdorben*, Zurich.

Wagner, Fritz, 1947, *USA: Geburt und Aufstieg der neuen Welt; Geschichte in Zeitdokumenten 1607–1865*, Munich.

Wallerstein, Immanuel, 1979, Aufstieg und künftiger Niedergang des kapitalist-ischen Weltsystems. In, Senghaas, Dieter (ed.), *Kapitalistische Weltökonomie: Kontroversen über ihren Ursprung und ihre Entwicklungsdynamik*, Frankfurt am Main, pp. 31–67.

———— 1983, Die Zukunft der Weltökonomie. In, Blaschke, Jochen (ed.), *Perspektiven des Weltsystems: Materialien zu Immanuel Wallerstein 'Das moderne Weltsystem'*, Frankfurt am Main, New York, pp. 215–55.

———— 1984, *Der historische Kapitalismus*, Berlin.

———— (ed.), 1983, *Labor in the World Social Structure*, Beverly Hills.

Walvin, James, 1982, *Slavery and the Slave Trade*, London.

Weggel, Oskar, 1983, 'Schlagt die Chinesen nieder!' Community-Probleme mit den Auslandschinesen in Südostasien. In, Italiaander, Rolf (ed.), *'Fremde raus?' Fremdenangst und Ausländerfeindlichkeit*, Frankfurt am Main, pp. 65–75.

Weiss, Ruth, 1978, Südafrika und sein Hinterland. In, Ripken, Peter, *Südliches Africa: Geschichte, Wirtschaft, politische Zukunft*, Berlin, pp. 252–63.
———— (ed.), 1980, *Frauen gegen Apartheid: zur Geschichte des politischen Widerstandes von Frauen*, Reinbek.
Wellmer, Gottfried, 1976a, Die historische Entwicklung des Wanderarbeitersystems. In, Wilson, F. et al., *Wanderarbeit im südlichen Afrika*, Bonn, pp. 9–34.
———— 1976b, Resettlement und Bantustans als Bestandteil der Politik der 'multinationalen Entwicklungs'-Strategie der Republik Südafrika. In, Wilson, F. et al., *Wanderarbeit im südlichen Afrika*, Bonn, pp. 35–60.
Werlhof, Claudia von, 1978a, Dritte Welt bei uns – Frauenarbeit und Kapitalakkumulation. In, *Alternative*, no. 120, vol. 21, pp. 181–5.
———— 1978b, Frauenarbeit: der blinde Fleck in der Kritik der politischen Ökonomie. In, *Beiträge 1 zur feministischen Theorie und Praxis: erste Orientierungen*, Munich, pp. 18–32.
———— 1980, 'Vereint wie eine Schar wütender Adler...', Frauenkämpfe und Machismo in Lateinamerika. In, *Beiträge 3 zur feministischen Theorie und Praxis: Frauen und 'dritte Welt'*, Munich, pp. 26–43.
———— 1983, Lohn ist ein 'Wert', Leben nicht? In, *Probleme des Klassenkampfes*, 50, pp. 38–58.
Werth, Manfred and Stevens, Willi, 1976, Mobilität in den Ländern der europäischen Gemeinschaft. In, *Mitteilungen aus der Arbeitsmarkt- und Berufsforschung 2/1976*.
Weyl, Ulrich, 1976, Wanderarbeit und Unterentwicklung. In, Wilson, F. et al., *Wanderarbeit im südlichen Afrika*, Bonn, pp. 179–230.
Williams, Eric, 1964, *History of the People of Trinidad and Tobago*, London.
Wilson, Francis, Wellmer, G., Weyl, U., Wolpe, H. et al., 1976, *Wanderarbeit im südlichen Afrika*, Bonn.
Wilson, Henry, 1969, *History of the Rise and Fall of the Slave Power in America* (reprint of the Boston edition, 1872, 1877), New York.
Winnie, William W., Guzman-Flores, E. and Hernandez-Saldana, Victor M., 1980, Migration from West Mexico to the United States. In, *US–Mexico Economic Relations*, Boulder (Colorado).
Wirz, Albert, 1984, *Sklaverei und kapitalistisches Weltsystem*, Frankfurt am Main.
Wöhlcke, Manfred, Wogau, Peter von and Martens, Waltraud, 1977, *Die neuere entwicklungstheoretische Diskussion*, Frankfurt am Main.
Wolff, Inge, 1964, Negersklaverei und Negerhandel in Hochperu 1546–1640. In, *Jahrbuch für Geschichte von Staat, Wirtschaft und Gesellschaft Lateinamerikas*, 1 (1964), Cologne, Graz, pp. 157–86.
Wolff, Richard D., 1972, Der gegenwärtige Imperialismus in der Sicht der Metropole. In, Senghaas, Dieter (ed.), *Imperialismus und strukturelle Gewalt: Analysen über abhängige Reproducktion*, pp. 187–200.
Wolpe, Harold, 1976, Kapitalismus und billige Arbeitskraft in Südafrika: von der Rassentrennung zur Apartheidspolitik. In, Wilson, F. et al., *Wanderarbeit im südlichen Afrika*, Bonn.
World Labour Report 1, 1984, *Employment, Incomes, Social Protection, New Information Technology*, International Labour Office, Geneva.
Yesufu, Tejani M., 1978, Loss of Trained Personnel by Migration from Nigeria. In, *Human Resources and African Development*, New York, pp. 333–50.
Zavala, Silvio, 1962, *The Colonial Period in the History of the New World*, Mexico.
Zwangsumsiedlungen in Südafrika, 1984. Published by the South African Council of Churches and the Catholic Bishops' Conference of Southern Africa, Hamburg.

Index